CALEDONIA LOST
THE FALL OF THE CONFEDERACY

WILLIAM D. MCEACHERN

Caledonia Lost: The Fall of the Confederacy
Copyright © 2017 by William D. McEachern

All rights reserved. No part of this publication may be reproduced, distributed, or transmitted in any form or by any means, including photocopying, recording, or other electronic or mechanical methods, without the prior written permission of the publisher or author, except in the case of brief quotations embodied in critical reviews and certain other noncommercial uses permitted by copyright law.

Although every precaution has been taken to verify the accuracy of the information contained herein, the author and publisher assume no responsibility for any errors or omissions. No liability is assumed for damages that may result from the use of information contained within.

Library of Congress Control Number: 2017946354
ISBN-13: Paperback: 978-1-64045-660-0
          PDF: 978-1-64045-661-7
          ePub: 978-1-64045-662-4
          Kindle: 978-1-64045-663-1
          Hardcover 978-1-64045-664-8

Printed in the United States of America

LitFire LLC
1-800-511-9787
www.litfirepublishing.com
order@litfirepublishing.com

CONTENTS

Acknowledgements 1
Author's Preface 4

Book I: Prologue 9
Chapter 1: Keeping Promises 11
Chapter 2: The Seeds of Our Destruction 19
Chapter 3: A Day at the Races 24
Chapter 4: Those Heady Early Days 27

Book II: The Play War-1861 41
Chapter 5: "No Stronger than a Horsehair" 42
Chapter 6: A Tale of a Flag: The Ghost of Glenfinnan 48
Chapter 7: Sullivan's Island 53
Chapter 8: A Letter Home 59
Chapter 9: The Birth of the Hampton Legion 62
Chapter 10: The Claremont Rifles in Camp 65
Chapter 11: Virginny Bound 69
Chapter 12: Measles and Mumps: A Plague Strikes the Camp 78
Chapter 13: Winter is Coming 81
Chapter 14: Fire Claims Memory 85

Book III: Hard War -1862 89
Chapter 15: Boisseau House 90
Chapter 16: Reorganization Breeds Disorganization 97
Chapter 17: Yorktown: The Stride of a Giant, Stumbles 100
Chapter 18: Seven Pines 108
Chapter 19: The Mills of God 121
Chapter 20: Marching to Maryland 133
Chapter 21: Blood Runs Red in the Antietam 136

Chapter 22: The Best of the War 142
Chapter 23: Don't Grow Too Fond of It 149
Chapter 24: Christmas 1862 152

Book IV: The War is Lost in a Night-1863 155
Chapter 25: A Side Visit 156
Chapter 26: The Bombardment.. 159
Chapter 27: Vows 163
Chapter 28: Wauhatchie... 174
Chapter 29: Wauhatchie Revisited... 194
Chapter 30: Another Siege 196

Book V: We Endure Beyond Endurance-1864............................207
Chapter 31: Silence 208
Chapter 32: I Jine the Cavalry.. 213
Chapter 33: At Home with Vicee 221
Chapter 34: A Gift 229
Chapter 35: The Horse March... 232
Chapter 36: Riddell's Shop... 236

Book VI: Breakthrough-The War Ends-1865 245
Chapter 37: 1865 Dawns 246
Chapter 38: The World Turned Upside Down.................................. 250
Chapter 39: The Dance Begins 259
Chapter 40: Cowpens Revisited... 264
Chapter 41: Lee to the Rear!.. 269
Chapter 42: Fire Strikes Again... 279
Chapter 43: Fire and Sword... 286
Chapter 44: Epilogue 291

Appendix I 299
Appendix II 301
Appendix III 303

Books by William D. McEachern

Caledonia Series
Caledonia: A Song of Scotland
New Caledonia: A Song of America
Caledonia: Free Trade and Sailors' Rights (Available 2018)
Caledonia Lost: The Fall of the Confederacy

Casting Lots Series
Casting Lots
The Life of Levi (Anticipated Availability 2018)

ACKNOWLEDGEMENTS

The author greatly appreciates the editing work done by Margaret L. McEachern. Her tireless efforts, her suggestions, and her questions greatly enhanced this work. I am deeply indebted to her.

The author greatly appreciates the editing work done by Richard A. Merkt. He was kind enough to read the manuscript and, from his vast knowledge of the Civil War, added many valuable suggestions and comments.

Any errors in this text are the author's and the author's alone.

For Kathleen, my one, and only, always.

This novel is dedicated to all who fought in the American Civil War.

AUTHOR'S PREFACE

This novel is based on the true story of a Confederate soldier: James Augustus McEachern. He joined his home militia no later than January of 1861. He had the honor, if one may call it that, of having served his home state of South Carolina and the Confederacy from the bombardment of Ft. Sumter through the surrender at Appomattox. He was wounded twice during the Civil War. He served in both the eastern and the western theatres of war: In the east in the Army of Northern Virginia under Robert E. Lee and in the west under Braxton Bragg in the Army of the Tennessee. He served under some of the most famous corps commanders, among them, Thomas Jonathan Jackson and James Longstreet.

James Augustus McEachern was a member of the Hampton Legion throughout the War, which for most of the War was part of the legendary Texas Brigade. The Hampton Legion is memorialized with the other regiments of the Texas Brigade (it was a regiment from South Carolina and the only regiment not from Texas) on a monument in front of the Texas Capitol Building in Austin, Texas. It was the Texas Brigade which gave Robert E. Lee his first victory of the War at Gaines' Mills. Under John Bell Hood, who would later lose both an arm and a leg during the War, the Texas Brigade charged down a hill, then across a swampy creek, and then up a steep hill studded with three entrenched lines of Union infantry to break Union General Fitz John Porter's corps, forcing the Union Army to retreat during the Seven Days Battles.

James Augustus McEachern fought in many of the major battles in both theatres. For example, he fought in Second Bull Run, Antietam, and Fredericksburg. Later, he fought in the Battle above the Clouds at Chattanooga and Missionary Ridge. He fought both as infantry and later as mounted infantry. He endured numerous sieges, being on the side besieging at Suffolk, Chattanooga, and Knoxville, and as the besieged at Petersburg. He avoided the great killers of the War: measles and mumps, because he had contracted these diseases as a child. He rose through the ranks until he was a 2nd lieutenant and the highest ranking officer of his company, when it surrendered at Appomattox.

His story, though, is not one only of war and battles. During the Civil War, he wrote letters home. In this book, I have reproduced several of them. In one of these authentic letters to his beloved Victoria, whom he called Vicee, written just days after the bombardment of Ft. Sumter, he asked her to marry him. Thus, this book is a love story of a man for a woman during the most trying times that anyone can ever face: the literal demise of an entire way of life in the midst of overwhelming destruction. Their love in the face of a world crumbling all around them is a triumph of will.

This novel contains the text of three actual letters written by James A. McEachern to Victoria Clifton Ham (known as Vicee) during the Civil War. These letters appear as Chapters 8, 12, and 29. They have been edited, because James A. McEachern, like so many of his time had an eccentric way of capitalizing words, and, among other things, he did not use virtually any punctuation. In the original, these letters are almost unreadable.

In the several appendices that follow the text of the novel, you can review the military records of James Augustus McEachern. You can read the real names of the men, who surrendered at Appomattox, in the Roster of the surrender. Finally, I have included many maps throughout the novel such that the details and location of camps, battles, and important places can be easily visualized by the reader.

The novel's setting deserves a few notes. The novel is set in approximately the 24 hours stretching from the morning of April 1, 1865 through the morning of April 2, 1865. It was during this timeframe that the most important battle of the Civil War was fought: The Breakthrough of the Confederate Lines at Petersburg. This Breakthrough occurred near the planation known as the Boisseau House or Tudor Hall, which is today preserved in Pamplin Park in Petersburg, Virginia.

At 4:40 AM on the morning of April 2, 1865, 14,000 Union soldiers rose from the ground from their advance positions only a hundred yards from the Confederate picket lines. During the night, they had crept forward almost a mile from their own lines in stealth and silence. With the dawn barely bringing forth light, in a charge, which was bigger than Pickett's Charge at Gettysburg, they stormed the Confederate advance lines, which were only 300 yards in front of the Confederate main lines. Within moments, they brushed aside the Confederate advance guard and stormed the main Confederate lines. At this point the courage of one Union Captain, twenty-year old, Vermont-raised, Charles Gould, almost single-handedly propelled the Union forces up and over the Confederate main line, breaking it. For this heroic action, he not only received two bad wounds, but also the Medal of Honor.

Thus, this is the story of that Breakthrough and the immediate consequences of it. The Breakthrough broke a nine month siege of Petersburg, which has to be viewed as Robert E. Lee's masterpiece of defense. Lee was able to keep Grant and his massively large Army of the Potomac at bay, while Lee's Army of Northern Virginia suffered severe deprivations, including cold and hunger. While one can appreciate the mastery with which Lee operated through the campaign, and the number of blows that he successfully parried, one must also appreciate the dogged determination of Grant, who engineered his own masterpiece of offense, stretching Lee time and again until Lee's lines snapped. As a result of Grant's successful siege, Lee was compelled to surrender within one week, on April 9, 1865, effectively ending the War.

With the Breakthrough, Richmond fell. Thus was lost was not only the Confederate Capital, but also the main industrial center of the South, producing most of the iron, cannon, and other munitions of the Confederacy. Like many other Confederate cities near the end of the War, Richmond burned to the ground, leaving to the conquerors only a vast sea of smoldering rubble. How this happened, and I think the how will astound you, is set forth.

I have written a story where everything I relate is as true and accurate as is possible, except for one thing. Company G of the Hampton Legion was not at the Breakthrough site of Tudor Hall. Otherwise, the story of the Breakthrough happened just as I have told it.

I should like to thank Pamplin Park for its hospitality and its assistance in the research of this novel. The Breakthrough took place on the site of what is now Pamplin Park in Petersburg, Virginia. There, one can see Tudor Hall, also known as the Boisseau House, just as it was before the Breakthrough as occupied by General Samuel McGowan and his staff. One can also walk the Confederate breastworks and find the spot near Arthur's Swamp where Captain Charles Gould almost singlehandedly assaulted the Confederate Lines. I would urge the reader to attend Pamplin Park to get a greater understanding of that momentous event.

Just south of Pamplin Park, one can also walk the Union lines which have recently been preserved by the Civil War Trust, including Forts Welch, Fisher, and Fort Gregg. From there it is about a mile's walk to retrace the attack leading to the Breakthrough.

Finally, during the writing of this novel, my friend and fellow Civil War historian, Mr. Richard A. Merkt, shared his insights upon the Civil War. One, which I find most compelling, asks a question which I have not seen discussed anywhere else during my nearly sixty years of reading about the War. To quote Mr. Merkt: "I often wonder what might have been, had Beauregard not fired on Ft. Sumter. Lincoln had a terrible political problem in early 1861, just as FDR had just prior to Pearl Harbor. If the South had just shrugged and walked away, how willing would the Northern states really have been to raise an army of invasion just to force the seceding states back in? We'll never know for sure."

June 14, 2017 – Flag Day
Palm Beach Gardens, Florida
152 Years Later

BOOK I: PROLOGUE

"It will be enough for me, however, if these words of mine are judged useful by those who want to understand clearly the events which happened in the past and which will (human nature being what it is), at some time or other and in much the same ways, be repeated in the future. My history has been composed to be an everlasting possession and not to win the prize of an hour."- **Thucydides**, *The Peloponnesian War*

CHAPTER 1:

KEEPING PROMISES

"Hold Five Forks at all hazards."
*-**Robert E. Lee** to George Pickett*

April 1, 1865 6:00 AM

Dear Vicee,
How many times have I uttered these words-Dear Vicee? I have thought of you virtually every moment of every day. I have begun thousands of letters to you. Each and every one of them has been interrupted. I start anew, and then something happens that cuts that one short, too.

The best that I can do are these mental letters. Now, all I have is the will to write you. I do not have the physical means to write.

I promised you that I would write every day, but I did not know then that I would not be able to fulfill that promise. This was not because of lack of desire; not because of lack of time; not because I have forgotten; not because of any one of a million reasons that a man might utter to his wife to cover why he had not done the one thing, which she has asked of him; no, not because of any of this. It is because my country has run out of paper, pencils, pens, and ink months and months ago. I know not whether the few letters that I have actually written to you with paper and pen have even gotten through the mails to you. I will still write these dream letters to you in my mind in hopes that someday I will sit with you again, and can pour of out my heart to you, and share some of these writings, if I can ever remember them.

This last winter has been horrible. Perhaps it is the worst I have ever known. I have been here in the midst of this winter camp for what seems to be forever. The blustery winter has robbed all of creation of its colors, except one; it has left grey, an endless vastness of unforgiving grey. We have built log cabins. They are sturdy, with barrels for chimneys. We have built a whole town of these things nestled on the grounds of what used to be a tobacco plantation.

Someone said that it used to be a very rich planation with 50 or 60 slaves. Now, I don't see a one. Now, it grows only gun emplacements and trenches. I look at the grounds of this planation and I see a fine home, white clapboard, green shutters, with a high, wide porch surrounding it. This is where the general lives with his staff. They have real beds to sleep in and real furniture to sit upon. Carpets soften the world beneath their feet. A roaring fire in the fireplace warms their backsides. The General is McGowan, a fine South Carolinian.

General Sam McGowan somehow detailed me and my company from the Hampton Legion, and has us as pickets beyond our lines near Tudor Hall Planation. We have carved a line of trenches beyond our main fortified position. The rain drizzles in, and the bottom becomes soupy with mud. We wait. We hear the Yankees somewhere beyond our lines cooking, washing, cleaning their guns, playing cards, rolling up artillery, and doing those one thousand and one things that men in camp do before a battle to get ready for the day, which will somehow someday come, but then sometimes seems not to come at all. We sit. We do not know if the battle will be today, tomorrow, or the next day, or never. We wait. That is all that we do. When we are off duty, we, too, do all the things which men do to make ready for war, as well as for daily life. But we can't wash, because we each only have one uniform, and if it were washed, it would come apart, because it is so threadbare. We can't really cook, because it is rare that we have food to cook. Sometimes a weevily lump of hardtack gets our way. Maybe a slab of bacon that is not too green to be eaten. We can't practice our aim, for we do not have enough ammunition. So, we wait. That is all we can do.

I am sorry. I have become too maudlin, even for my own tastes. I cannot write you too much. It is too depressing and distressing. Still, you must know that I adhere to the faith that we will prevail. I know not how; I know not why; I know not when, but I still believe that we will prevail. If I do not believe this, then I will fall apart.

There is too much on my mind and heart for me to give in. My men depend upon me. They look to me for guidance and leadership. If I give in, I will break their hearts. I have seen it happen. Too many times, some officer will give up and when he does, the men of his command melt away in the dark of night. Desertion is rampant. We have lost easily twenty-five percent of our men this rainy, soggy, spring. Few will sit in a trench that fills with rain water, watching the mud swirl around their feet. They will not stay, because they are cold, hungry, and without a change of clothes.

Again, I say that desertion is rampant. You would be shocked, Vicee, to learn that our friend Sidney F. Cole deserted. You know his wife, Frannie, who lives in Timmonsville. He was in the Manning Guards, which is Company C of the Legion. He was a gentle man. Although he was some six years older than I, both of us having come from the Clarendon region gave us a brotherhood. He had become a real friend. You might recall that I told you of how he nursed men with the fever back in the fall of 1861 at Brentsville Hospital. He acted as a nurse several times - he had a gift for it, and many men credited him with their recovery. The man had gone through a lot. He had been wounded at Seven Pines, just like me. But at Seven Pines, he had been captured and was a prisoner of war in a Yankee camp. Later, after he was exchanged, he fought again, only to be wounded in the head. He went to Chimborazo Hospital from the fall of 1862 throughout the spring of 1863. Thereafter, he was ill at least two times that put him in the hospital for two or three months at a time. The man had had enough. It was just too much of a strain. But while I blame him, I absolve him of any sin. To desert now - actually Thursday March 30th-when it is clear that the war might end any day, is perhaps the act of a sane man facing an insane situation. This is a route that I myself cannot take. I must stand fast.

We look out over the ground, the barren ground, which separates us from the Union Army. All we see over there is their gleaming rifles and bayonets, smell their real coffee cooking, watch them reading a newspaper printed just a day or two ago. They sleep under warm blankets-yes they have blankets! Everything we lack, they have. What can you ask of men who have fought battle after battle and have suffered each and every deprivation? Can you ask them again to charge over the top of the trench unto the face of the abatis of the Union? Can you ask them to risk their lives going through the Union cannon fire of canister, shot, and shell? Can you goad them to charge into the teeth of the Union lines knowing some are armed with repeating rifles? What can you ask of me who has done it all time and time again? Can you ask for one more time? If I can't ask myself, can I ask them? And if so, for what?

I can't give in for me too. What have I done? Have I spent four years chasing a dream? Does this dream cannibalize my soul? Does it gnaw at my feet and fingers? Does it rot away my body, my heart, and my soul? This is just too much. My heart is breaking.

What I thought I'd do, Vicee, is try to tell you all that I am thinking of in this War at this time. I will try to tell you my story so that maybe something will make sense. I know that this is but an imagined conversation with you, but it is all that I have. It is the only way now that I can communicate with you.

I have vowed to you that I will come home to you. Do you know that every day, in every way, I am doing all that I can to fulfill that promise to you?

So Vicee, all of our recent troubles began on the evening of March 29, 1865. The heavens had opened up with mighty fury, if not Biblical fury. Rain fell in torrents and continued to keep falling for 36 straight hours. Rain, heavy rain, fell from the sky with no letup, no cessation, and no diminishment. This rain filled the creeks and made them overflow their banks, with raging cascades and cataclysmic waterfalls. Every road became a quagmire of mud, sucking boots off the feet of men as they marched.

For us, this was a welcome respite from the relentless western push by the Union forces. Month after month, Grant's siege has tightened its grip on Petersburg, slowly strangling our army. Now, Grant has massed what some say is 55,000 infantry on our extreme right behind the stream called Hatcher's Run, beyond our right flank. How do I know this? The Petersburg newspapers print everything, and what they don't print the Yankee newspapers do, so we know everything.

Just southwest at Dinwiddie Court House, named for Robert Dinwiddie the Royal Governor of Virginia during the French and Indian War, Grant has placed Sheridan's force of 10,000 cavalry. They are poised to exploit the breakthrough of Lee's lines, once their infantry does their job. The rain has flooded Hatcher's Run and their attack has to wait for the flood waters to recede. We know it will come, but we did not know when. We only know that it will come, when the rains let up.

We know that Bobby Lee has to counter this move for, if he does not, the South Side Railroad Line, which wends its way from the west into Petersburg and then turns north to Richmond, will be severed. This is our last, and our only supply line south.

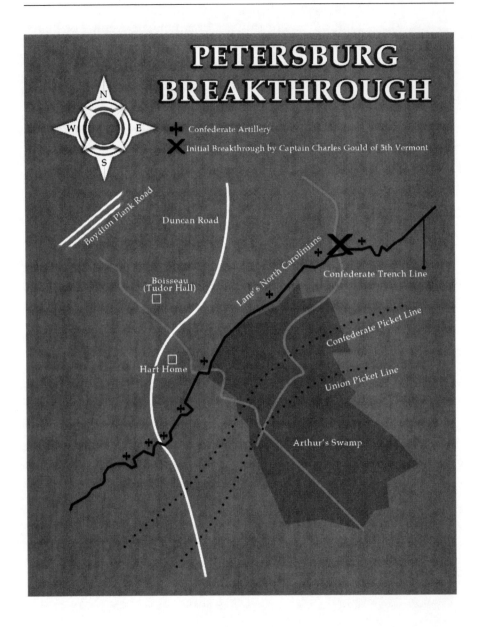

The Southside Railroad runs west towards Tennessee. Around fifty miles or so to our west, it makes a junction in the town of Burkeville with the Richmond and Danville Railroad. This is our true last connection with the South. Every morsel of food, every slice of hardtack, every strip of bacon, and every grain of wheat moves over that railroad line feeding our ever starving grey army, which is strung out from west of Petersburg, below it, and then east of it, turns northwards to then encircle Richmond on its north side. We are 30,000 men holding over 30 miles. The South Side Railroad line is also our last and only escape route, if our lines around Petersburg break. Five Forks, the area where they are threatening to break this railroad, has to be held, for otherwise there is no hope for our army. But Bobby Lee has never let us down. Oh, I know some think that at Gettysburg he let us down. Nothing seemed to work then. Thank God I was not there. I was on reserve duty guarding Richmond. Otherwise, I would have been in Pickett's Charge. Vicee, I am glad that I was not in that fight. I know that if I had been, then I would have been killed, and that would have been my end.

I have fought on so many fields and been so many places. I never thought that, as a boy from South Carolina, I would see so many states- Virginia, North Carolina, Georgia, and Tennessee.

After months of countering each of Grant's moves, all Lee has to meet this latest move are George Pickett and some 11,000 men, who are stationed at the crossroads of Five Forks, which, if held, would thwart Grant's infantry thrust. Lee's order to Pickett was simple: 'Hold Five Forks at all hazards.' This order by Lee rankled Pickett, because he still nurses the emotional wound he suffered in the frontal assault at Gettysburg, and he still holds great resentment against our commanding officer for that frontal assault. For 11,000 men facing some 65,000 men, this was an order of suicide. 'All hazards!' Each man is to die to hold a square of ground. To sacrifice one's self, so that the rest of the army could survive. But if Pickett and his men lay down their lives, who would be there to bar the door so that Grant's and Sheridan's men would not come flooding in? Is Pickett supposed to kill each and every one of them?

On March 31, the day dawned bright and clear. The rain had stopped. Grant ordered his men forward. Pickett did well that day. He attacked Sheridan and drove him back. I cheered when I heard that. "Pickett held!" I shouted.

Then Grant's other attack under General Gouverneur K. Warren, the hero of Gettysburg and who led the Union's V Corps, also did not fare well. "Thank God!" We all sighed with the most profound relief and gratitude.

But Grant would not give up. He is as bull-headed as a man could ever be. Once he has got in his mind to do something, he will do it and do it again, until it works. Have we learned nothing from Vicksburg?

Grant ordered Warren the next day to join up with Sheridan and to push forward at Five Forks. But April 1st always has its ways of embarrassing people. April Fools!

CHAPTER 2:

THE SEEDS OF OUR DESTRUCTION

On the same day Jesus went out of the house and sat by the sea. And great multitudes were gathered together to Him, so that He got into a boat and sat; and the whole multitude stood on the shore. Then He spoke many things to them in parables, saying: "Behold, a sower went out to sow. And as he sowed, some seed fell by the wayside; and the birds came and devoured them. Some fell on stony places, where they did not have much earth; and they immediately sprang up because they had no depth of earth. But when the sun was up they were scorched, and because they had no root they withered away. And some fell among thorns, and the thorns sprang up and choked them. But others fell on good ground and yielded a crop: some a hundredfold, some sixty, some thirty. He who has ears to hear, let him hear!"
-Matthew 13: 1-23

April 1, 1865 6:45 AM

I am sitting around a campfire. I am drinking what we call coffee, although it is but some roasted chicory, what you might call a blue dandelion with some roasted grain, if we have some.

Vicee, as a child I had a map of the United States. All the vacant land to the west stretching until one reached California was shown on that map. As each new state was added to our nation, I would outline the borders of that new State upon my map. I was thrilled that our country was growing and expanding. It seemed to me that we had endless possibilities. Our vistas were panoramic. I wanted our country to reach from ocean to ocean and span the continent. We were to be the greatest nation in the world. I saw nothing but the greatest of all human achievement, as our destiny, as each new State was added.

But this was not what everyone saw, as they saw this growth. Each state that came in was balanced by another state: one free and one slave. It was the addition of the slave states that agitated some. Each new slave state enflamed their passions, ripped at their guts, and tortured their souls.

Where I saw greatness in our nation becoming bigger; they saw nothing but evil being spread across the map. Where I saw an ever more magnificent nation; they saw nothing but chains binding men to servitude and degradation. Where I saw the hand of God guiding us to a new and wonderful future; they saw the abomination of the devil's spawn spreading the apocalypse.

It was a tale of two nations. And it was not just of one that was slave and one that was free. It was a nation divided by what vision of the future it would pursue. We thought their way of life, defined by factories, smoke, grime, and the voices of foreign immigrants, was somehow vulgar, cheap, and lacking in refinement. They saw our plantations spreading across the land as decadent, effeminate, and prisons debauching families of blacks and whites alike.

These twains would never meet. As the years went on, the North went further and further its own way, while we pursued our life beneath magnolias, Spanish moss, whispering pines, and live oaks. We saw our lives as gentle, as built around the family, and in harmony with the earth. We saw their lives in the North as the relentless pursuit of money, trade, and power, and lacking in all harmony. We built few, if any, factories, for we did not want to despoil our land and our harmony with nature.

Besides they, the North, could provide what we needed in exchange for our cotton, our tobacco, and our rice. Could we not live in peace, yet still go our separate ways? Would not our Constitution protect us and our way of life? Would not the hand of God preserve us?

So I thought I would try to think through this War for you Vicee. I thought that I might put all of what I have seen, heard, and experienced together in one long letter to you. Yes, I know that this is just words flowing through my mind and that this might never really get written down, but at least once I would have tried. I know not whatever else that I can do, but at least I can try to get this in some semblance of order, in chronology, for you, such that maybe then you might understand. If it never gets written, then at least I will have gotten it all straight in my mind why I did this and why I left you. For in my heart, here and now, if I had it all to do over again, I doubt that I would have bowed to the pressure of friends and family, and gone away. I should have stayed with you. I should have never left you. For I am afraid that all that I have done, I have done for naught.

We were at Ft. Moultrie. None of us could forget that we stood upon the very site where the mightiest navy in the world had been defeated by a few rebels behind a ragtag fort of palmetto palm logs that seemed magically to repel the finest iron cannon balls ever cast. Our freedom as a State, our identity as South Carolinians, our spirit of never bending to the knee of an oppressive tyrant had been tested and found strong in that crucible. Now, we stood here again. Would we as men be able to stand as tall as our forefathers? Many of us had grandfathers or great-grandfathers, who had fought in the War of Independence. In some cases, those ancestors still 'lived' with us, for some of us carried a knife or a sword which that revered ancestor had carried. Would our cowardice betray their legacy? We had no choice but to stand tall and do our duty. The whole world, we were told, was watching us. Our fellow States in our new nation were watching us to see if we would and could stand up to the tyranny of those who had of late been our own nation.

Even the youngest boys among us could recite, chapter and verse, the depredations that had been inflicted upon us by our supposed brothers in the North. First, there had been the protective Tariffs. In the summer of 1826, South Carolina was aflame about the amount of the tariffs, which the North had put in place to protect the fledging industries of the North. The General Assembly did little to cool the fevered brow, issuing a mildly worded resolution merely urging that "the State Legislatures be watchful, and to remonstrate with Congress when necessary." That remonstration became necessary, when the next spring, Congress passed what was called the Tariffs of Abomination of 1827, which taxed goods coming into our nation, which the South needed, at 50%, compelling us to buy Northern goods, which were inflated in price to be just below the cost of foreign goods when the tariff was added. Fiery Robert Barnwell Rhett demanded action: succession if need be!

Then there had been John C. Calhoun's plaintive action. While he was serving as Vice President, he drafted a sixty page report with a well-reasoned argument against protective tariffs. He branded Protectionism as being "a breach of a well-defined trust" creating a system which was "grossly unequal." He declared that it was up to the Sovereign States "to determine, authoritatively, whether the acts of which we complain be unconstitutional; and, if so, whether they commit a violation so deliberate, palpable, and dangerous, as to justify the interposition of the State to protect its rights."

Calhoun went to the South Carolina General Assembly which, after study, accepted Calhoun's report with only minor changes made. Wade Hampton II voted in favor of the Assembly's Report. The General Assembly begged other states to join South Carolina in her fight against the tariffs. Calhoun approved of the Assembly's half-hearted action but urged further steps. In particular, he urged that South Carolina suspend enforcement of the collection of the tariffs within her borders, with the hope that this act would bring about the change we wanted: the repeal of the tariffs. Calhoun called this "nullification."

The crisis continued to fester. Finally, South Carolina stopped talking, negotiating, pleading, and begging: she acted. On November 24, 1832, the General Assembly heard the clamor of the people and voted to nullify the tariffs. With this, the crisis continued to boil, but was not yet threatening to spill over.

John C. Calhoun resigned as Vice President as a further step of defiance. The South Carolina General Assembly made him South Carolina's Senator. So Calhoun stayed in Washington. That is, until Henry Clay suggested the Compromise Tariff, which passed Congress and seemed to mollify South Carolina.

With this second great compromise, brokered by Henry Clay, John C. Calhoun, and Daniel Webster, the tone of the next almost thirty years was set. Provocative action by the North had to be met by near force by the South resulting in a compromise. The only problem was that with each compromise, both sides felt that they had given up more than they should and vowed to give up less the next time.

CHAPTER 3:

A DAY AT THE RACES

When I bestride him, I soar, I am a hawk:
He trots the air; the earth sings when he touches it;
the basest horn of his hoof is more musical than the pipe of Hermes.
*-**William Shakespeare**, Henry V, Act 3, Scene 7*

April 1, 1865 7:30 am

Vicee, you might ask me when did my War begin.

In my mind, I think it all began that day in the fall of 1860, when I went to the horse races. If I had never met him, maybe I would have never fallen under the spell of God and Country. Maybe I would have never signed up to leave you, my Vicee.

I was looking forward to the races. I had thought about nothing else. I loved horses and had stayed with my father and made carriages, because of my deep love of the creatures! But it was at the races that I could watch them at their finest.

The crowds at the start line of the races milled with activity. Voices were raised in proud salute to the event. Men came from miles around to race, to bet, to drink, to brag about their horses and their riders, and to preen in their best clothes, finer than Sunday. Their conversations encompassed words such as "Pass me the flask, but don't let my wife see,' or 'I've got five gold dollars on the bay, who'll take it?' and 'Johnnie MacDonald is the finest rider in five counties!' While the women, clustered yards away from the horses for safety of their dresses, whispered words of fashion. 'Paris' here, 'London' there; 'silk' and 'crinoline'; 'latest' and 'best'; followed by words of desire: 'want', 'love', 'must have', and 'must buy.' With these words, came the questions: 'Where did you get that?' Some were impudent: 'How much did that cost?' The questions were often accompanied by whispered comments behind gloved hands shielding the words spoken from the one about whom they were spoken: 'How could she ever wear that?'

So two beehives of activity were created, and, like two distant galaxies were composed of stars, dancing side by side, but never really interacting, these beehives were separated by gender, interests, and distance. The two galaxies spun around their respective axes of gravity, but then again these two had a third center which rotated around the races.

So little did these galaxy worlds have in common, but still they shared the essential necessity of sexual desire and mutual need against the harshness of a world that could steal a soul with a fever, or claim a woman in childbirth, or a man in a duel, seemingly faster than the race could be run.

The afternoon sun beat hot and heavy upon the crowds, while the horses snorted and tossed their heads. Some of the horses pawed their hooves against the ground fighting to race and race now. The smell of perfume started to fail to mask the odor of horse and sweat.

The men patted the necks of their chosen horses. Inspecting fetlocks and lifting lips to look at teeth, the men extolled upon the virtues of one champion over another. Some horses had larger shoulders than others, or had grace of line, or lightness of step, or beauty in the toss of a head, or some other attribute that caught the bettor's eye and was proof of racing superiority, causing money to be bet in ever larger amounts.

I bet on the bay, because he was a beautiful horse that looked strong and powerful. I waited for the races to commence with visions of winnings dancing through my mind. I thought that I would buy you a ring, Vicee, and ask you to marry me, revealing my true love for you.

It was then that I saw him for the first time, the richest man in South Carolina, Wade Hampton III. He was truly a magnificent man. All knew of his family. His namesake had fought honorably in the Revolution. Like many men after the fall of Charleston in 1780, he had signed an oath of allegiance to the Crown. He was a merchant and had wealth. But with British General Clinton's proclamation that all men had to fight for the Crown coupled with Clinton's repudiation of the paroles he had just granted, the first Wade Hampton had taken up arms against the Crown and had fought alongside other patriots. No less than General Nathanael Greene had called him a "Valuable and Intelligent Officer". At Eutaw Springs, at the height of the Battle, he had taken over command from the fallen Colonel William Henderson. He rallied the men when their hearts were flagging and were ready to run, and he had won the Battle. After the War, he had prospered so much that, when he died, his estate was the astronomical sum of One and One-Half Million Dollars! Now, before me stood his grandson, State Senator, planter, and moderate voice in the heat of the debates on the question of Secession. I shall never forget that first glance at the man who would become so important in my life. I never suspected that in just a few short months, we would be at War and he would be my commanding officer. I remember how gracefully he navigated the crowds. He seemed to know every man and woman, calling them by name and seeming to remember details of their lives, their likes and dislikes, and always a smile upon his face. It was just a few moments, but I felt that the sun had shone upon me.

I am sorry to say that the bay lost and so I did not win the money to buy you your ring. But that day, the sunlight, the horses, the activity of the crowds, and the smile of that man are forever etched upon my memory.

CHAPTER 4:
THOSE HEADY EARLY DAYS

"Let me tell you what is coming. You may alter the sacrifices of countless millions of treasures and hundreds of thousands of precious lives, win Southern independence, but I doubt it. The North is determined to preserve this Union. They are not a fiery impulsive people as you are, for they live in colder climes. But when they begin to move in a given direction, they will move with the steady momentum and perseverance of a mighty avalanche."
- **Governor Sam Houston**, *1861, just a few days after the Texas Ordinance of Secession was passed.*

April 1, 1865 8:30 am

Father had asked me to take the newly finished landau to Columbia for delivery to its new owner. Until then, I had labored upon the landau, unaware of who had commissioned it. I had sanded, smoothed, painted, and then added a second coat of paint to my father's exacting specifications.

"Paint with the grain! Smooth and easy," my father said, as he glided the paint brush across the wood. "Fill your brush, but then pull it down along side of the paint can to get a proper finish on the wood. Not too much. Not too little." He made sure that I knew exactly what he wanted.

He told me time and time again that I had been listed as a painter and not an apprentice on the 1860 Census. "You are becoming a man. I should accord you proper respect."

I was pleased that he had honored me in this manner, but I still felt that, in many ways, he treated me as a child. Here, now with this task to drive the new landau to Columbia and turned it over to its new owner, he was giving me real responsibility.

I was thrilled to be going to Columbia. In the last several weeks, big doings had been going on at the Capital. The Legislature was debating Secession. The Minute Men had been doing everything they could to bring about the dissolution of the Union. There were parades, speeches, demonstrations, and even nightly, fireworks were being shot off. I had heard that the atmosphere was like a carnival, feast, and an annual Church picnic rolled into one, but many, many times over. I would be going to the Capital, doing a man's work, where there were men, real men, debating the future of our State. It was truly heady stuff.

I hitched a team to the landau, waved good bye to my mama, Caroline. I heeded my father's last minute words of warning and encouragement, jumped on the seat, and was just about to crack the whip, when my father delivered his final instructions, "You are to meet John Preston. Give the landau to him and no one else. Deliver my bill and await his response to it." He waved to me and I was off.

The landau was pulling away from our house, when I thought to check to see if my bag was there. I had brought things for a couple of days' journey. I clicked my teeth and the horses responded with a little more speed. Columbia was about 70 miles from Darlington. I intended to stay away for about a week and then ride the team of horses back home. Little did I know that I would be gone for longer than that - far longer.

The ride to Columbia went well. The horses easily pulled the new landau which seemed to glide so nicely over the road. I took great pride in my father's work. Someday, I imagined, the sign over our shop would read in big, bold letters, writ in scroll work, *"Daniel McEachern and Sons, Inc. - Carriage Makers"*

*****

I had read in the newspapers that the local elite in Columbia, as well as other towns and cities had formed local militias. Of course, the elites somehow usually came to serve as the officers. These militias were men's clubs that were in reality nothing more than social gatherings and they certainly were not true military establishments. Darlington was a little town, barely on the map. We had lost our chance for glory, when we were not chosen as the state Capital. But we were a proud town.

I knew that Darlington had been settled by Scots, Scots-Irish, and Welsh in the 1750's. My great-grandfather, Daniel, had fought in the Revolution, like so many others. He had fought in the battles of Kings Mountain and Cowpens at the side of the great Daniel Morgan. Later, he had gone north with Nathanael Greene and finally helped to corner the English at Yorktown. After the war, he had settled near Jeffries Creek and farmed. My father was the first to forego farming and try his hand at something else. He had become a master craftsman of carriages and had risen to the lofty height of being one of the best carriage makers in the State. The fact that we got commissions from the rich men who lived in or near the Capital was proof enough of his fame and his reputation.

I grew up in an ideal world or so it seemed to childish eyes. Darlington was a lovely town. Like Stateburg, it prided itself (or more likely deluded itself) on the fact that but for a few more votes, it would have been the Capital of South Carolina. But it was the Granby's Ferry on the Congaree River that won the election, when it was decided to move the Capital from Charleston to a place more inland and centrally located. Then Granby's Ferry renamed itself with the loftier sounding appellation of Columbia.

At that time, the area was still being cut out of the wilderness by axe and steel. The great trees were felled and the first settlors built the first homes. My great-grandfather, James McEachern, who had fled Scotland in 1750, was one of the first to go there. He was joined by others who walked the Great Wagon Road from Pennsylvania through Virginia and North Carolina and finally settled by the Congaree River. For the longest time, it was called the High Hills of Santee. There, James McEachern joined Thomas Sumter, who had become famous in the Revolution.

We were a land of verdant pastures and farmland, but still the grandest of boulders, some truly monumental, would be planted smack in the middle of a field. The summer nights burst forth in an abundance of lightning bugs, who in their lime-yellow flashing, danced throughout the night, darting and dashing hither and fro. Sometimes the summer nights were broken with the crash of thunder sounding like a rumbling cannonade that shook the house and made the china rattle. It might be followed by rushing wind that threatened to strip the house of its gambrels or by torrents of rain that might flood the floors.

It was from this land that our ancestors sprang. They were men; almost it seemed, from the moment of their birth. They were larger than life. They were men like Daniel Morgan, Daniel Boone, and Captain Anthony Hampton. Captain Anthony Hampton, who fought in the French and Indian War, led his family to South Carolina just before the Revolution.

Anthony Hampton was a pioneer near Ninety Six, South Carolina, his land abutting the Cherokee Nation. The name Ninety Six is one that is shrouded in mystery. Some said it was because it was Ninety Six miles from the nearest Cherokee settlement, which it wasn't. Some said that it was Welsh for dry gulch, which again it wasn't.

Still, the jagged peaks of the hazy Blue Ridge Mountains lay to the west. The Carolina Upcountry was land which seemed to come out of the mists of time. During the 1770's, it had just begun to hum with the swing of axes, the thud of the fall of trees, the sway of fast notes threading full and fine from a fiddle in a country reel, and the cry of new born babes. In the dark forests, the roaring sounds of big cats shattered the night. The land was rugged and wild, with giant boulders peering out of the hillsides surrounded by clay so red you would have sworn it had been burnt by giant fires. These same hillsides brought treachery in the fall, when the rains fell for days, and the mud became man's worst enemy, ready to suck boots off feet, leaving trouser legs reddened, and splattered with clay-muck that clung tighter than octopus tentacles clutching prey. The blustery winters were brutal with knee deep snow. But the summers were graced with magic, as sparks of lime-colored light danced in the night, spun and swirled, floated and darted, hither and fro, with nary a sound, as the lightning bugs made their way to find their life's true soul and love and create a new generation. But lightning bugs oftentimes were precursors to true lightning that swelled in great arcs from the billowing, folding, and enlarging anvils that sailed upon the soaring drafts like the sea crows floating aloft on drafts of heated air which were winging their way up to the heavens in spirals, gyres, and circles. Upon the horizons, the lightning loomed at first, their white zigzags spiking earthwards without a sound. Then, in time, the distant rumbles began. The wind picked up and the smell of ozone permeated the wind wet with aqueous vapor. Then, with a sudden rush, the storm crashes upon one.

But now, we were caught up in the fervor of a different kind of storm. When it was announced, in late 1860, that Darlington would have its own militia, we boys joined. I had joined the Claremont Rifles out of my home town of Darlington. I had been too late to enlist with the Darlington Guards. The local boys joined the militia, got uniforms, and we drilled each Saturday afternoon for about an hour. Most of us joined because there was so much patriotic music playing, the uniforms looked great making us look manly, and all the girls were urging us to do so. Each girl seemed to say while she batted her eyes, "Protect us you strong, big, boy! I love how you look in uniform!" What were we going to do? Refuse the chance to impress the girls? Be shown up by every other boy? Look a fool before all the leaders of the town? We were pulled along like the seaweed, and tossed like flotsam and jetsam in the waves of the tide, which pulsated along the shore back and forth under the mysterious push-pull force of the silvery moon.

Little did we know that much more was going on around our State. Forces, of which we boys were totally unaware, were fomenting rebellion. Deals were being made. Men who might be able to provide things that armies might need were finding ways of providing those things at the cheapest possible cost and the greatest possible profit. Great political groups were forming. Undercurrents of politics were swirling and whirling. Men's lives were being caught up in the eddies, vortices, and gyres of these undercurrents.

During the fall of 1860, two groups began to agitate for South Carolina's Succession from the United States. The first was the 1860 Association. The 1860 Association held meetings, beginning in September of 1860, in anticipation of the election of Lincoln as President. They roared to much greater life on November 19, 1860, when it was clear that Lincoln was to be President. That night their meeting in Charleston was the talk on everybody's tongue. Although prominent names joined and led the organization, they saw their duty solely as being education through the use of pamphlets. Soon, too soon, many saw them as just another useless men's political club.

"Ain't no use in another d'bating society!" cried nameless voices in the streets of Charleston.

"We need action!" answered just as many other nameless voices.

"Action now! South Carolina must secede!" Both sets of nameless voices cried out loud together.

While Charleston may have started the movement, it gained its force and character in Columbia. There the other group vying for men's attention gained prominence. This other group was known as the Minute Men. They felt that demonstrating for Secession was their route. They took action in the streets. People saw them taking action and their numbers swelled.

Minute Men groups formed throughout the state in such cities as Greenville, Columbia, Charleston, Laurens, Newberry, Camden, and Limestone. The men joining the Minute Men had to swear a signed oath of allegiance to the group's Constitution, pledging "our LIVES, our FORTUNES, and our sacred HONOR, to sustain Southern Constitutional equality in the Union, or, failing that, to establish our independence out of it." The Minute Men, as in the early days of the American Revolution, began drilling.

Members had to procure an approved firearm. Wearing their uniforms, they engaged in their favorite activity of torchlight parades and other agitation.

Nightly, as the Legislature was meeting in session in Columbia, they held demonstrations carrying signs such as "South Carolina is Expected to Lead" or "Prepare for the Issue!" Over the course of November and December 1860, the mood of our people swung more and more in favor of secession.

Then one night, States Rights Gist, the brother of the Governor of South Carolina, returned to Columbia from his self-proclaimed diplomatic mission to the other southern states. "I have assurances from the other southern states that, if South Carolina leads, they will follow. If Carolina follows secession, then secession will follow elsewhere!" Gist cried from the podium, knowing his words were kerosene thrown on the fire.

It was that night that Wade Hampton and his brother-in-law, John S. Preston, attended the meeting of the Columbia Minute Men. With great solemnity, Preston and Hampton signed the Constitution and became members. The Militia which Hampton commanded, the Richmond Light Dragoons, voted unanimously to offer their services to Governor Gist.

It was then, that very same night, that I met that magnificent man I had seen some while ago at the races. Well, actually, I bumped into him. I had just tied up the landau outside of the hotel. I was entering to register and to secure stable space for my team of horses and the landau. I was going in the hotel, and he was coming out. I wasn't looking where I was going, and I don't think he was either. He was six feet tall - so a little taller than I. What was most striking was his posture. It was so straight and so perfect, that he appeared to be regal. His eyes were so benign and pacific that I immediately felt at ease. I instantly recognized him for he was literally the man of the hour, the man for all Columbia, if not South Carolina. People were awaiting his return from his plantations in Mississippi. He was unassuming and incredibly polite and soft spoken.

"You are Wade Hampton, aren't you?" This is not perhaps the most intelligent question I could have asked.

"Yes, I am." He doffed his hat to me. "What can I do for you, young man?"

"I am here to meet your brother-in-law, Mr. Preston. I am to deliver to him his new landau." I halted for I knew not what else to say. I pointed towards the landau. The gaslight reflected so brightly off the polished wood.

"You are, are you? Mr. Preston is my brother-in-law. I can accept delivery for him."

I bowed low. "No, sir. My father said not to deliver the landau to anyone but Mr. Preston. It is right there," again I was saying was not the most intelligent thing that I could say.

"I like a man who follows orders. However, you are wrong, sir."

"Wrong, sir? How am I wrong, sir?" I was perplexed. I would follow my father's orders, no matter what the 'man of the hour' said.

"Yes, wrong, sir! Mr. Preston was acting as my agent in buying the landau. I was in Mississippi and I asked him to act for me. So you can deliver the landau to me. It is a present for my wife." He stared at me. Then, he grasped his chin with his left hand. "Perhaps, I should know if Mr. Preston paid you? You deserve payment for your work."

"No, sir, he has not. But my father says that Mr. Preston can pay our bill either now or as he pleases."

"Then I shall pay you, now." He pulled something from his inner jacket pocket. "Well, I would think your father would much prefer to be paid now. I presume you have a bill." His eyes lighted up and seemed to smile at me. "How much does my brother-in-law owe you?" He laughed as he said this.

It struck me as odd, very odd, as very gallantly odd, that he was concerned whether I had been paid. This man cared for me.

"Yes, sir. Here's the bill." The bill was all crumpled from being in my pocket. "I am sorry that bill is in such sad shape." I unfolded the bill and smoothed it before handing it to him.

Mr. Hampton scrutinized the bill and then started to write. "Here. This is a draft on my bank. You just present it to them tomorrow morning, and they will pay you the full amount in gold or currency, as you desire. I must say, your bill is quite reasonable for the landau is extraordinarily beautiful." He rubbed his hand along the polished wood. "It is an exquisite masterpiece."

He handed over the draft, and then he said, "I would like your father to make a new Victoria Carriage for my family. If you will undertake the commission." He looked directly into my eyes, while he handed over the draft. I felt as if he were looking right into my soul and measuring whether I was worthy. After a few moments, I felt that I had passed the test and I felt so close to him, even though we had just met. He commanded my respect instantaneously.

"Thank you, sir." I took the draft. "You are quite kind. I am sure my father would be honored to construct the Victoria carriage for you." I started backing away and as I did so, I kept bowing and bowing. I did not know how else to pay homage and respect to this incredible man.

*****

On December 17, 1860, the Secession Convention met at the Baptist Church in Columbia. The day was raw and wild, because a hard rain was blown by a strong northerly wind. The delegates, some 169 strong, filed into the Church, which was built in the Greek revival style. However, it was odd that the four Doric columns holding the white entablature were made of red brick. The spirits of the delegates were bright and cheery, contrasting deeply with the dankness and darkness of the day.

When it came to a vote, the delegates had but one voice: South Carolina would secede. However, there was a smallpox epidemic rampant in Columbia at the time, so the Convention adjourned to Charleston to write the Ordinance of Secession, which was enacted on December 20, 1860 in St. Andrew's Hall. I wasn't there, but a more fitting name and a more fitting Saint could not have been chosen to lead the people of South Carolina to throw off the shackles of tyranny and oppression represented by the United States. St. Andrew, the first called, whose name means brave, was crucified on a cross that resembled an 'x' at his own request, because he did deem himself worthy to be crucified on the same type of cross upon which Our Savior had been crucified. We could take a great deal of learning and spiritual refreshment from St. Andrew, the patron saint of Scotland.

When the Conventioneers came out of St. Andrew's Hall with their Ordinance completed, Wade Hampton waved the newly - enacted law high above his head. The crowd clapped and cheered as he did so. The bells of nearby St. Michael's Church pealed, spreading the news of secession. Flags bearing the Palmetto Palm were unfurled, and their fluttering filled the sky with billows of cloth. Gadsden Flags, with their bright yellow fields and coiled rattlesnakes, ready to strike, sprouted from the crowd like so many stalks of corn growing in the summer sun. This alone should have brought fear to the hearts of South Carolina's foes: "Don't Tread On Me!" As cannons from The Citadel roared, Hampton yelled, "The Union is Dissolved!" While the crowd was still gathered in front of St. Andrew's Hall and St. Michael's Church, boys began to sell an extra edition of the Charleston Mercury, the headline of which proclaimed: "Passed Unanimously at 1.15 o'clock P.M. December 20, 1860, An Ordinance" in small font, but in a font twenty times or greater in size: "Union is Dissolved!"

*****

Later, making his way home in the new landau, Wade Hampton felt that the world was somehow very different from what it has been just a scant few hours before. The streets of Columbia were filled with cheering men and women. Flags were waving everywhere. Men had put a blue cockade in their hats to symbolize resistance. As I said, it was as if the State Fair, Carnival, and the great summer Sunday picnic had erupted throughout the Capital. But where most people saw a joyous party, Wade Hampton saw the start of something far more serious and deadly.

*****

Meanwhile at High Hampton, Sally Baxter Hampton was writing a letter to her parents who lived in New York "I am no Southerner heaven knows, & at heart if not abolition at least anti-slavery but I must concede that the tone of the South has been most firm–calm-manly & decided. It is with great sadness that within days, this great nation will cease to have existence. Yet with all this, is mingled, a calm-self-determination & heroic bravery one cannot but admire."

*****

In Ohio, one old college roommate was visiting his friend seeking the answer to a question that perplexed him. The friend was a prosperous railroad executive. In fact, he was the President of the Ohio and

Mississippi Railroad. Their friendship had withstood the greatest a blow a male friendship can: the railroad President had not only wooed the same woman as his friend, but also had won her.

The old college roommate entered the office of the railroad President. "Good morning, Mac. Thank you for seeing me."

Gesturing towards a large leather winged back easy chair, the President offered his friend a cigar. "I think you will like these. I get them direct from Virginia."

The college roommate, elegant in his full dress military uniform, sat down carefully, swinging his sword out of the way as he sat. Nervously, he repeated what he had said before. "George, thank you for seeing me." He took a puff on his cigar. It was clear that he did not know where to begin.

"Captain Hill…Ambrose, we have been friends since West Point. What can I do for you? You said you had an urgent question for me. What is it?" George McClellan sat back in his office chair. His desk was filled with papers, but all was neatly arranged, with piles marked by little labels titling the contents of each pile, as well as the importance thereof. The President was meticulous and organized.

"Well, Mac, I wanted your opinion on something. But where are my manners? How is your wife? Your wedding in New York was simply spectacular. It was without a doubt the social event of the season." Captain A. P. Hill puffed on his cigar. "This **is** a mighty fine cigar."

"Thank you. I was glad you could come and serve as one of my groomsmen. Thank you for making the trip. I know coming from Washington, D.C. is a trip. Thank you. It was a pleasure to see you then, and it is pleasure to see you again." President McClellan puffed on his cigar. "I am sure that Mrs. McClellan will appreciate your regards."

Hill started to ask his question, but then said, "I am sorry that you were unable to attend my wedding, in Lexington a year ago July. I am sure that you would like Dolly very much. Her brother, John Hunt Morgan, served as my best man."

George leaned forward. "Ambrose, I feel as if I know your Dolly. You wrote to me so often about her and your love for her, I feel that I do know her. I wish you only marital bliss. You deserve it, my friend."

The room was now enveloped in silence while Captain A. P. Hill mused about the best way to put his question.

There was a knock at door to the office, which then opened and a clerk entered. "Sorry to interrupt you, sir, but I have a letter from your lawyer, I mean the president-elect now, Mr. Lincoln about that lawsuit…" It was then the clerk saw Captain Hill. "I am sorry sir; I will wait until you are ready for me." He bowed and backed out of the room.

Hill now saw his opening. "Actually, it is about President Lincoln that I have come." He eased back into his chair and let it envelope him for a moment. "I am thinking of resigning my commission," Hill began, taking another puff on his cigar. "I cannot fight against my native state of Virginia."

After a few moments, during which the mantle clock above the fireplace chimed, McClellan responded, "Hill, I am truly sorry that you are going to leave us; but to be frank I cannot blame you. If I were in your place, I would do as you are about to do, but I am an Ohioan and will stand by my state, too."

McClellan got up, extended his hand and the two men shook hands. Then McClellan came around his desk and embraced his old friend. "I am not sure that we will see each other again in this life. We are divided by events that are larger than either of us. May you go with God."

"My friend, may you, too, go with God."

Ambrose P. Hill turned and left the room. He did not look back. But both men had a tear in their eyes as they parted.

BOOK II: THE PLAY WAR– 1861

CHAPTER 5:

"NO STRONGER THAN A HORSEHAIR"

The works "...would have been impregnable if defended by any adequate force, but ...in fact were occupied by a mere skirmish line."
*- A **North Carolina Soldier**, commenting on the strength of the Petersburg Defensive Lines*

April 1, 1865 10:00 AM

I saw him, Vicee, from afar. I wondered about General Hill being ill, and I could imagine his thoughts as he stood there, still, inspecting his battle his lines, taking it all in, or was he?

Ambrose P. Hill sat upon his horse. He cut a graceful seat upon a horse. Everyone had always told him this ever since he had been a small child. He had one of the best seats in all of Virginia. And while that may have once been true, was it now? While he wanted to cut an exquisite military figure, erect, boldly looking out into the teeth of the enemy lines just over a mile away, he knew in his heart that this was not the truth. In actuality, he felt quite ill. He had been wracked by fever, chills, nausea, and vomiting. This had left him quite frail. How many times would he suffer this? It seemed to be hitting him harder each time it came, and it came more and more frequently. He hadn't been this ill since Gettysburg, where he could not even sit upon his horse.

'Well, at least I am a little better this time,' he thought as he patted his horse's neck.

He felt the mental confusion that came with 'the illness', as he styled it. He did not want to show it to anyone, but he knew in his heart that Sergeant George Tucker knew what he was going through. Tucker knew that the General had suffered with typhoid fever, yellow fever, and malaria in Mexico, and that one of them, or all of them seemed to come back time and time and time again. But Tucker did not know about the Mercer Street illness. In fact, no one did. George Tucker, the faithful courier, who seemed always to be at A. P. Hill's side, was always ready to ride off with some message for some officer under Hill's command. Hill rode usually with one or two couriers and maybe an officer of his staff. Today, he was only with Tucker.

Hill had thought of asking General Lee to relieve him. He felt bad about asking for this relief, because he had just gotten back from a furlough due to illness. He had asked Lee for that just yesterday, but Lee had said, "No, I need you, Powell. We all need to make sacrifices now. It is our Duty to stand by now and help the men get through whatever Providence has in store for us." It was some consolation that Lee, unlike just about everyone else, did not call him 'Little Powell'.

So now, Ambrose Powell Hill felt much, much older than his thirty nine years. The isolation of command, the burden of his disease, the coming demise of his beloved Confederacy, all this and more weighed him down. He coughed and pulled his long coat around himself tighter. "Can it be that I have just returned from a sick leave?" he asked of no one. He stared and the morning's cold and dampness surrounded him more. He hardly noticed that Tucker rode with him, because he was so debilitated. He did notice, however, the sound of the firing, which was coming from the direction of Five Forks. His steel grey-dappled horse also noted the rising artillery and shied away from riding in the direction of the noise. The General patted the neck of his horse again to calm him down.

He scanned the lines of trenches, which his men manned as it stretched for about eight miles. 'Too few men, too long lines,' he thought. He rode from east to west and everywhere it was the same. First, there was Thomas' Georgia Brigade, then there was Lane's North Carolinians, next was McComb's, followed by Joseph R. Davis' and, finally, Cooke's North Carolinians. There were some 8,300 men, but only some 1,000 or so a mile, which meant that Hill had only one rifle every two yards or so. "This is but a skirmish line, where in the past, men stood shoulder to shoulder." He muttered. He could see the men were whispering to themselves about what the sounds of firing from the Five Forks direction meant. He wondered, too.

He didn't know how it had happened, but it just did. His mind wandered. In his confusion, he saw the long lines of his men as they surged forward toward Beaver Dam. It was 1862 again. He admired the men of his division, the largest division in the newly minted Army of Northern Virginia. He had named it the Light Division, even though it was so large - the largest in the Army of Northern Virginia, because he wanted to convey the thought that his men would move quickly, almost at a breakneck speed. It was June 26, 1862 again. Lee was leading the newly styled Army of Northern Virginia for the first time. Hill felt that all was enthusiasm and confidence. Although Stonewall Jackson from the Valley had not yet arrived, it would be any minute when he and his battle-hardened veterans would come storming down on the left of where Hill was urging his men on. Hill rode along the front of his lines and his men saw him out ahead of them leading them into battle. They could not miss him, for he wore his red flannel battle shirt. He relished every moment of battle. The Union flank would be attacked by the relentless Jackson and it would break. Hill just had to push his men on and keep Porter occupied until Jackson's stealth force surprised the Yankees.

Hill knew the plan. When he heard Jackson's cannon fire shortly after dawn, his Light Division was to advance to Meadow Bridge, clear the Union forces, which were thought to be only pickets, and then attack the Beaver Dam Creek. Though Jackson's guns hadn't fired, Hill had become anxious as the day wore one. The morning became afternoon, and now it was late afternoon. Wouldn't Lee's plan misfire unless he went now?

'But Jackson didn't come,' Hill shook himself awake, 'and the Union forces were not flanked, and my men went into battle as a frontal attack.' He whacked his hat against his right arm to shake off the wet. 'Porter still retreated, so it all worked out.' Hill could not, even today, shake the conviction that Lee was not wholly pleased with his performance that beautiful June day, but still Lee hadn't ordered him to go ahead? Lee had always said he was proud of what Hill had accomplished, but Hill still could not shake the lingering doubt.

Now, Jackson would never come again. So many others would not come again. "Gotta shake this sense of foreboding," he admonished himself.

"What's that, General?" asked George Tucker, the faithful courier, who seemed always to be at A. P. Hill's side.

"Nothing." Hill enjoyed Tucker's company, but that didn't mean that he had to answer every one of Tucker's questions. Tucker knew when not to ask a question again. This was one of those times, and Tucker knew it.

Tucker was a man who understood the value of silence. He, too, had had his share of both glory and hardship in this war. First, he had been arrested by the Yankees in May of 1861 as a spy. Finally, when he was released in late summer of 1862, he immediately joined the 12th Virginia Cavalry, Co. F. He had joined just in time to fight at Sharpsburg in his beloved native state of Maryland. Hill had rushed his division to Sharpsburg just in time to hit Union General Ambrose Burnside's corps in the flank and save the day for Lee's army. Hill had seen Tucker in action that day and thought that he was both "active and fearless". From then on, Tucker was Hill's courier, later rising to be the head of Hill's couriers. But before that happened, Tucker was captured at Chancellorsville, as he guarded the two wounded Generals,

Hill and Jackson. Sent to Capital Prison, he managed to obtain release within a week and was able to rejoin Hill in time for Gettysburg. He was wounded in the thigh at the Wilderness in 1864 and was nearly captured for a third time. He recovered in Chimborazo Hospital in Richmond. Like his beloved General Hill, he received a medical furlough on June 10, 1864 and had recently come back to the army.

The firing from Five Forks way was growing. "What the hell could that mean?" A. P. Hill said to no one in particular.

Hill wanted to know if what he was feeling was the same general feeling of his men standing in the cold mud of the trenches. He bent down over his horse (a move he instantly regretted because of how queasy it made him feel) and asked one of Lane's men, "How are you today?"

He looked down at a private standing in the goo of the trench. The private instantly recognized the General, even though the General was not wearing his uniform, just an old overcoat with some colonel's stars on it. Yet, everyone recognized him. His diminutive stature of only five foot, nine inches, his slight physique, for he weighed only 140 pounds, his gaunt sunken cheeks, and his flaming, curly red beard, and, of course, his red flannel battle shirt marked and identified him to anyone and everyone.

"Well, General, I think I speak for all the men that there's a feeling of unrest and unease, not only among us men, but even in the animals. We haven't been able to sleep the last couple of days, for we feel the Yankees over there as if they're acoming any moment. The rain has been miserable. I ain't got no recollection of having spent a more thoroughly disagreeable day."

The General sat slouched on his horse. He was now so sick to his stomach that he wanted to throw up and cancel the rest of his ride, but he knew he must go on. He had to inspire his men to the extent that he could. He had to let his men know that their commander was enduring the same hellish conditions that they were. So, he continued on his extensive and exhaustive inspection. "What better way is there to spend an April's Fools Day?" He laughed as he turned to Tucker to see his reaction.

"No better way, General, no better way." Tucker laughed too.

CHAPTER 6:

A TALE OF A FLAG: THE GHOST OF GLENFINNAN

Tandem Triumphans! (Triumphant at Last!)
-Bonnie Prince Charles' Banner of Glenfinnan

April 1, 1865 10:30 AM

With all the hoopla that went on around the State of South Carolina in the month following our Declaration of independence, the day that the Claremont Rifles became an official militia unit stands out in my mind.

It seemed as if all of Stateburg was there to cheer us on. Certainly all the ladies, but one, were there. They had made us a flag. We knew nothing of the details of the flag for the ladies had worked upon it in complete secrecy.

Captain Spann had us come to attention as a formation. "Men, today, you stand before me as the defenders of your town, your state, and your homes!" We cheered wildly.

"You cannot go into battle without a banner to lead you, a banner which will remind you of your homes, your womenfolk, and your sacred duty to defend them!" Again, we cheered wildly. Captain Spann turned to the assembled crowd, and raised his drawn sword squarely to his face.

"This day, such a banner is to be presented to you by the women of Stateburg!" As he said this, Captain Spann wheeled to the assembled crowd, and thrust his sword high up into the air. The assembled crowd and all the men broke out in wild cheering and threw their hats into the air.

"Men, I give you Dr. Nelson Burgess, who shall do the honors!" The stately and portly old gentleman, who stood now before us, had cradled in his hands a white silk flag about three feet by three feet, with a golden metallic fringe encompassing the flag's perimeter."

I was standing in the ranks between Robert MacDonald and his twin brother, Douglas MacDonald. These two men had been my childhood friends, and our close friendship had endured to this day. Robbie MacDonald leaned over, and whispered to me, "Dr. Nelson Burgess is a relative of Dr. Warren Burgess, Sr., who owns Enfield Planation." Enfield, as everyone called it, was a planation of about 500 hundred acres and about 80 slaves. Like so many plantations hereabouts, its main crop was cotton.

Then Dr. Burgess gave a speech about defending the womenfolk of our town whose hands had sewn this flag such that we, "the brave boys of Stateburg", could "carry it high above our heads with honor as we fought for Glory, South Carolina, and our Mothers, Sisters, and Wives!" His speech, as did many of the time, droned on, and made up for its lack of originality with length. So we stood there in the sun in our wool uniforms with all of or gear, which must have weighed 40 or more pounds, on a Saturday for what seemed like hours. The day was spring-like so we all sweated as we stood in the ranks. The fervent wish of all the men, and me especially, was to be done with the ceremony, and to have some of the cool lemonade that sat on the tables next to the cakes and pies.

Then Dr. Burgess started to talk about slavery, and why it was essential to the economy of the South, and, thus, worthy of our blood and treasure.

It was then that a lot of us stirred in the ranks. Now, many of us in the Claremont Rifles were from families that did not own slaves, and had never owned slaves. My family was one of them. I had actually little contact with blacks, whether free or slave. When people said we were fighting for slavery, the men of the Claremont Rifles would correct them. "We are not fighting for slaves or slavery, we are fighting against aggression. This war is a war against northern aggression. They want to have us pay all the tariffs, and we did not get any of the benefits." I wanted to correct the fine Doctor, but I held my tongue. Besides, Vicee, I was really fighting to protect and defend you.

I was upset that you were not there to see this ceremony. You had explained your reasons, and had cast aside my protestations to the contrary. "I can't stand to see you in uniform. I can't stand to think that you will fight. You might get killed or wounded. I can't stand the thought of you being hurt." But I still think you should have come.

Then, Dr. Nelson Burgess unfurled the flag. On the obverse side, the Palmetto Palm stood tall and defiant, and was done in natural colors that stood out on the field of white ringed with golden braid. The motto, which undulated like waves, above the Palm read: "WHERE HONOR, LIBERTY AND OUR STATE CALLS." We cheered as the flag was shown to us. To us, the motto spoke our hearts. Words like honor duty, liberty, and responding to the call of our home state of South Carolina spoke directly to all that was idealistic, right, and true within our souls.

Then the good Doctor showed us the reverse side of the flag. Looming in the center was an embroidered single golden star. Above the star the name "Claremont Rifles" was arched, while below the star the words "January 1861" were embroidered such that the effect was that the words partially encircled the star. Our cheers rang out with one mighty voice. I was so proud. Proud to be in uniform, proud to be in the Claremont Rifles, and proud to be fighting for my home and South Carolina!

After that, we were all invited to partake of the pies, cakes, and lemonade. Robbie and I were devouring food, but Doug had a somber cast to his face. "What's the matter?" Robbie asked his brother. Doug was the more intellectual, more brooding of the twins. Robbie and I were the more daredevil and devil-may-care ones.

"I think I want to be alone." With that, Doug went off, and pulled out his whittling, which told us that he had something to think over.

I shrugged my shoulders at Doug. Robbie and I returned to our celebration by eating more cake and lemonade.

It was later in the day, after the festivities had died down. We were walking home three abreast.

"Did you think it out?" I inquired of Doug.

"Yeah, I guess." He slowly replied.

"Well, what was it that was bothering you?" I prompted.

"I was thinking about our new flag."

This wasn't that helpful, so I prodded him, "What about our new flag?"

"How similar it is to the one of Glenfinnan." At that name, both Robbie and I stopped. Every Scot knew that it was at Glenfinnan where the old and nearly crippled Marquis of Tullibardine, hobbling on his cane, came forward, and after a slight bow to Bonnie Prince Charles, unfurled, and held aloft the silken Bratach Bhan - the Crimson and White banner. Its motto, Tandem Triumphans! (Triumphant at Last!), had brought cheers to the assembled mass of Highlanders who had just vowed to restore the Stuarts to the throne of Scotland and their allegiance to Prince Charles. With that the Rising of 1745 had begun. No matter how hopefully it had begun, every Scot knew how badly it had ended: The catastrophic loss at the Battle of Culloden; the Highlands Clearances, in which tens of thousands of Scots had died; and the Black Hand of William, the Duke of Cumberland, with the burning of Scottish villages, churches, and castles; the rape of Scottish women; and the transportation of children. With that thought, all three of us, had a shivering tingle move down our spines.

Doug wasn't finished. He barely whispered the next words. "And if that isn't bad enough, doesn't anyone think it looks a lot like a flag of surrender?"

CHAPTER 7:

SULLIVAN'S ISLAND

"I could not fire the first gun of the war."
-Noted Secessionist Robert A. Pryor

April 1, 1865 11:00 AM

While I am going about my duties, my mind wanders. I think back to that April long ago now, or so it seems, when this War first roared to life. I was there, Vicee. But you know that.

I was standing near Ft. Moultrie waiting for our company captain, Captain Spann, to inspect us. I felt very important being the 2nd Corporal of the Company. I puffed up my chest, threw back my shoulders, and drew in my stomach. I was as spiffy as I could be. I had also done all I could do to get my men into order. I was not going to have any let down of standards on this day. It was clear that action was going to occur soon. I wanted to be ready for it. But I had thought that action was going to occur at any time for days. My men were tired of my kicking them into shape with the incessant calls to arms which were only false alarms.

Vicee, I was thrilled to be in Charleston. To be drilling under the shadow of Ft. Moultrie, where my State of South Carolina repulsed the British in the Revolutionary War and helped to win freedom was intoxicating. So much history bound up in this one spot.

We were at attention. Captain James G. Spann stood before us. He waved his arm towards the brick fort behind us. "Men, to think that right here, General William Moultrie with his four hundred men stood firing their cannon as the British fleet lashed out to destroy their little fort. The palmetto palm logs caused the round shot of the British ships to bounce off doing little or no damage. They won our Independence from the British, and you are going to win our Independence from the Yankees!" The men cheered.

Let me give you an idea of where I am. Ft. Moultrie is on a point of Sullivan's Island jutting south into Charleston Harbor. Sullivan's Island is on the north side of the harbor. To the southwest of our position in the middle of the harbor stands Ft. Sumter, where Anderson and the Yankees are separated from us by water of about a mile and a quarter. About another mile and a quarter southeast of Ft. Sumter is Morris Island. We have batteries there, as well as on Pinckney Castle Island to the west of Ft. Sumter, Mt. Pleasant Island, which is just west of Sullivan's Island and on James Island, which is just west of Morris Island. On Sullivan's Island facing Ft. Sumter from west to east we have arrayed six batteries: Point Battery, then Enfilade Battery, Mortar Battery No. 1, Ft. Moultrie, and, then, Mortar Battery No. 2, and, finally, Maffitt's Channel Battery. The Mortars throw a very heavy cannon ball in a high arc in the air that then falls down to earth with great force. The rest of the batteries fire was aimed directly at the Fort.

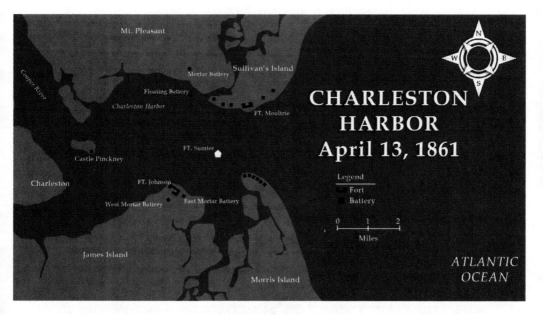

Truly, Vicee, I still cannot not conceive of how years ago the weight of the great British Navy was unable to destroy that small American Rebel contingent and blast that small fort of palmetto logs into oblivion, but stand it did!

Now, I was there on that self-same Sullivan's Island, right beside the walls of the latest incarnation of that famous fort about to watch it and others around the Charleston harbor begin their bombardment of iron and gunpowder to fight once again for South Carolina's freedom and independence. I soon would know the heroic uplifting of victory which Moultrie and his men felt as they fired at the circling British fleet.

Charleston is an intoxicating city. Yes, it had that the sense of great history made present, poignant, and personal. It also had the scent of luxuriant flowers filling the air during the day and the night. By day the white broad flowered gardenias ruled the breezes, while in the night, the air is sultry and liquid, and is the domain of the night blooming jasmine. The jasmine aroma is fruity and sweet, which beguiles you with its calming, exotic, but romantic bouquet. The gardenia, as a flower of the day, is stronger, earthier, and more sensual that the jasmine, but both share that floral note which most white blossomed flowers seem to have. The gardens of Charleston seem to have large bushes of both flowers. Each bush is a green with white flowers, which contrast nicely with the red bricks of the homes. But the bushes differ. Gardenias have much larger leaves and blossoms. The jasmine is more delicate with tiny leaves and tiny flowers. Forever after, I shall always associate Charleston with these scents and colors: red, white, and green. This shall be forever the most romantic of places. The only thing spoiling it all is that you, Vicee, are not here to share this heaven upon earth with me. But still I will associate this with you, because it was here that I began to know my heart and began to want you more than anything.

Those early days held such heady euphoria. Nothing it seemed would be impossible. The aroma of women's perfume, mixed with the smell of freshly fried chicken, the warmth of fresh cornbread, the burning taste of raw whiskey, blended with the martial music wafting on a pleasant evening breeze, which hinted of spring and made the Spanish Moss beards sway, while the magnolias bloomed as a full moon rose over the dark blue Atlantic Ocean formed a silver stairway that shimmered, oscillated, and undulated serpentinely, inspired the romantic in each man's soul. It also almost banished from one's mind that this scene would soon be rent by the booming of cannon flaming and flaring in a burst of bomb and explosion to crumble the fort that stood in the middle of the harbor as a poised mocking face of Union defiance.

Charleston was a city built upon the might of the sea. Merchants trading with the world exported goods and made money. Rice and tobacco, cotton too, went on swift ships following the warm currents of the Gulf Stream to waiting ports, like Glasgow, where merchants there became tobacco kings. In time, as the 1730's and 1740's melted into the 1800's, the prosperous merchants moved their families from above waterfront offices, or stores or sometimes warehouses into handsome homes they built for their families, while the community built soaring church steeples, nestled behind protective seawalls. The fashionable homes lined streets with names like Ashley, Meeting, and Montagu. The salt breezes whipping off the sea waves were enhanced by newly planted bushes of jasmine and gardenia.

The city grew. The planters brought their harvests by boat to the pond by Queen Street. The Cooper River side of the city, that is East Bay Street, became heavily populated by sailors and stevedores. The harbor was a forest of masts. One could feel the vibrancy pulsating in the pace of the city. Ships laden with cotton seemed to leave multiple times daily as if the world was eating up cotton. But the ships which left with rice or cotton or tobacco were replaced at the same frantic, frenetic pace by ships from England bearing English wool, or rum from Jamaica, or linen from Ireland, or plaids from Scotland, or silk from Spanish Barcelona. The women of Charleston called out for bonnets to be brought to them by the crateful, while the men prayed for hogsheads of ale, wine, and liquor, the quantity of which were only outstripped by the barrels of wheat, the crates of fine cherry wood furniture, and the libraries of books that flowed into Charleston to fill the plantations and homes of the rich and soon-to-be rich.

When one first views Charleston from afar, it is a splash of colors pastel accented by gleaming whites that pleases the eye. There, behind the immense seawalls, the steeples of many Churches soar over the graceful houses of red brick, displaying the wealth of the merchants, rice planters, and ship owners. The sea breezes tantalize one's nose with a salty bracing smell which carries with it the exotic aromas of cargoes of various expensive woods from around the world, for example, mahogany from Honduras and ebony from India and Ceylon. Other goods came from far away, such as wool from Britain, rum from Jamaica, linen from Ireland, but they were all mixed with scents more known to the nose such as live oak from Georgia (one could still imagine the Spanish Moss hanging from its boughs) and rice from South Carolina.

But I have digressed, Vicee, from what I wanted to tell you. The wind carried the hint of a little drizzle, while the temperature hung in the 60's as the wind whipped across the water, making little white-caps, and blew into our faces, disheveling our hair. We faced forward at attention and waited for the review to begin. I saw the little skiff of a boat carrying two of our officers towards the great fort that dominated the harbor. What were they doing? Was this the time that they were going to demand the surrender of the fort? Would this demand be refused, leading to the commencement of the bombardment?

It was late afternoon and the night would soon be upon us. I figured the 'Elephant' would show itself tomorrow or the next day. But as one of my men had said, 'If we'd had a penny for each time we thought we'd agoing to see'd the elephant, we'd have enough money for the whole circus, now!' What would it be like for our nineteen batteries to open fire upon that island fortress? What would happen? Maybe the better question was: when was that going to happen?

It was April 12, 1861 at 4:30 am, Vicee. A giant mortar shell fired from James Island across the harbor to the south of us drew a great fiery arc across the sky and burst right above Ft. Sumter.

Being without you, facing possible death, it was here that I began to see that the only thing that is real in life is the love we give to others. I came here to Charleston with a crush upon you that ripened into real love, the kind of love which will sacrifice all, if necessary, for the beloved.

CHAPTER 8:

A LETTER HOME

'FORT SUMTER, S.C., April 12, 1861, 3:20 A.M. - SIR: By authority of Brigadier-General Beauregard, commanding the Provisional Forces of the Confederate States, we have the honor to notify you that he will open the fire of his batteries on Fort Sumter in one hour from this time. We have the honor to be very respectfully, Your obedient servants, JAMES CHESNUT JR., Aide-de-camp. STEPHEN D. LEE, Captain C. S. Army, Aide-de-camp.'

April 1, 1865 11:30 am

I can recall almost word for word the letter I wrote you from Ft. Moultrie. I wanted to burn into my brain my proposal to you, for you are the most important person in the world to me, Vicee. I think I did it quite poorly now upon reflection, but at least I did it. I think I can recall it:

Sullivan Island April 20th 61
   Dear Vicee,
   I drop you these few lines to let you know that I am well & am in a great deal Better Quarters than when I wrote you last for we have a nice bed now. Well-furnished, carpeted - I am a Beau Brummel now & we have a cooking stove to cook in & have as good fare as I could wish for.

I would be very well satisfied If I did not want to see you so bad for it seems that I have Been down here six months already. But I will be up Just as soon as I can get off and I want us to get <u>married</u> then, if you are willing, for I think that I could Remain Better Satisfied for you Know hard days and expectation keeps me fearful. Then you could come down and stay a week or two at a nice place. I could get a good place for you to stay for several of the men are talking of bringing their wives down. But I don't know whether they are so earnest or not, But I am willing to do any way that you think is right. For my mind is so distracted that I don't know hardly what is Best for us to do. I dream of you all the time.

You must write. I would not grieve, if I could hear from you every hour. It would be all the consolation I need. This will make Three letters I have written you and have not received a reply from you. I want you to answer as fast-you get them, if not faster.

I heard today that the Darlington Guards were going to Virginia. I have seen George Cole today & he was agoing to Charleston. John Powers and Jim Blackburn left here to go home. They will Return Tuesday. But I had Rather wait awhile longer & stay a week or more when I get there. I will know Better, when I will come up when I get an answer from the Captain.

I heard today that's you was in Timmonsville. Mr. Sansburg wrote to Cowans to tell me that you was there. You must get Clifton to find out how they are getting on with our house for Father will not Write me much when he writes. For he is not one to write long letters nor me rather only when I get to writing to you & him.

Give my Best respect to Mrs. Clifton & Clifton & all of your father's family & tell Gustus howdy for me & send me general news when you write for there is nothing here that interests me. Tell your Step Mother to send me that classic bread recipe for I want to cook same.

For you ought to see how I am improving in cooking. But I don't Know how I will come out when I get to washing. But I will soon learn.

You ought to hear us sing for we all are improving fast our Chaplin is agoing to Preach to our Regiment tomorrow and I am agoing to attend. There are agreat many sons of Temperance in our Company from necessity, But I have seen the most of our sons at home taking some of the spirits. But I came sober don't intend to take any. There is very much real bitterness in our company, but most of them are complaining from Being sore from drilling & carrying our heavy muskets. But I think that it is the Best thing that I can do. I have no doubt but that it will make me stronger for I can stand more now than I could before.

You must give my best Respect to Old Dame & tell her God Bless hers & not be uneasy about old souls for he is faring well. I must close for I know you will get tired of reading my long trashy letters. I can't help writing, when I start. But you must bear. I Remain yours most devotedly until death

J A McEachern
Sullivan Island
Near Charleston, SC
In camp Capt. Owens
8 Reg

CHAPTER 9:
THE BIRTH OF THE HAMPTON LEGION

Lt. William Campbell Preston fired a gun from Ft. Moultrie which brought down Ft. Sumter's flagstaff. When his grandmother, the widow of the first Wade Hampton and a woman who was described as "the mildest, sweetest, gentlest of old ladies," heard the news, she fired off a telegram that praised her grandson, "Well done, Willie!"

April 1, 1865 12 Noon

For some weeks, Wade Hampton had contemplated how he could help his home state of South Carolina, now that war had come. Although he had been in Mississippi tending to one of his plantations when the bombardment of Ft. Sumter occurred, by the third week of April of 1861, he was back in Charleston, his plan fully formed in his mind. He approached General P. G. T. Beauregard and then he approached Governor Pickens to explain his plan. With their agreement and armed with letters of introduction from both of them, he sped off to the new Confederate Capital in Montgomery, Alabama to meet President Jefferson Davis.

"Your Excellency," he began, bowing down to the new President, not being sure of the correct protocol, "I should like to thank you for the opportunity to speak to you about a plan I have in mind. I have discussed the particulars with both General Beauregard, and Governor Pickens such that I can assure you that I have carefully considered my proposal and that I have sought the best counsel I could obtain upon my endeavor." He stood erect now.

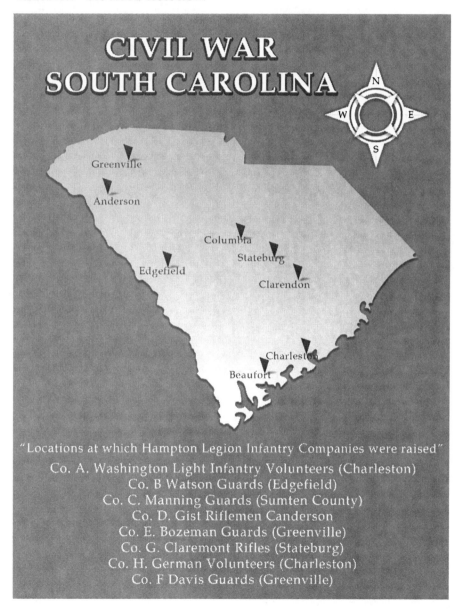

Davis looked at the planter he saw before him and thought: 'How can I gracefully end this conversation sooner rather than later?' He smiled weakly. "Yes, Colonel Hampton, what can I do for you?"

"Your Excellency, it is I who want to help you. I propose to raise a Legion of one thousand men, composed of infantry, cavalry, and artillery, deployed as an independent command."

Hampton took a breath of which Davis took advantage. "Colonel, I am sure that you mean well, but our finances of this new nation do not admit themselves to such an endeavor at this time…"

Hampton raised his hand to indicate that he had not finished. "Your Excellency, I meant not to burden the Government. I plan to recruit the men, equip them, uniform them, arm them, and train them, myself."

At this Davis, became animated. "You would equip a thousand men at your own expense?"

"Yes, your Excellency. It would be my gift to the Confederacy."

"Please come back tomorrow. I would like to have you meet my Secretary of War, Leroy Pope Walker, to further discuss this idea of yours." President Davis smiled broadly.

CHAPTER 10:
THE CLAREMONT RIFLES IN CAMP

Mavourneen, mavourneen, my sad tears are falling,
To think that from Erin and thee I must part!
It may be for years, and it may be forever,
Then why art thou silent, thou voice of my heart?
It may be for years and it may be forever,
Then why art thou silent, Kathleen, mavourneen?
-Lyrics of **Kathleen Mavourneen** *(Mavourneen means 'my darling'), a popular song of the Civil War*

April 1, 1865 12:15 pm

We had languished after our service at Ft. Sumter. We went back to Columbia awaiting orders that would send us somewhere useful. The summer was upon us. Our forces had been victorious at Bull Run. We were sure that we had missed our chance in the War or would, if we continued to wait in Columbia. Waiting is difficult, especially for impatient young men. We want things and we want them, now. So the Claremont Rifles were drilling and drilling to become as smooth and well organized as any company could be in hopes of catching someone's eye who would be in a position of power to get us where we wanted to be: in the forefront of battle.

Rumors abounded in our camp. Some said that Wade Hampton was back in town looking for reinforcements for the Legion. We had all heard how the Hampton Legion had gained glory during the Battle at Bull Run. The heroic story told of the Legion fighting its way up Henry House Hill and resisting charge after charge of Federals until the Legion was joined by Jonathan Jackson's men. But the victory had come at a steep price. The Legion had been decimated and needed men.

But this rumor was but one of many. While I wanted to join the Legion, because I had seen that majestic man Wade Hampton before, others felt that maybe it wasn't such a good choice, because "If he was such a good leader, how comes he lost so many men?"

But no matter what, it wasn't up to us. It was up to the Governor of South Carolina, the dour faced, Francis Wilkens Pickens. He was a famous man in his own right and as a double descendant of men who had served South Carolina well in the past. His grandfather on his paternal father's side was General Andrew Pickens, who had served under General Daniel Morgan at Cowpens, where my great grandfather, James, had died after making a marksman's shot killing an aide of Colonel Banastre Tarleton. Further, his father, also named Andrew Pickens, had been a Governor of South Carolina. His fame did not end there, for on his maternal side, he also had names that were glorious and highlighted with honor. His grandmother was a cousin of the fire-eater, John C. Calhoun. He was also a cousin of Floride Calhoun who was John C. Calhoun's wife. His son-in-law later became General Matthew C. Butler. So much of the history of South Carolina was attached to his families' names that some said South Carolina flowed in his blood.

The Governor, of course, knew Wade Hampton from his days in the Legislature. Unbeknownst to us, Stephen D. Lee, no relation to Robert E. Lee, was trying to finagle a way to a combat command. Lee had come from a wealthy family in Charleston. This had led him to serve as an aide-de-campe to General P. G. T. Beauregard before the firing upon Ft. Sumter. With that position, came a promotion from Captain to the impressive title of both Assistant Adjutant General and

Assistant Inspector General, but this was still not enough to satisfy his ambition. Besides, it was a position behind a desk and not in the field. Stephen Lee had been the one to announce Beauregard's ultimatum that the Confederates would now fire upon the Fort in one hour, when he had been authorized to allow up to three days for the evacuation. This 'miscommunication,' as Lee termed it, had led Beauregard to request that the pesky Lee be reassigned soon after the bombardment. Lee had gone back to the South Carolina Militia where he had languished for the last several months.

"Governor, I would be willing to accept any command which would allow me to see action," Stephen D. Lee had told the Governor, while he bowed respectfully.

"Anything you say?" The Governor tilted his head downwards and looked through his bushy eyebrows at the young man.

Gulping, Stephen D. Lee answered, "Yes, sir. Anything…"

"Well, Colonel Hampton has a position open commanding his artillery. It is two light sections…" The Governor quickly turned silent.

Stephen D. Lee thought. 'He might not have anything else available. If I turn this down, what might I be assigned to? Further, the Washington Artillery in the Legion is composed of many of my friends from Charleston's finest families. It might be a great lark. Then there's the fact Colonel Hampton was born in Fitzsimon's Home at 54 Hasell Street in Charleston and, thus, is from one of the best of Charleston's neighborhoods, Rhettsbury. Our families know each other, although he is 15 years my senior.'

"Your Honor, I have experience with artillery. As you may recall, I was educated at West Point and studied artillery extensively. I would be honored to assume that command, assuming that a commensurate rank went with the appointment…" Now, it was Lee's turn to go silent. 'Let him think about that,' Stephen D. Lee thought

The Governor, not sure that he liked the horse trading that was going on, but also aware that he did not have a better candidate for Hampton, decided quickly. "Why, of course, a promotion goes along with this command. You would be a Major."

Stephen D. Lee thought that he would play his hand a little further. If Hampton's Legion were to be increased with infantry, there might be an opening for him to command infantry there. "I passed a rather fine company drilling just outside of the Capital. I know that Colonel Hampton is looking for more men to reinforce his Legion after his costly victory at Manassas. I think the Claremont Rifles would be just the thing."

CHAPTER 11:
VIRGINNY BOUND

"We talked the matter over and could have settled the war in thirty minutes had it been left to us."
- Unknown Confederate Soldier referencing a meeting he had with a Union soldier between the lines.

April 1, 1865 12:30 pm

We were camped just outside of Columbia. Captain Spann had us drilling, as if there was nothing else to do, when he rode up. I saw Colonel Wade Hampton riding his horse sitting in the saddle fully erect and cutting an almost regal figure of an officer. He dismounted as gracefully as only the most experienced riders can. He was extremely tall. His luxuriant and handsome light brown wavy hair framed his large gray eyes. While he was broad shouldered, he still had a deep chest and a most narrow waist. His full beard was topped by a wide and carefully combed mustache which flared across his face almost ear to ear. Unlike most officers, not only did he not smoke or use tobacco in any form, but also he drank rarely. His body betrayed great muscular strength. Our eyes followed his form as he dismounted, walked up to Captain James G. Spann, saluted him, and then vigorously shook his hand. With a wave of his hand in our direction, we gathered that Colonel Hampton had asked Captain Spann to put us through our paces.

Now, all the drilling and training came to fruition. We were as smart as any company of men had ever been. We dressed our lines and stood as tall as we could possibly do. We were preening as if this was our first date at a country dance, and the lady, we liked the most had intimated that she wanted us to ask her to dance. Every skill we possessed, we showed off.

After an hour of close order drill, the Captain had us fire, reload our weapons, and then commence volley fire upon order.

It was clear that Colonel Hampton liked what he saw, for his eyes betrayed a twinkle that made several of us later remark that he almost looked like Old St. Nick. Colonel Hampton shook hands with Captain Spann. He then turned and smiled at us.

"Gentlemen, you are some of the finest South Carolina boys I have ever seen in drill. I want you to know, although there is much to do to make this official, that I welcome you to the Legion! God bless you, and God bless our Confederate States!" Colonel Hampton then snapped a salute to us. To this, we responded in kind.

Within days our orders came. We were ordered to take trains from Columbia for northern Virginia. We were not only joining the Hampton Legion as Company G, we were joining Joseph Johnston's Army. It was Private Douglas MacDonald, whom I have known since childhood, who had learned somehow that the Legion was in camp on the right of the Confederate line which stretched in front of Centreville, Virginia. We were going to be closer to Washington than the old line before Manassas had been. The Legion was bivouacked at Camp Wigfall on the Occoquan River, just above where it joined the Potomac River. We were bivouacked with the Texas Brigade. Our Camp was named for the famous Fire-Eater, Louis Wigfall, from Texas. He had been a Senator before the war. At one point, he had acted an as emissary for Beauregard to Major Anderson demanding the surrender of the Fort. So, he had been in Charleston during the bombardment of Ft. Sumter. He was described as being the happiest man alive, while shot and shell rained over the Fort. Later, apparently, he had become a Colonel of the 1st Texas regiment. Soon, he became a General based solely upon his celebrity.

Our Camp was on the Telegraph Road which reaches northeast from Dumfries, Virginia. While we were not on picket duty, we did various other things. Obviously, we had to cook, and clean up the camp, but for amusement, some of the men (but not me, Vicee) would play cards, often for money. Of course, we spent a lot of time foraging for food and other necessities. Sometimes, we would go to other camps to visit friends, and share news over coffee.

We were with the Texas Brigade. Some of the men built what they called "The Lone Star Theater," which became the home of "Hood's Minstrels." So many nights, we had performances of plays, or the brass

band would play songs, and we would sing along. Many of us, including me, joined the choir, and we would sing hymns that we all knew by heart. A couple of times we had performances by the famous banjoist, Sam Sweeney. He was often joined by the man who wrote the lyrics for "The Bonnie Blue Flag," Harry McCarty.

Little did we know that this camp would be our home for the next seven months. Little did we know that all our dreams of being active, of being in the war, and of fighting battles would not come true for over seven months. Finally, little did we know that we would not go home, even when our State of South Carolina was invaded and needed us.

The letter I received from you, Vicee, was heartbreaking.

> "November 21, 1861
> My dearest James,
>
> I am sure that you know that our sacred soil has been besmirched by the foul tread of the unholy invader. Just days ago, Yankee gunboats attacked Ft. Walker and drove away Beauregard, the hero of the Battle of Manassas, and his men. We are so dismayed that the heathen foot could fall upon our land. Can you not with your men come back and protect us? We need you here. You should be here to protect your mother, your father, all your sisters, and your brothers.
>
> I cannot tell you how very much I miss you. I do want to marry you so and I wish we were married already. I cannot stand being apart from you. You are my world, my moon, and my stars. I am so very lonely. I truly ache for you.
>
> Now with what has happened, I need you not only to satisfy my soul and my love, but to staunch my fears. I have awakened at night thinking or dreaming that Union soldiers in blue are coming in my windows and doors. I am

so afraid. I cannot stand the dark. I tremble at the thought of each night's descent. I long only for sunlight. My step mother says that I should write you and tell you of my fears. But I am afraid that what I might write you might break your courage.

I know that you have your duty, but if you can, please talk with Captain Spann. He is older than you are by some 14 years. He is married. I know because I asked around Stateburg when I last went there. His wife is the former Elizabeth Eveleigh Richardson. She is known as a God-fearing woman. They were married in the Church of Holy Cross. While they are Episcopalians, I am sure that he would understand a cry for help made by you even though we are Baptists. Tell him I have begged you to come home. You must come home to me.

I have seen your father recently, and he is fine. He told me that your family is well. He says to tell you that he is proud of you, as am I. But being proud of you does not prevent my heart from calling out to you.

Know that I love you, and I ask you only because I love you so. Your loving, Vicee"

This is the hardest thing in the world to do: To stay here in Virginia, when my heart tells me to be in South Carolina. Is what I am doing here protecting my kinfolk in Darlington?

For the longest time, I kept this letter, as I did with all of your letters in a little packet near to my heart.

During those seven months we were camped near the Occoquan River, we saw much of Colonel Hampton. He attended to every detail concerning the Legion. We came to know a great deal about him.

I had been elected a 2nd Corporal in the Company. I was very proud that the men had singled me out to be one of the men that led them. Of course, I knew nothing about being a Corporal or even what a Corporal did. I figured I would learn as I went along. I knew that I would make mistakes, but figured that those above me in rank would point them out, and I would learn. I had been my father's apprentice, and I had learned from him, so I could learn from the men above me. Elisha Scott Carson, Jr. was the 1st Corporal, so he immediately outranked me. I was 20, but he was only 18. For a time, it rankled me that a man younger than me outranked me. Especially, as when we were the Claremont Rifles militia, he had been the 5th Corporal, that is, ranked lower than me. But after a while, I got used to the idea. I had to give it to him for Corporal Carson, however, really knew how to be a Corporal, because he had graduated from King's Mountain Military Academy in June of 1861. This was the first time I would become acquainted with the King's Mountain Military Academy, which would figure quite large in the life of the whole Hampton Legion. But the tale of Jenkins and Law is best left to a later time, even though it almost destroyed the Legion.

Another man above me, who also deserved to be ranked above me, was William Bowers Councill. He had been a doctor and was 11 years my senior. A nicer man you could not have found. He had been with us at Ft. Moultrie. He was the 3rd Sergeant. He was also a Stateburg resident.

Of course, the real leader of our Company was Captain James G. Spann. He owned two plantations in Sumter District and another one in Lowndes County, Alabama. At first, I thought he was just another rich man who got his rank by his wealth. Unfortunately, nothing that he did while he commanded our Company did anything to dispel this notion. He had made his brother, Ransom Davis Spann, his 1st Lieutenant. The men thought that Ransom had no credentials or ability to be in such a lofty position. This feeling tainted anything and everything Captain James Spann tried to do with the Company. Eventually in April of 1862, when the Company, the Legion, and the Army were reorganized, the men voted out both Captain Spann and 1st Lieutenant Spann. Both of them went on to serve on the staff of Major General Richard H. Anderson. At Weldon Station in August of 1864, Captain James G. Spann, who then held the rank of Inspector, Adjutant General, was killed in action, and his brother, who was then a Captain/Assistant Adjutant General, was seriously wounded in action. Maybe, I had misjudged them.

Captain Spann did one good thing for me: he ordered me to read Hardee's Rifle and Light Infantry Tactics. This book had become, as he told me, the standard manual of arms for West Point in 1855. When the revised and expanded edition came out in 1862, Spann bought several copies. He gave them to his subordinates, and then ordered us to read and memorize it. From this work, I learned what a Corporal was supposed to do. I read at night, often only the night before, what the men were to learn the next day. I was exhausted reading late at night and drilling by day, but it made me better in the long run, and for that I have to thank Captain Spann.

But, Vicee, I was talking about Colonel Hampton. He came from a very educated family that prized learning. Everyone remarked upon his family's library, its size and its quality. He had been educated at the South Carolina College in Columbia, which had beautiful Georgian style red brick buildings with giant white columns with large shade trees. It was only three blocks from the Capitol building. Upon his graduation from college, he was appointed Lt. Colonel and an aide-de-Camp to the Commander in Chief by Governor Pierce Mason Butler in the South Carolina militia. So he had years of experience, or so we all thought. I took a wait-and-see attitude, for I thought again, that he might be another rich man, who got his rank by wealth and not by talent.

One day in the fall of 1861, while we were on the Occoquan River line, Lieutenant Ransom Spann shouted an order, "Quiet in the ranks. The Captain is going to speak."

Captain Spann stood in front of us. He was quiet and paused a moment to let all talk die down. "Men, you need to know the mettle of the man who leads us all. I want to tell you this to quell the incessant rumors that are going around the ranks. These rumors do great disservice to a man who is truly worthy to command you." He coughed there to emphasize, that what he was about to tell, us we needed to hear, and, thus, we needed to pay attention.

"Some of you know that Colonel Wade Hampton has paid for the weapons, uniforms, cannon, and other equipment for this Legion from out of his own pocket. We should respect him for that alone, if he did nothing else for our command."

He looked at each member of the company passing from one set of eyes to the next. The minutes went by slowly as he framed what he would say next.

"And I am sure that many of you know that he wisely and competently led the Legion in Battle at Manassas before our Company joined the Legion. He was on Stonewall Jackson's right flank, and joined the attacks which broke the Union artillery line, and pushed their infantry off of Henry House Hill. This alone again would be enough to deserve our respect, but…" He paused there and let his words sink in. "…some of you men question this man's courage. Shame on you." He paused again. I could see out of the corner of my eye that some of men were looking around the ranks thinking, who was the one who had ratted them out to their commanding officer.

"I need not name who those might be, but I assure you that Colonel Hampton is braver than many of you, and, maybe, most of you." The Captain was clearly enjoying telling us this story.

He started pacing up and down. The words poured out. He began to smack the back of his right hand into the cup of his left hand to emphasize the rhythm of what he was saying. "He was in Columbia (smack) when a fire broke out (smack) in a blacksmith's shop (smack). The fire spread quickly (smack). Buildings from Plain to Taylor Street (smack) were burned in the conflagration (smack). Hampton without thinking of his safety (smack) climbed to the roof of one (smack) of the buildings (smack) and began to fight the fire (smack)."

He paused again and stopped pacing, as well as he stopped smacking. "He was joined by a sailor named Neville. The two of them saved the building! They stopped the fire's expansion! When they came down from the roof, the crowd greeted him with a husky cheer. Hampton and Neville presented a sad appearance when they came down from that roof, hair and whiskers singed, clothing soaked with water, blackened and burned."

"Lieutenant, do you have anything to add?" Captain Spann cast his gaze upon his brother, but did not break the proper decorum of addressing his brother by his rank and last name.

"That is the character of the man under whom you serve. How many men would have done what he did? Would you have done the same? Maybe if it were your family, or your blacksmith shop! But a complete stranger's establishment? A man that you didn't even know? Would you have risked your life, the life of the wealthiest man in all of South Carolina to save a much poorer man's business?" Lieutenant Spann barked, "I don't think so!"

"One thing more, stopping the fire had spared his church: Trinity Episcopal Church. The corner stone contained both a Bible and Common Book of Prayer. When that cornerstone was laid, Dr. Shand had prayed: 'Here may worldly anxieties and worldly strife find no entrance-the passions of our corrupt nature be hushed into silence.' That is good advice for us all," Lieutenant Spann finished.

Captain Spann then ordered, "Lieutenant, dismiss the men!"

CHAPTER 12:

MEASLES AND MUMPS: A PLAGUE STRIKES THE CAMP

And I saw another sign in heaven, great and marvelous, seven angels having the seven last plagues; for in them is filled up the wrath of God.
- ***Revelation 15:1***

April 1, 1865 1:00 PM

Camp Butler Sunday November 10th, 1861
My dear Vicee,
I received your letter of the other day & was glad to hear that you were well & all of Sister's family. I would have answered your Letter Sooner But I had just written to you & thought that I would wait awhile to have Something to write to you. But we have not Been away from Camp Since I wrote to you.

I am well as I Ever were & I think the health of the Legion is Improving fast, since we have had Plenty of beautiful white frost which seems to have stopped the mumps and the measles. I fear though that we will Still have some warm days. We have not wanted for Rain. Lately you wanted to know when I had the fever. I never had it. But I am still taking Quinine anyway.

But if I get sick I will be very apt to let you know it. I know that all of you at home think it horrible thing for one to Be Sent to the hospital, But if I get Sick I want them to Send me there. For one thing, the Soldiers that go there are well attended to & get everything to Eat-that Suits their appetite & it looks like everyone that goes there, tries to stay as long as he can. Jim Stephens had Been there for weeks with the Yellow Jaundice. He is well now & looks Better than I Ever Seen him. We have all of our Sick at the Hospital as it is in Better Place for them than our Camp.

Jarrot Sansberg, old Daniel Sansberg's Brother, left here last week, as he got a discharge. You said Something about me getting a furlough. You might as well talk about getting everything else in the world, as about getting a furlough. I don't think there is any Chance for a leave. But I know the Chance will not come after we get into winter Quarters. But I don't know yet when we will go into winter Quarters or whether we will attack the Yankees. But I don't think we can do it. But I hope that I can let you know all about it in my next letter.

I am glad to hear you say that you are well Satisfied at your Sister Mary's. Say hello to Mary for me. But I am sorry to hear you Say that you get dispirited. You ought not to. You should keep up your Spirits. You should not look at the dark Side of anything more than you can help. For Everything will Peaceable in a Short Time, I hope. I hope there will come a time when we as a nation can forget all our Past Troubles. I hope for the future.

It is Reported in Camp that the Yankees landed in Alexandria, But we don't know whether to Believe it. But if it is So, then I mean to carry the Legion Back and fight them.

I have not Read a letter from father Lately, But get News Papers most every day from him & judge from that that they are all well as home.

I Seen Sidney Cole yesterday & he Said that his wife at Timmonsville is coming on a visit. He is Still at the Hospital waiting on the Sick & he looks Better than I ever Seen him. He seems to enjoy nursing others and is good at it. If his wife were to come to See him, then I damn well think I should be able to get the same reward & have you come, if you want.

They have not Paid the Legion off, yet I think they will this week they will. I want to send the most of my Money to you and to father for your Expenses. But if you need any more, you must not hesitate to tell him. Know that you can get it every time you need it for I will repay him, for I love you.

You must get my Shawl from Mrs. Wingate when you go to the Village. You can use it & I know you will take care of it for me.

Looks like the officers Expect a fight any day now. And when they do, they will send for the Hampton Legion. In the past, we have gone by the train, but when we get there, the Yankees have gone back across the Potomac. We now have ten cannons in the Legion. We have now two artillery companies, the second one being the German Volunteers that joined us Some time ago with four pieces.

You must tell me how your father's family is all getting along. I expect to write to father today. Give my love to Georgie and Sister Viola & all the children & tell all that I am well & howdy for my mother But remain yours as ever Till Death J. A. McEachern

CHAPTER 13:
WINTER IS COMING

"This is the most atrocious & unnatural war ever waged, & if it does not soon cease its horrors will exceed those of any previous war recorded in history. It is fearful. And the sights after a battle are too horrible to think of. I want to see no more of them."
- **Wade Hampton,** *after the Battle of First Manassas*

April 1, 1865 1:30 PM

The chill of fall spread across the northern Virginia landscape. So too, the little tents of the Legion spread their wings around the idyllically named little hamlet of the Maple Valley and near Bacon Race Church. There the Legion would remain through this first winter of the war.

Wade Hampton guarded his prerogative of being an independent military unit, so that the Legion was not brigaded with any troops. This did not please Earl Van Dorn to whom Hampton and his Legion were first assigned as part of Van Dorn's division, and so the Legion became a party of James Longstreet's division.

General Hampton thought first and foremost about his men. Longstreet had assigned him a long stretch of the Occoquan River to defend. Hampton personally patrolled the river both on horseback and in a little boat, observing all of its little intricacies that might yield a better line of defense. From his observations, he discovered a new ford. He constantly spoke to his subordinates on all levels on how to make the River more defensible.

"I am issuing orders that the Occoquan River continue to be fortified, because I don't want any surprises from the Yankees," Hampton told Captain Spann. "I want your men to take all measures to guard themselves against any attack." As he spoke, the two men could hear the federal camp across the River as their drums, bugles, and brass bands played to rally the spirts of the northerners. But while giving his men hard work to do, Hampton saw to their health and welfare, by insuring that the commissary kept the men plentifully supplied with rations.

Nonetheless, morale fell as news of the Federal invasion of South Carolina spread around the Camp. Captain Spann spoke to us, "The capture of Port Royal this November has created a calamity for our State. I know that each and every one of you wants to go home, and fight for our homeland, our wives, our families, and our children. I can assure you that General Hampton has tried every possible means to obtain our reassignment from here in Virginia back to South Carolina, but it has been in vain."

Captain Spann stroked his newly grown beard, and then spoke in a more hushed tone, "I don't know if I should tell you this, but the General shared with me his feeling about our Governor. He said, and I quote, 'I have looked for nothing but disaster since that fool Pickens was elected Governor. It will be only through the mercy of God that we get over our troubles safely, if we do get over them.'" The men laughed because Pickens was not very popular.

One of the men said, "We should go home to fight them, and we should run up the black flag!"

"What's that mean - a black flag?" I asked.

Captain Spann spread his arms to hush the company. "We aren't going to say to the enemy that no quarter will be asked or given. It ain't humane. It ain't Christian. There will be no black flag, as long as I am in command! If we beat them, we will treat their wounded, and we will bury their dead. If they surrender, we will honor their surrender. Not a Yankee will be slain except according to the rules of civilized warfare!"

*****

Just a few days later, a different flag arrived in Camp Lee, near Bacon Race, Virginia, another one of the Camps in which the Legion was ensconced. It was a Christmas present to the whole Legion. A group of ladies in Matanzas, Cuba, just outside of Havana, I think, who were sympathizers of the Confederacy, in general and the Legion in particular, sent a silken banner through the blockade on the blockade runner, Theodora. The Theodora brushed right past the blockade near Key West, skirted the Keys, then went up the coast until she made land somewhere in South Carolina. It was a beautiful Confederate flag, Vicee. It was the first national flag style, with eleven stars on a field of blue, flanked by two broad red stripes separated by one board white stripe. The workmanship was exquisite. The silk was soft and smooth to the touch. It was the stars and bars done by the hands of beautiful black - eyed, mysterious senoritas, or at least that was what we all imagined.

The General called for a general assembly to welcome the banner. "We shall cherish it for their sakes, and, if need be, defend it with our lives!" To that the men cheered and threw their hats in the air.

Christmas 1861 came. For the General, it was a day marked by a magnificent gift. Commanding General Joseph E. Johnston sent Wade Hampton a finely wrought sword. Hampton held it in his hands. 'I shall tell the commanding General that this is a beautiful sword. I trust it will do good service whilst in my hands. I shall treat this as a loan and shall return it to the General after we have won the war untarnished.'

For the rest of us, Christmas, no matter how lively the men tried to make it, was lonely and depressing. All of us were thinking of our families at home. Throughout the day, someone somewhere was playing "Home Sweet Home" on a harmonica, a guitar, a banjo, or else a Yankee band across the river, which was answered by our brass band. Every one of us wanted to be back in South Carolina. We wanted to talk with our mamas, sisters, fathers, brothers, and our sweethearts.

"I can smell the ham roasting right now." Robbie MacDonald said to me. "I can taste the yams and corn bread."

His brother, Douglas MacDonald, always the quieter of the two, only smacked his lips, and then he said, "I can see mama." He was quiet then, and Robbie stopped his reminiscing.

Those of us who sat around the fire also grew silent. I took this as a good moment to thank God for Christmas and the miracle of the birth of Jesus. I was grateful I was well. But thinking of my health reminded me of so many of the men who were ill with mumps and measles. So many of the young men who had these diseases died. I thanked the Good Lord, Vicee, that I had had both of these diseases as a child and, thus, was immune to them now. We were miles away from our sweethearts and wives. Our native land of South Carolina was being besmirched by the foot of an evil invader. There was little to cheer about. Especially, as we looked forward now to three months of cold, snowy winter in northern Virginia.

We watched the day fade into the grey of night as a chorus of voices, northern and southern, joined in singing "Home Sweet Home."

CHAPTER 14:
FIRE CLAIMS MEMORY

"...supplies within the reach of Confederate armies I regarded as much contraband as arms or ordnance stores. Their destruction was accomplished without bloodshed and tended to the same result as the destruction of armies. I continued this policy to the close of the war. Promiscuous pillaging, however, was discouraged and punished. Instructions were always given to take provisions and forage under the direction of commissioned officers who should give receipts to owners, if at home, and turn the property over to officers of the quartermaster or commissary departments to be issued as if furnished from our Northern depots. But much was destroyed without receipts to owners, when it could not be brought within our lines and would otherwise have gone to the support of secession and rebellion. This policy I believe exercised a material influence in hastening the end."
- **U. S. Grant**, Personal Memoirs

April 1, 1865 2:15 PM

It is inconceivable to me that most of Charleston was destroyed by fire on December 17, 1861. When I was on Sullivan's Island, it was before that great conflagration. We had to march through the city to get to Sullivan's Island, and I was struck by the immense beauty of the city.

Now, the oldest and most beautiful haunts of the city are gone. Homes that housed those great figures of our American Revolution are lost. They are hulks of wrecks. Piles of bricks and other rubble are all that remain. Nothing stately or hinting of grandeur stands. Streets such as State and Market no longer exist. The ancestral homes of some of the most illustrious families of South Carolina are no more; the mansions of such families as the Pinckneys, the Middletons, the Laurences, the Heywards and the Haynes are leveled to the ground without a whisper of their former glory around to recall them. Block after block near the Battery, where I had walked one day on a leave, which was so beautiful and had such a panoramic view of the harbor and its many forts, the Post Office, the Hall, all of Wentworth Street, the oldest and most sacred areas of the city lie in desolation. The great Cathedral of St. Finbarr on Broad Street with its mighty steeple and its soaring Gothic flying arches is a ruin. Oh, that it existed but a bit over seven years! Women despair as they comb the debris for some lost keepsake, such as a lock of hair, of a departed one. Children cry inconsolably. Some four or five thousand people out of the city's population of 40,000 were homeless. What remains of Charleston is magnificent and brings tears to one's eyes that so much was lost.

Within days, throughout South Carolina, but, particularly in Charleston, people were asking themselves whether the destruction of Charleston by fire was the Hand of God visiting judgment upon the Confederacy for having seceded from the Union.

"Have we sinned against God in some way that He would visit this upon us?"

"Wasn't it just exactly a year ago today December 17, 1860 that the Secession Convention convened in Columbia and voted unanimously, 169-0, to declare secession from the United States?"

"Why yes it was! You don't think?" And so the unthinkable became the thought.

People prayed to God, "Dear Lord, guide us, your people! If we have offended Thee in any manner, show us the errors of our ways such that we may repent."

Churches filled with mourners, sinners, and repentant worshippers begging for mercy.

This all happened over three years ago. Little did we know then that this vast conflagration would be but the first of many. Vicee, I truly think the history of the Confederacy is written in flame. Did Sherman burn the city of Atlanta? Whether or not he did, when he left, wasn't the industrial district but a smoking shell? They say that over 40% of the city has vanished! Did Sherman burn Columbia? Certainly! Wade Hampton and his cavalry tried to prevent it. But nevertheless, on February 17, 1865, (Was it so recently, Vicee?), liquor flowed through the streets and fire followed thereafter. You cannot let men, who have not had a drink in ages, be allowed to drink uncontrollably: it leads to chaos. But the next day, no matter what, Sherman's men did their work destroying all of value: railroad depots, machinist shops, warehouses, arsenals, and railroad track. Sherman certainly burned our home town of Darlington. It is not legend, is it? Didn't Sherman send one of his engineers, J. L. Klickner, to burn our town? It is fortunate that Klickner had been an architect before the War. He had built the home for Colonel Samuel Hugh Wildes in 1857 in Darlington. Bobby said that his pa had written him that the Federal forces were about to burn down the Wildes house, when Major Klickner suddenly recognized his own creation. He was able to intercede and the house was saved. But the rest of the town was not so lucky. Vicee, did they burn down the Traxler Plantation?

I know that Petersburg and Richmond will share the same fate, if Grant has his way. That is one of the many reasons we still fight. We know what they will do, and what they will do, will be catastrophic for the South. We fight because we must; there is no other choice.

The burning of Richmond might be the bookend to the burning of Charleston. And if it comes about, then I think those who thought that the burning of Charleston was God's punishment upon us for our actions, may well be proven right.

BOOK III: HARD WAR –1862

CHAPTER 15:

BOISSEAU HOUSE

*All the world's a stage,
And all the men and women merely players;
They have their exits and their entrances,
And one man in his time plays many parts...*
-**William Shakespeare**, *As You Like it*

April 1, 1865 2:30 PM

Dear Vicee,
You wouldn't believe what happened to me today.
I was walking to the Boisseau Home; I'll tell you all about that home later. (Don't you notice that I no longer use words like agoing, awalking, athinking, and areading! I am learning.) I was going to visit James Fitz James Caldwell; he's the writer who is writing the history of McGowan's brigade. He's been teaching me about reading literature. He loves Shakespeare. He's always talking about the Romans and spouting some Latin motto. He has been giving me books and teaching me. I want to become a better educated man. I'd like to be more like James Caldwell. James says it's all the fault of General Sam McGowan.

I saw General Hill was riding back along the lines as he neared the southern branch of the stream known as Arthur's Swamp. His men love him, because he sees to their every need. He shared the danger with them along the lines; he visited them in the hospitals; he knocked on the doors of their winter cabins to make sure they were warm; he sat around their camp fires on cold nights; he always seems to be able to find supplies and especially provisions, when it appeared that all had been consumed.

As his weary horse walked along, General Hill saw me, a lowly 2nd Lieutenant, beginning the long walk from the picket line in front of the main line. The slogging through the mud sucked at my boots and pulled one off. I don't know'd why, but he turned his horse and rode out to the back to me, just a young officer.

"Lieutenant, can I be of assistance?" Tucker heard the General say to the surprised Lieutenant as Tucker rode up.

The Lieutenant stared at the General and seemed dumbstruck. "Why, no…I don't…think…uh, so, Sir."

"Come rest your hand on my horse, as you get that boot back on. I'll keep him still." The long flowing curls of the General's red hair and beard waved in the wind. I placed my hand on the horse's side and tugged on my boot.

"Why, thank you sir."

"What are you doing out here?"

"Well sir, my company, Company G of Hampton's Legion, is assigned picket duty along the north branch of Arthur's Swamp. "I'm…"

"You're part of Hampton's Legion? What are you doing here? You should be with the rest of your regiment." Hill turned to Tucker. "What the fool hell is a company of Hampton's Legion doing here in front of the Third Corps? Isn't the Legion down by Nine Mile Road, east of the city?"

Without thinking, I responded, "Well, General Sam McGowan ordered us to be part of the pickets and cleared it with General Gary."

General Hill wheeled around, "He did, did he? You have some sort of special relationship with the good General McGowan?"

"Begging the General's pardon, I do. General McGowan has sort of taken me under his wing, so to speak. All winter, he and a member of his staff, James Fitz James Caldwell, have been educating me like a gentleman. I've been reading Shakespeare, studying Latin, reading the Bible and…"

"Even so, he put you and your men out here on the picket line, only three hundred yards or so from our main line…"

Hill was interrupted by Tucker, "General, speaking of being close to the Yankee lines, I think we should move closer to our lines. You're a fetching good target."

Hill rubbed his beard. "I don't think so. My old black slouch hat and worn surcoat doesn't mark me out to be anything important." He turned back to me. "Besides, Lieutenant, McGowan and his men have been moved south towards Hatcher's Run."

"Still, General, I think we should go." Tucker tried to grab the reins of the General's steel-grey dapple horse, but missed.

"Lieutenant, report to me later such that we can discuss this matter further." The General twirled his horse around with beautiful adroitness.

Well, Vicee, I ain't never met a Major General before. I'm thinking I handled the situation well, don't you?

*****

Vicee, as I go through my day, you are never far from my thoughts. You are my constant companion. I talk to you all the time.

This winter was so long and so boring. I would not have made it through were it not for your occasional letter and the time I spent with General McGowan and James Fitz James. The General's Headquarters were set up in the Boisseau Home. It's big home and stands over two and half stories high, 'cause the basement, which you can partially see, is part out of the ground and part in it. The basement is built of red brick like two massive chimneys at each end of the house which finally soar over the roof. The house, though, is a white clapboard affair, with green shutters framing each window. There were porches with a ramp of stairs leading to both the front door and the back door. The house is framed by ancient, giant trees that date back to colonial times.

The Boisseau family had farmed here before the War, raising vegetables and grains as crops. Long years before that, this was a sprawling tobacco planation with 60 or 70 slaves. The Boisseau folk named their home 'Tudor Hall', although I now know that this home is not an example of Tudor architecture at all. When we came, only two fields to the west of Duncan Road were being cultivated. The fields to the east, towards where the Yankees are, have been fallow for some time. Every tree that was on the grounds has been cut down, except for a few right near the house. That's the doings of Commissioner Boisseau, whom I'll tell you about later.

So, with all the trees cut down between us and the Yankees, we can see the Yankees, even though they are about a mile and so away. We are often without a fire, for we have to go a long ways away from our camp to cut timber to make fires. McGowan did his best to have logs cut each day and brought to us, but the trees have ever gotten further away. He has been good to us to take care of us this way.

General McGowan took the home for his headquarters, and he and his staff have had the run of the place since last fall. Joseph and Ann Boisseau moved out last October, when McGowan and his staff moved in. The Boisseaus are in Petersburg living with some relatives. I know Mr. Boisseau had gotten himself appointed to be a Commissioner to meet with Confederate military authorities to curtail the 'wanton destruction being wrought by the Confederate soldier in occupation of private residences and businesses'. I was there in the parlor, when Mr. Boisseau came in his official capacity to lodge a protest with General McGowan as to how the South Carolinians were treating his house and his lands.

"General, I must protest, in the strongest possible manner, the disregard, neglect, and wanton destruction that your men are visiting upon the lands of Tudor Hall." Boisseau bellowed.

General McGowan is a theatrical sort of gentleman. To entertain his staff, he allows them to recite lines of poetry, or read from books aloud, or to present plays. The General is particularly fond of Shakespeare, so there are many performances of soliloquies. The General himself joins in occasionally. He made a fine Hamlet equivocating as to his course of action. Thus, it was fun when he imitated Mr. Boisseau drawn up in his finest commissioner pose trying to intimidate the General, played by my friend, James Fitz James, who is an aide-de-camp to the General.

"Generrrral," McGowan rolled the 'r' endlessly, "I most", mispronouncing the word to mimic the Commissioner, "prrrrrotest," rolling the 'r' again, "in the strongest possible mannerrrrr, the dis-regard, neglect, and wanton de-struction that yourrrrr men are visiting upon the lands of Tudorrrrr Hall." McGowan as Boisseau bellowed.

Throughout, Fitz, playing General McGowan, rolled his eyes at each iteration of rolling 'r's', sighed heavenwards as if in complete pain in listening to the 'Commissioner' and otherwise making light of the plaintive plea.

When the performance was over, the men were rolling on the carpet, holding their sides as the General bowed low to the ground and swished his hat from left to right, as if he were one of the Wilkes receiving a standing ovation after Hamlet. He turned to his co-player, Fitz, beckoning him to likewise take a bow.

The parlor is filled with the General's staff, as would befit a brigadier. There are two Majors, the alliterative Harry Hammond, the Brigade Quartermaster, followed by the Master of the Commissary, Andrew Bowie Wardlaw, whom I did not find lived up to his fearsome knife-like name, and then multiple Captains who seemed to come and go with the seasons, including the staid Ralph E. B. Hewetson, Assistant Quartermaster, and another Assistant Quartermaster, Captain Robert L. Caughrin, who resigned, John Gibson Edwards, Assistant Commissary, Langdon Cheves Haskill, Assistant Adjutant General, who was replaced by James W. Riddick. The brigade also had a surgeon, whom I came to know and love, Dr. Thomas Alexander Evans. Finally, the General had a flock of lieutenants and second lieutenants around him, in which James Fitz James and I were numbered. I did not get to know all of these men well, but some will live forever in my memory.

We so often would sit around the parlor of the Boisseau Home, and tell tales of our adventures during the War, or read favorite passages of books aloud, or act out a play. Many times a serious play would soon be parodied and the names of Yankee Generals would appear as villains.

Orderlies and clerks moved through the house as orders were copied and distributed, maps reviewed and re-drawn, crises encountered and solved. Around the Headquarters were the guards protecting the busy officers within, whether they were engaged in work or play.

Besides this, a flood of humanity came to Tudor Hall to confer with the General. Officers who outranked him, such as Generals Henry Heth, who started the battle of Gettysburg, and Cadmus Wilcox, the man whose brigade was credited with breaking the Union line on Cemetery Hill on July 2nd, 1863, but was unable to stay there, graced the walls of the Boisseau house. Others who were the same rank came and enjoyed the festive atmosphere, such as William MacRea. A lot of these officers came because Sam McGowan was known to be a sharp player of Whist, and they could not resist a good game of cards. Others came because they, too, enjoyed recitations of Shakespeare or Milton.

It was a good place to spend these windy, weary, winter months. I'm tired now, Vicee. I haven't slept much. I'll take a nap.

CHAPTER 16:
REORGANIZATION BREEDS DISORGANIZATION

Reorganizing is a wonderful method for creating the illusion of progress while actually producing confusion, inefficiency, and demoralization.
- **Gaius Petronius Arbiter**

April 1, 1865 3:30 PM

Vicee, life is full of those moments when people think they are doing the right thing, and it turns out that it is the wrong thing, even the worst thing. So it was with the Legion in the spring of 1862.

We marched out of Ashland down the Peninsula through Williamsburg, and camped upon the old Revolutionary War battlefields of Yorktown. We were to be the reserve of the Army on the left.

In Camp, we had to deal with the new law that Congress had passed. Because many troops were starting to go home as their year-long enlistment period was expiring, the Confederate Congress saw the Confederate Army, which was to protect the Capital, melting away. Our enlistment was up in July, but we were never to get to see that period expire.

Congress passed the Conscription Act, which not only said that all men between the ages of 18 and thirty-five were subject to conscription, but also that all men already in the Army were to be given the choice: either reenlist or be subject to conscription. Of course, the reenlistment was for the duration of the war. The Conscription was also for the duration of the war. So why reenlist, you might ask, Vicee? Because Congress also said in the Act that if you reenlisted, you could choose your own company, and you could elect your own officers. After all this time, the boys of the Claremont Rifles wanted to stay together. And, we wanted to elect our own officers. For some time now, the Spann brothers had been universally disliked in Company G, the Claremont Rifles. Captain James G. Spann had been our leader, and his brother, Ransom D. Spann, had been our first lieutenant. This seemed to be too much power in the hands of the two brothers. While I had gotten on well with each of the brothers, many of the Company found them overbearing and too condescending. Now, under the Conscription Act, those who disliked the Spann brothers had a means to get rid of them.

The elections were held on April 25th. Only two men who were captains were not reelected to their commands, James G. Spann and Brown Manning of the Manning Guards. In Brown Manning's case, it was simple why he was not reelected: he was too ill to command, and withdrew his name from contention. So in reality, only Captain Spann was voted out. But so, too, Ransom D. Spann was not reelected. As they were not reelected, they were dropped from the rolls of the Legion and were forced to find other assignments.

So, here we were on the very cusp of fighting in a big battle, and we were under new and untried leadership. Our handicap was greater however than that. The Company had elected Isham Moore as our Captain. Isham had been our 2nd Lieutenant and had been fairly well liked. He seemed a decent and a fair man. There was only one real problem with Isham: he was ill when he was elected and was on a medical furlough. So everything fell on the shoulders of James J. Exum, who had been our 1st Sergeant before the reorganization and after was our 1st Lieutenant. I, too, had been promoted from 1st Corporal to 3rd Sergeant. So lots of us were in positions with which we were unfamiliar.

This was true for our company as well as every other company of the Legion. Our elections had rendered us ineffective and disorganized. And this was when we were the rear of the army; we were the ones to protect everyone else, when we retreated.

But during the night of May 3-4, 1862, we were ordered to retreat. We pulled back from Yorktown and were the last troops to move through Williamsburg. We were the tail of the army with only Jeb Stuart's cavalry behind us to shield us from the Yankee onslaught.

CHAPTER 17:

YORKTOWN: THE STRIDE OF A GIANT, STUMBLES

"I can do it all."-**General George B. McClellan** *to President Lincoln upon being named Commander in Chief of all Unions Forces*

April 1, 1865 4:30 PM

General George McClellan had brought his army of some 130,000 men by water to Fortress Monroe at the very tip of the Peninsula of Virginia. This feat had demonstrated his mastery of logistics, organization, and administration. It was an achievement worthy of Napoleon to whom General McClellan was often compared. General McClellan had been nicknamed the 'Little Napoleon', which was usually shortened to 'Little Mac.'

Little Mac's vision to go by water to attack Richmond was inspired. It avoided the long over land approach where General Joseph Johnston, leading the Confederate Army of Virginia, would have the edge. The terrain that would have been necessary to be traversed was cut by rivers, wide rivers, which flowed generally west to east, providing the Confederates with ready-made defensive line after defensive line. The movement over water of 121,500 men, 44 batteries of artillery, 1,150 wagons, and 15,000 horses, as well as tons of supplies, tents, ammunition, and food, was called the Stride of a Giant by a British military observer.

But McClellan's campaign up the Peninsula demonstrated another facet of his personality: his great timidity. McClellan had faced at first only 10,000 men under Confederate General John Magruder, but Little Mac didn't know the size of the opposition. Prince John, as General John Magruder was known to his men, was famous for his acting abilities. His nickname grew out of his thespian achievements. He staged plays at his headquarters, usually Shakespeare and other classics. Prince John had put to military use his acting abilities. He had his men march in a circle where there was a break in the woods through which the Confederates were visible to the Union forces. Prince John ordered his rebels to make as much noise as was possible as they marched by the break in the woods. They complied; they marched stomping their feet with trumpets blaring and periodically carrying different battle flags. General Magruder had other troops sweep the ground with branches to raise dust, and officers yell orders at unseen (and imaginary) regiments and divisions, mimicking thousands of reinforcements marching to support the Confederate defensive line. In addition to his acting abilities, Magruder added another element to foil McClellan: strong defensive entrenchments. He had built a defensive line along the Warwick River which was really quite impressive. So, McClellan, who had assumed that he would have an easy time of it marching up the Peninsula, found he was faced with a strong defensive line he had not known existed and an unknown, but apparently quite strong, army defending it.

McClellan halted. He thought. He decided. His decision was to bring up heavy siege artillery, which would take a couple of weeks to get there, and then he would lay siege to the Warwick line. So, unknowingly, McClellan was bringing up his heaviest guns to brush aside a defensive line, which a fly swatter would have crushed. Prince John had managed to not only stop General McClellan, but also had thrown fear into Little Mac. Prince John with fewer than 10,000 men had scared an army thirteen times its own. For two weeks, two crucial weeks, Prince John kept McClellan at bay, giving General Johnston time to build up the main Confederate army.

Ultimately, the timid McClellan crept forward, and Prince John had to pull back. But by then, Johnston had reinforced Magruder on the Peninsula. I was there.

Johnston ordered a retreat. As the Confederates retreated through Yorktown, McClellan ordered an attack on the tail of the Confederate column. Jeb Stuart and his cavalrymen were there, and held on as long as they could. Once it became clear that the horsemen could not hold, Johnston detached part of his army to halt the advancing Union forces. Johnston turned to Longstreet, who turned to A.P. Hill. Hill's men rushed into the confrontation.

May 5, 1862 had dawned to reveal a gloomy and dank day. The cold rain fell from the heavens in downpours. The rain fell so hard that campfires sputtered and flared trying to get going. The men awoke with aches and pains of lying upon the cold, damp soil as their bed. Visibility was poor with the mist and rain obscuring men's vision. Everyone was drenched to the bone.

We were just west of Williamsburg with its majestic College of William and Mary. Doug MacDonald leaned over and told me all about how Queen Mary, a rabid Protestant, had deposed her father, James II of England and VII of Scotland, from his throne such that she and her equally rabid Protestant husband, William of Orange, could succeed her father upon both the thrones of England and Scotland. James II's reign was short-lived, three years, but bloody as he tried to kill the Covenanters throughout Scotland who agitated for a Presbyterian king upon the throne of Scotland. James, a devout Catholic, was just another member of the dysfunctional Stuart family that included Charles I, who was beheaded, and Mary Queen of Scots. I could always trust Doug to know his Scots history.

The terrain, as we had just passed through it, was clear in my mind. Just east of Williamsburg, ran our main defensive line. It spanned from north to south across the Peninsula, river to river, blocking McClellan's westward movement. Anchoring the whole line was Ft. Magruder. When you think fort, I am sure, Vicee, that you have visions of turrets and towers, palisades and moats. Actually, this was just a bigger, grander entrenchment on the road to Yorktown. On either side of Ft. Magruder, there were square, earthen works, with abatis, rifle pits, and felled timber adding to its defenses.

Hill's men sat in the mud awaiting the call. The fighting started at 7:30 am, but it was a whole hour later before they were called. By then the whole line was in jeopardy of collapsing. Bluecoats were clambering over the sides of all of our earthworks. It seemed that the whole Union army was breaking through everywhere along our line. Fortunately, the rain provided not only our torture, but also our salvation. Union artillery, of which they had unlimited amounts, was being brought up. Our army, having just marched over the selfsame roads, had churned them up so much that they were swamps of mud or really just goo, which functioned as quicksand. The Union artillery, which would have been devastating, was stuck up to its axles in muck, and was going nowhere.

The rumble of battle was over the ridgeline. As time passed, Hill became more and more restless. Contrary to his usual battle habit, Hill was not wearing his famous red battle shirt. He was clad in a dark blue, loose fitting blouse. His waist carried his sword, while his slouch hat tried its best to protect his head from the rain. He was on his horse, named Prince, which many of the men had thought had been named in honor of General John Magruder. Hill reached over the neck of Prince, and ripped a sprig of a pine tree off, and put it in the band of his hat. The men of his Light Division, seeing him do this, also grabbed sprigs of pine, thinking that it might aid them in the identification of friend from foe.

Then Longstreet's plea for reinforcements came. "Double quick on me, men!" cried Hill. He pulled out his sword, and pointed east down the road back to Ft. Magruder. Hill's Division sprang into action and galloped back the three miles to the fight.

In a hollow perpendicular to the Yorktown Road, Hill formed his battle line. It was now 10:00 am. The Confederate line was a shambles. Longstreet could see that to continue to fight in a defensive mode would only lead to the utter and complete destruction of his force. He also saw that, were he to withdraw now from the contest, his supply wagons and artillery, which were struggling through the mud and gunk of the Yorktown Road, would have to be abandoned. General James Longstreet sat bolt upright on his horse, bringing his six foot tall frame fully erect. His cold-steel eyes more grey than blue became fully focused. He pulled a cigar out of his breast pocket, and tried to light it up, but the rain and wind conspired to deprive him of this delight. After a couple of tries, one of his couriers rode up.

"General might this help?" asked the courier as he gave the General the stump of his cigar such that the General could light his cigar.

"Thank you." General Longstreet, although called "Old Pete" by his men, was not much liked by them. Longstreet pulled on the cigar, and felt the smoky warmth spread through his body. He surveyed the scene before him, not moving, and not saying anything.

"General, don't you think we should do something?" The courier slouched back on the back of his chestnut horse. The horse's breath came out in swirling, massive clouds, one to each side of his snout.

"You're right. Ride to General Hill, and give him my compliments. Tell him to attack those Yankees hitting Ft. Magruder, and drive them back at all hazards." Longstreet pulled on the cigar again. He held the tangy smoke in for a long time, before letting it out slowly. He tried to puff a smoke ring, but the wind destroyed it before it was born.

The courier did not move. All hazards meant that Hill was sacrifice his entire command, if need be, to drive the Federals back. Such an order was a death sentence. "Uh, General... all hazards... Hill... Ft. Magruder...?"

Longstreet turned, and looked the courier straight in the eye. There was nothing in his demeanor to hint that he felt the slightest compunction about the deaths of the several thousand he was ordering. "Get going Sergeant. Tell Hill to drive the Yankees back. AT ALL HAZARDS, if need be."

The courier, knowing that everyone in the army suspected Longstreet of having it in for Hill, thought 'Hadn't he ordered Hill to undertake that impossible task of emptying water out of the trenches, when everyone knew it couldn't be done? He might be sentencing him to death just out of spite.' With that, he spurred his horse to a gallop to get to Hill as soon as was possible.

*****

"General Hill, General Longstreet sends his respects, and orders you to prevent the Yankees from taking Ft. Magruder at all hazards!" The courier breathlessly yelled from the back of his winded horse.

Hill saluted the courier, "Tell General Longstreet that the defenders of Virginia's sacred soil shall do as he has ordered!"

Hill wheeled on his horse, Prince, and ordered his regiments, the 1st, 7th, 11th, and 17th Virginia Infantry, to advance to action against what had now been identified as General Joseph Hooker's Union forces.

Hooker's men had taken the time to take strong cover behind the trees and in the thickets that covered Ft. Magruder. Hill's men advanced against the unleashed volleys of Hooker's fighters. The Confederates could see little due to the falling rain, the smoke which hung like a drape over the battlefield, as well as the thickets and trees that hid the Yankees.

Hill dismounted, as he often did in the thick of battle. Off obliquely to his left some troops were just coming out of the mist. Hill ordered, "Hold your fire, until we know who they are!"

Through the mist came the form of Hill's boyhood chum, Colonel James Kemper, commander of the 7th Virginia. Hill and Kemper pulled out their binoculars. Hill's eyes identified them first, "They're Yankees! Give it to them!" Kemper repeated the order. The 7th Virginia roared as one gun as they unleashed a crushing volley.

Hill, waving his pistol in the direction of the Union forces, ran towards them, crying back over his shoulder, "Follow me men! Charge!"

As one man, the 17th Virginia followed Hill. Kemper, too, took up the charge, and as he did so, the 7th joined the charge with the 11th not far behind them. The 1st had swerved far to the left, and was embroiled in its own fight. The sweeping rain beat their faces as the three regiments charged. They jumped a farmer's fence and then slid down a small slope, through the zip, zip of a hail of bullets that swarmed around them, and on and on into the mist. The fight was at close quarters. The enemy were kneeling or sitting on the ground, hidden by bushes and thickets, behind trees or rocks. The grey line surged forward, and the blue line faded before the grey surge.

Finally, the enemy found a strand of fallen timbers which gave them an extensive and excellent defensive position. The two lines were separated by only 40 yards or so as they fired, reloaded, and fired again and again, as a half hour passed, and then an hour, and finally two hours. The battle flag of the 7th Virginia was shot through with 23 holes as the battle raged. Then the ammunition started to be exhausted.

Hill walked the line encouraging his men. He stood bolt upright amid the thunder of battle and the smoke of hell, and pointed to the fallen timbers. "Clean 'em out, boys!" he yelled.

A private was huddled in the mud quivering and afraid of the battle. The uproar was great, the cannon were booming, the men were yelling, and the rain beat down. Hill saw the young boy. He bent down, and, without a word, began to stroke the young man's cheek. They looked at each other: The General, a rich target for Union guns, and the fearful boy crying in the slime. Hill finally said to the boy, "I know son that this is hard, but you are from Virginia, and we, Virginians, do not give in. I will help you up." With that Hill took the boy's hand and placed the boy behind a tree. "Load your weapon, son," Hill calmly said. "You can do it. You do not want to let down your hometown."

The boy obeyed and loaded his musket.

"Son, now you must fire your weapon," the General again said calmly.

The boy hesitated a second, then he looked at Hill, and then he aimed his musket and fired.

"There. That's better." The General nodded to the boy, and the boy meekly saluted in return.

Finally, the ammunition was almost gone. Hill looked at the Yankees holding their position in the timbers. He raised his sword, and pointed to the timbers. "Give them the bayonet!" He jumped out in front and led his men, who rose up with a yell. That was the first time I heard it -the rebel yell. It was like the yelping of dogs in a fox hunt mixed with an Indian war whoop with the strong overtones of the guttural cry of the Clans charging across the moors in Scotland, when they were about to kill Englishmen.

The Union line broke, and the blue clad soldiers ran in retreat. Hill's men captured 160 Union soldiers, 7 battle flags, and 8 cannon. Hill had lost some 67 men dead, 245 wounded, and 14 missing, but had inflicted some 334 dead, 906 wounded and 330 missing upon the Union forces they had faced for seven long hours.

It was almost dusk then, and the battle dribbled out.

CHAPTER 18:

SEVEN PINES

*"How would you enjoy sleeping if it had to be effected out in the woods, in a driving rain, with a soggy, spongy soil for a bed, and no covering for a blanket? I have waked up at midnight under such circumstances and found half the regiment standing silently and gloomily around camp-fires, while now and then the barking, hectic cough of some afflicted soldier preached a sermon on death."-**Confederate Chaplain***

April 1, 1865 5:00 PM

We had retreated all the way up the Peninsula from Yorktown and Williamsburg to the outskirts of Richmond. The spires and towers of Richmond loomed above the trees. The chimes of the clock towers and the bells of the churches could be heard in the distance. It would have been an idyllic scene, Vicee, but here I was with the Legion, my back to Richmond and my face to the damned Union troops, who were now only seven miles from Richmond. The damned Yankees could see, hear, and almost taste our Capital city, the objective of their long march up the Peninsula

The Federals were close, too close, exceedingly close to our first city. If they took Richmond, then the War would be over. We could not survive without the manufacturing of the city, the textiles, the foundries, and the Tredegar Iron Works, where the bulk of our cannon were cast, and all the other myriad services and goods which were produced there. The loss of our Capital meant more to us, because without our Capital, we would suffer the greatest drop in morale. Further, a country that can't defend its Capital, cannot defend its people. We were facing complete extinction; the Yankees were close to complete triumph.

The long trek up the Peninsula had not produced a single battle that was decisive for our cause.

The Union behemoth slinked closer and closer to its quarry, ready to strike and kill.

The pressure on Commanding General Joseph Johnston was great. Daily, the President of the Confederacy tried to prod his Commanding General to action. Some days he rode his horse out of Richmond to personally confer with Johnston; other days he sent him a telegraphic inquiry; still other days he sent an official to query him, such as the Secretary of War, George Randolph. He kept up the pressure by writing him letters, and, finally, by asking Robert E. Lee, his military advisor to find out when Johnston was going to do something.

'Doing something' was an element of his personality that Johnston seemed to lack. Procrastination seemed to rule his psyche. The story circulated that Joseph Johnston, who was reputed to be the best shot in the Confederacy, had been invited to a weekend of hunting quail. He went out each day to hunt, but each day he returned to his host's home not only without a bird for his efforts, but also without having fired his shotgun. It seems that every time a bird or a flock of birds was spotted, something was wrong with the shot, so Johnston did not shoot - either the wind was too strong from the side, or the birds rose too suddenly, or there was a beater who might be hit, or his gun was unloaded, or some other excuse. Everyone suspected, but no one said, that Johnston feared taking a shot, because, if he missed, then his reputation as the best shot in the South would have been destroyed. He'd rather not shoot, than fail at a shot.

This same fear was now staunching his abilities as a commander. For now, he bore the reputation that he was the best general in the Confederacy: it is better not to fight, then fight and lose, or so he thought.

But now, with the Union hosts of 130,000 upon the doorstep of Richmond, that is being only seven miles away, there was no more room to which to retreat. If Richmond was given up, the war was over. He had to fight now and here, because there was no future, and there was nowhere else.

By the end of May, 1862, McClellan had moved his forces to the Chickahominy River. His logistics base was at White House, a beautiful plantation home on the banks of the Pamunkey River. There, the Richmond and York River Railroad bridged its name sake River as it made its way almost in a straight shot to Richmond. This railroad, thus, was crucial to the Yankee effort to take Richmond.

Johnston was looking for McClellan to make a mistake. All the way down the Peninsula and now to the banks of Chickahominy River, McClellan had moved flawlessly. Still, Johnston had run out of time. Then, as May was ready to pass into June, two things conspired to enable Johnston to attack. First, the weather smiled upon the Confederates as rain began to fall. The Chickahominy River became swollen. Then, McClellan made a mistake. He pushed a small portion of his forces across the Chickahominy River. This force might be isolated, and certainly could not be reinforced quickly being across the River from the main Union forces. Johnston saw his chance, and he made preparations to attack this small force. The night before the attack, Mother Nature unleashed her fury in the form of a tremendous thunderstorm which made the Chickahominy River burst forth from its banks turning from a little placid stream into a raging torrent. Although McClellan's pioneers had built bridges, they were swept away with the flood.

Johnston devised an overly complex plan to attack the Yankees. Two Union corps were across the River. They were centered on the small hamlet of Seven Pines. The Fair Oaks Railroad Station of the Richmond and York Railroad was about a half mile or so northwest of Seven Pines. Four major roads converged at the Seven Pines and the Railroad Station area, making it a road hub of strategic value. The spokes of this wheel of roads radiated in such a way that three of the four were in our hands. The first one, starting with the one coming in from the northwest, was known as Nine Mile Road. The second one, the Williamsburg Stage Road, came from the west but hooked around such that it entered Fair Oaks Railroad Station from the south. A third road approached from the southeast, and joined the Williamsburg Stage Road just about a quarter of a mile short of the Railroad Station. Finally, the fourth road, which came from the northeast, led to the Grapevine Bridge, and was the main and only connection to the Union Army north of the Chickahominy River, some two and a half miles away.

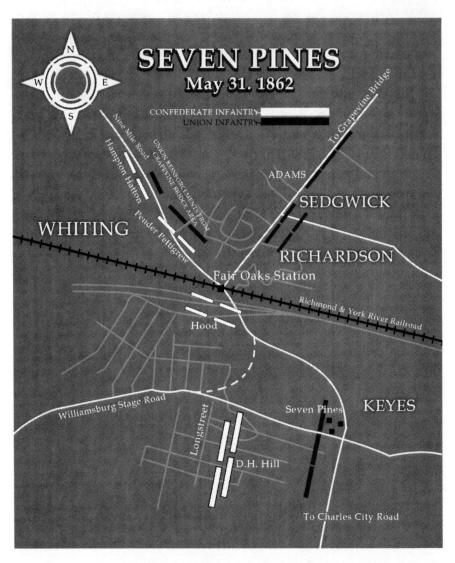

Johnston spread a map out on the table in front of General James Longstreet. "My plan calls for a diversionary attack by General A.P. Hill and Prince John Magruder's forces on our left against the Chickahominy River. I intend by this diversionary attack to distract the Union forces as to where the real attack will fall, and to pin Union reinforcements by the River such that they will not come down the Grapevine Bridge Road to the Seven Pines-Fair Oaks area." He paused a moment, and then repeated, "I hope to pin them in place on the Chickahominy River." He pointed to the area of River that Hill and Magruder would hit. "Do you see this General?"

"Yes, sir," Longstreet crisply responded.

"Now General, I want you to lead the attack." Johnston looked Longstreet in the eye to see his reaction. Longstreet's board smile told Johnston all he needed to know.

"Thank you, sir," Longstreet could barely contain his ambition for glory and honor.

Johnston continued, "You are to hit one of the Union corps, which we believe is Keyes Corps, on this side of the Chickahominy River from three different directions simultaneously. You will be in tactical command of the attack, even though Generals Smith and Huger outrank you. Do you understand?"

Longstreet's smile could not have stretched further across his face. His head bobbed up and down in gleeful anticipation. He thought, 'Finally, I will get the chance to prove myself, and be covered with glory.'

"You are to march down the Nine Mile Road, whereas D. H. Hill, the brother-in-law of Stonewall Jackson, will march just about due east on the Williamsburg Stage Road to hit Seven

Pines head on. You will deploy your forces on Nine Mile Road, and hit Seven Pines from the northwest. General Benjamin Huger will take his forces across the Williamsburg Stage Road to the Charles City Road, and attack Seven Pines from the southwest." Johnston's finger traced the three roads one at a time, as he spoke.

"Is this all clear to you, General?"

Longstreet nodded affirmatively.

"Thus, General, there will be three prongs hitting the Yankees, one frontally, led by D.H. Hill, whose job it is to pin them down. Your prong and Huger's will hit them in both flanks, you north, Huger south." Johnston pointed out the directions of all three prongs slowly on the map. "Are you getting this General?"

Longstreet again bobbed his head up and down, perhaps, a little too animatedly.

Johnston continued, "Whiting and Smith will be the reserves for the attack, and they will hang back near my Headquarters. Whiting will be the reserves for you and Smith for Huger or Hill, as needed." Johnston thought about asking Longstreet to repeat the orders to make sure that he had them, but then he realized that such a request would demean Longstreet, for Longstreet was a very vain and ambitious man.

"I will give orders to the others about the attack. It is important that everyone know their role and execute it properly. Do you have any questions?" Johnston looked at Longstreet carefully. 'Should I give him an exhortation as to how important this attack is? Should I appeal to his vanity? Should I issue written orders? But what if my orders are captured?' He dismissed these thoughts from his mind, and added, "General, the fate of the Confederacy rests upon our actions. I will pray for your success."

As May 31st, dawned, Johnston stayed in his Headquarters with Generals Smith and Whiting nearby. Johnston thought that he would know the right time to throw in the reserves. He walked back and forth as the morning slowly progressed. Often, he stroked his nearly bald head, blotting away the perspiration that formed on his forehead and pate. He was immaculately attired in his dress uniform. His van dyke mustache and beard were perfect to the hair. Like so many of the high-ranking officers of the Army of Virginia, he was a Virginian. But unlike many other officers, he was not from the first families of Virginia. In fact, he was just a third generation Virginian, his grandfather having emigrated from Scotland in 1726. His grandfather had married well in that he married a niece of Patrick Henry. Also, his grandfather had fought in the American Revolution. So Johnston was proud of his heritage.

The daylight hours whittled away, and still Johnston did not hear the sounds of battle coming from Seven Pines. Johnston did not know that the battle sounds could be heard in the streets of Richmond some seven miles from Seven Pines, but, for some reason, they could not be heard at Johnston's Headquarters, which were only two miles away.

Noon came, and then the sun started to slant to the west in the spring sky. Johnston wondered why all he heard was some occasional musket fire, which he dismissed as normal picket exchanges along the line, but did not think to send out any staff officers to inquire why the assault had not started.

General Gustavus Smith asked, "What time is it General?"

"About four o'clock, I think."

Just then in burst a courier from Longstreet. He was panting from his breakneck ride to Headquarters. "General, I bring the compliments of General Longstreet." The courier took a couple of gulps of water from an offered canteen. Then he resumed his report. "Longstreet urgently requests that the reserves be put into the battle. He told me to say to you that he had been engaged for hours, and he is making some progress, but the Yankees are throwing in more and more men. Again, the assistance of Whiting's reserves is urgently needed, he said."

Johnston looked out of the frame door of the Headquarters, and saw the courier's lathered horse tied up outside. "I just don't understand why I haven't been able to hear anything."

"I think it might be an acoustic shadow," General Smith answered.

General Johnston saw that his grand plan had fallen apart. Bypassing General Smith, who was right by his side, Johnston issued orders to the brigades of Whiting to march double time down the Nine Mile Road to support Longstreet. He also ordered Wade Hampton to follow behind Whiting. He also ordered General John Bell Hood's division to the Confederate right.

What Johnston did not know was that Longstreet had not followed his plan at all. If Johnston had ordered a reconnaissance, he would have learned that Longstreet had marched down the Williamsburg Stage Road, not the Nine Mile Road.

The grand attack of three prongs had become only one prong, and that prong was a frontal attack prong upon an entrenched enemy. In addition, Longstreet had ordered D. H. Hill to precede him, so instead of an attack coming from three sides, the attack had in fact just been a frontal assault on Seven Pines. Only Hill's men were in the attack. There was no prong down the Nine Mile Road, because Longstreet had not obeyed orders or had misread his map. And because Huger's men had farther to march, and had a much worse road to traverse, the southern prong did not materialize. The piling up of Longstreet's men, and Hill's on the same road only slowed these two forces down. Given the amount of rain which had fallen over the course of the last couple of days, Longstreet's force, which was behind Hill's, faced a churned up road of muddy slop which consumed far more time to negotiate. Thus, the attack had come off both late and in the wrong place.

Longstreet would later tell Johnston that he altered Johnston's plan. Unfortunately, Longstreet told no one of his change in the plans, and, thus, Johnston now was throwing reserves to places where the fighting wasn't even going on. Also, because Longstreet had not marched down Nine Mile Road, the Union had been freely able to reinforce Fair Oaks using the Grapevine Road, which Longstreet's forces should have been blocking.

So, as General Whiting men double-timed their march along the Nine Mile Road, they encountered Yankees in great numbers just north and east of Fair Oaks Station. Whiting reported this to Johnston, who cavalierly replied, "Oh! General Whiting, you are too cautious!" Whiting was ordered to attack and disperse these forces. Thus, Whiting's men would not be able to reinforce Hill or Longstreet.

Whiting turned to his lead brigades under two men whose names would become synonymous with Pickett's Charge at Gettysburg a year later, Pettigrew and Pender. Dutifully, they went in, and were repulsed with heavy casualties. At this, Whiting added Hampton's brigade, and renewed the attack.

As 3rd Sergeant, I helped to line up the men to attack. We had to slice through dense underbrush and thickly wooded terrain that undulated greatly. The soil, having been soaked with rain now for days, was muddy, and our feet sunk in with each step, making a sucking sound. The order came down, and we charged a strand of woods where we could see some puffs of grey musketry fire blending in with the grey mist of the rain that fell. As we charged through the thickets and dense underbrush, the rebel yell rang out loud and clear. Still, the shot, shell, and musket fire of the federal forces was overwhelming. We were repulsed again, leaving many friends and neighbors behind. We regrouped and tried another charge with no change in the outcome. We were hunkered down after having made our second charge, resting. We were winded and thirsty. The results were horrific as I surveyed my Company. I could not find either Robbie or Douglas MacDonald, the twins of my childhood.

Then a man in elegant civilian attire rode up to my company. I had my men, as I was now 3rd Sergeant, huddled by some fallen timbers, which I thought would act as kind of a wall behind which we could shelter.

"I say, is this Hood's Texas Brigade?" asked the handsome civilian, with a distinct Texas drawl.

"Sir, I am 3rd Sergeant McEachern of Hampton's Legion. Who are you?" I asked not sure what to make of this man, and wary as to his intentions.

I looked at him. He had coal black hair that he combed straight back, I guess to tame the curl in his hair which was apparent. His black mustache disappeared into his black full beard. Although he was nattily dressed, he was a quite a stout man.

"I am Postmaster General John Reagan of Texas, and I'm looking for my boys!" He shouted back, somewhat indignantly. "I have just left General Lee at Johnston's Headquarters. I am aiming to join the Texans in this here fight."

"Well, Postmaster General, sir, I don't think that would be a good idea…" I was going to argue with the man, but he cut me off.

"Look Sergeant, I know what I am doing, and I will find Hood whether you help me or not." With that he rode off.

The shelling increased, and we lay there huddled against the earth for shelter.

The smoke of battle added to the cloudiness of the day reduced visibility to virtually nothing. Suddenly, General Johnston, with Major Banks and other members of his staff, rode through my company. They were apparently riding up to the Fair Oaks House to make that a sort of forward Headquarters.

They disappeared into the haze, smoke and clouds, only to be replaced some ten minutes or so later by President Jefferson Davis, his military advisor, General Robert E. Lee, and General Magruder. It seemed to us that the whole government of the Confederacy was on the field. I feared that one of them might be shot, killed, or wounded that day. They stopped by us for a few moments, when Postmaster Reagan appeared again. He started to yell at the President, "Your Excellency, I must protest your unnecessary exposure to the dangers of war!"

With that, a courier came up from our left, and announced that General Hampton had been wounded. He had taken a bullet to his foot.

General Hampton ordered his staff to leave him alone. "I will stay on the field!" he protested. Surgeon E. S. Gaillard was nearby. Hampton's men urged him to let the Surgeon examine the foot.

"I can remove the bullet right here. You will not have to lose the foot!" Surgeon Gaillard quietly said to the General.

"Then take it out, and let me get back to my men," Hampton cried.

Gaillard removed the bullet right then and there. Although Hampton refused to leave the field, eventually the blood loss compelled him to leave. The day was not going well for us at all.

We had barely recovered from the shock of this news, when a second courier, panting after his hard ride, screamed at us that General Joseph Johnston had been killed. We all reeled from that news, which was followed up moments later by a stretcher bearing what we thought was his lifeless body.

President Davis turned to General Lee, "You are in command now of this Army. May God grant you success, for if you fail, Richmond will fall!"

Lee saluted the President, and then said to the President, "Sir, as my first order, I must order you to leave my battlefield. You must seek shelter and safety. The Confederacy cannot stand the loss of you on the same day as its leading General!"

The only fortunate thing that happened that day is that dark fell upon us, and the battle fizzled out.

The Legion went into this fray with 384 men, only to leave behind 24 dead, with 134 wounded, of which 16 were mortally wounded. The Legion suffered a staggering 41% casualty rate. It was 47%, if you included the 21 men we lost as prisoners.

The next day, the battle continued, but with no better results than the day before. I really don't know too much about that day, for within a half hour of the fighting resuming, I was shot through the lungs, fell to the ground, and blacked out.

CHAPTER 19:

THE MILLS OF GOD

Though the mills of God grind slowly;
Yet they grind exceeding small;
Though with patience He stands waiting,
With exactness grinds He all.
-**Henry Wadsworth Longfellow**, "Retribution", Poetic Aphorisms, 1846

April 1, 1865 6: 00 PM

Part I: Loss

I awoke in a start. I instantly turned my head from side to side looking for the Yankee attack. "Are they here?" I cried out.

"No, Lieutenant, they ain't here yet." Douglas, faithful Douglas, answered.

I rubbed my eyes. I was still not fully awake.

"I thought I had lost something…" I stammered.

"You lost what?"

"I don't know. It seemed so important at the time…in my dream…"

"Seems like we're always losing something, don't it?" Doug asked.

"I lost my Daguerreotype of Vicee. This is one of the greatest losses I could have ever suffered." I looked at him. Doug had not been with the Legion when this had occurred. For some reason I felt compelled to tell him the story.

"We had to strip off our haversacks, and our knapsacks, as well as the rest of our equipment, blanket, coats, and so on. The whole company left all of our things together and went forward to form the battle line."

I settled back and told him the whole story, Vicee. "It was Gaines' Mill." I remembered it as if it were yesterday. "I was just back from being wounded at Seven Pines. Bobby Lee had just taken charge after Joe Johnston had been wounded at Seven Pines. We were now the Army of Northern Virginia. Lee had decided we were going to attack and drive them away from Richmond. Little Mac had brought the Union Army of the Potomac within seven miles of the Capital."

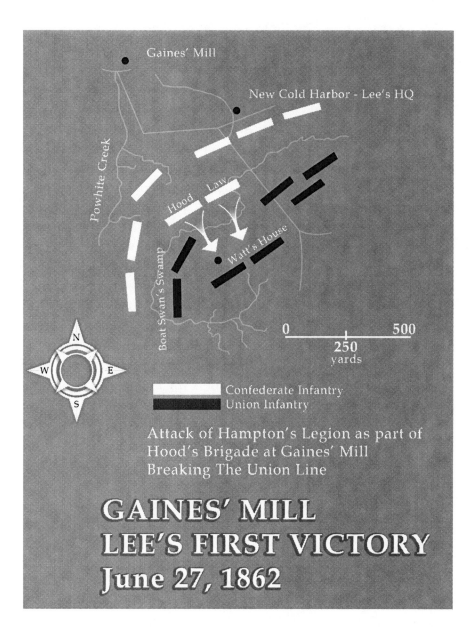

Doug piped in, "I understand they could hear the chiming bells of the churches and see the spires."

"Yes, that is true. First, D.H. Hill had come up with his men. They got nowhere." I was drawing in the dirt with a stick a map of the battle.

"Next came Maxcy Gregg of A.P. Hill's boys. He and General Hampton are close, childhood friends. His was the lead that day. All afternoon, the men of the Light division under A.P. Hill had tried to batter General John Fitz Porter's V Corps off of the ridge behind the swampy creek known as Boatswain's Swamp. Hill was in the fury of battle. He wore his red battle shirt, but no amount of battering had been successful so far."

I was reliving that battle-we called it Gaines' Mill; they called it Boatswain's Swamp.

"We were with the Texas boys under General Hood. Old Jack had brought us to the battlefield late in the afternoon. Bobby Lee asked Stonewall and then he asked Hood himself, if we could take the top of that ridge. Hood said, 'If my boys can't do it, then it can't be done.' He looked down at his boots for moment, and then he looked at the swamp before the ridge, and then the ridge itself. 'We can do it.' We stood in line for a long while, and even though the afternoon was getting late, it was a hot day in June in Virginia. We sweated as we stood in our wool uniforms.

Some sharpened their knives or their bayonets. Others tried to finish a letter to their wives, girlfriends, or mothers. Others, like me, kneeled and prayed."

"Oh God, I know that I have done some bad things. I gambled when I promised you, I wouldn't." Then I added, "I will read my Bible and try to follow your Holy Word."

"While I was apraying, I heard the rumors that Powell Hill was to beat Little Mac because of a woman." I don't know why I started gossip. Maybe it was all James Caldwell's doings. That Fitz seemed to gossip all the time. I guess that's what a regimental historian does.

Doug stared at me, disbelief shone in his eyes. "A woman? What woman?"

"Well, it seems that A.P. Hill, after he graduated from West Point, fought in Mexico as did so many of his classmates. After Mexico, he fought Seminole Indians in the swamps of Florida. From there, he was posted to the Texas frontier. Then he was posted back to Florida, this time to Key West. There he had contracted yellow fever, which forced him to leave Florida and recuperate at Culpepper, Virginia, his hometown."

Doug interrupted me, "Oh, come on! What's all of this got to do with a woman?"

"I'm getting to it. Once he was fit again, he requested a transfer, which was granted by no less than Jefferson Davis, as Secretary of War, to the Survey Office in Washington. In that office, he triangulated the Hudson River between Albany and New Baltimore. He improved the printing operations of the Office which improved the distinctness of the maps produced by the office."

I could see that Doug was becoming bored.

"Okay, while in that Office, the young officer Hill fell in love with Ellen B. Marcy. Miss Nelly, as she was known, was a woman of unspoken beauty. Blonde, blue-eyed, the daughter of Captain and Mrs. Randolph B. Marcy, she set many-a-heart aflutter. One such heart belonged to that of George B. McClellan, Hill's best friend and West Point roommate. Little Mac initially held the upper hand, because he had served under Captain Marcy on Marcy's Red River Campaign."

Doug had perked up. "Well, did Hill marry her?"

"No. Let me tell the story. George had promised to leave the military to take position as an executive of the Illinois Central Railroad, which also pleased both Captain and Mrs. Marcy, who wanted their daughter to climb socially and not merely marry an Army officer."

Doug had that disappointed look on his face again.

But he brightened up when I said, "Still, somehow, Hill managed to ingratiate himself with Miss Nelly. She turned down Little Mac's marriage proposal. Now, Miss Nelly was seen constantly in the company of Powell. Captain Marcy wrote long, well-argued letters to his daughter from his post in Laredo, Texas, pointing out the moderate financial status of the Hill family and the hardships a life as an officer's wife would be. He also pointed out how rich Little Mac was and what high society he was."

"Did she give in?" Doug asked wide-eyed.

"No, Miss Nelly at first did not relent. The letters from her father continued, until under pressure, she gave in to her father's wishes. Hill reacted quite vigorously to the situation and wrote to Captain Marcy. Although his letters implored, begged, and cajoled, they were to no avail. George McClellan was chosen by Miss Nelly. And that's why they say Hill fights like the demons of Hell when he faces off against Little Mac."

We became quiet. I thought about my lost Daguerreotype of Vicee. It pained me that after the battle, we came back to where our things ought to be, and nothing was there. Someone had stolen all our haversacks and knapsacks, leaving us without anything. They had taken our food, our cooking pans, our tent flaps, our extra shirts, our wives kits, and anything personal we had left for later recovery.

II. Gain?

I was still thinking of Gaines' Mill. How we charged down the ride, across the creek and then up that steep hill, breaking three lines of entrenched Union infantry to carry the day. I didn't know if I wanted to restart the story with Doug and he seemed to be content just lying there on his back with a sprig of grass in his mouth. I watched the sprig switch from side to side in his mouth. It twirled and then it started to get shorter and shorter.

"You becoming a cow?" I teased.

"Yeah. I reckon." He pulled up another sprig of grass and planted it in his mouth.

The afternoon wore on.

"When do you think it happened?" I asked Robert MacDonald.

"What happened?" He had no idea of what I was asking.

"I'm sorry. I was thinking back when we were camped along the Occoquan River."

Robbie interrupted me. "You mean way back at the beginning of the War?"

"Yeah, way back then," I replied.

"Yes, I remember. We had just come up from Columbia on the train after we was inducted into the Legion." Robbie was chewing a blade of grass, which twirled in his mouth as he chewed. The stalk was getting shorter with each gyration of his jaw. "What about it?"

"Well, back then the Yankees were camped just across the river from us. Each night, after dark, as the camps slunk off to sleep, our bands and their bands would alternatively play music back and forth over the river. They'd play 'Johnny Comes Marching Home', and then we'd play 'Dixie'. Back and forth, one song after another, until at some point both banks played 'Home Sweet Home,' and we'd all be sad and teary-eyed thinking about our wives and sweethearts at home, and wonder when we'd see them again." I paused a moment.

It was then, Vicee, when I understood it all, or at least I thought I did. I continued. "We'd trade with the blue fellers. Maybe our newspapers for their coffee or something like that. We'd fight them like hell, and, then, the night after a battle, we'd be playing songs and singing songs across the river and trading stuff like we were old friends or brothers. There was a civility to it then. Do you remember?"

Robbie was now lying down in the grass. He was selecting a fine tender stalk to chew upon. "Yeah, I remember it."

"Well, what happened? When did that all end? When did we stop playing songs to one another, and when did the civility stop?"

Robbie rolled over. "I don't rightly know."

"Well, I do. It ended when Grant came east. From then on, it all became a killing business. Before then, it was a war between men of the same country and experience. We may not have agreed with the Yankees on everything, but we shared the same experiences. We had fought the same war against the British to win our independence. And then we had to fight them all over again, to re-win our independence in the War of 1812. We all fought the same Indians and the same French. We all shared in the Declaration of Independence and fired off the same fireworks each Fourth of July. But when Grant came, something changed, and now we all fight to kill each other, and get this damn thing over."

*****

I stopped for a moment. The sun was setting. Robbie stood up, and looked for his brother, Douglas.

Douglas came at his brother's call and stood over us. While Doug was standing there in the orange sunlight, its glow framed his face. I could see the little hairs on the side of his face bathed in orange. I saw his profile and remembered how he looked as a boy, when we used to play together. Douglas was the shyer, quieter one of the two brothers. He always seemed more thoughtful and cautious. Robert was the daredevil, who was always ready to try anything anyone challenged him to do. It seemed as if a million years had passed since we played as boys in Stateburg. Back then we were the Scots fighting against the English. We brandished our wooden claymores and howled in rage against Edward Long Shanks. Of course, Robert was Robert the Bruce. I was William Wallace, and Douglas was Andrew Moray. We ran, waving our wooden swords, and cried our Clan motto at the top of our lungs: "Per Mare, Per Terras!" (By Sea, by Land!) It was as if the yelling of the motto would thrust aside our foes, and carry us to victory.

If we were not playing Scots against the English, then we were the Americans against the British. Everyone we knew had had an ancestor who fought in the American Revolution. We all knew how it was the Scots and the Scots-Irish of South Carolina, banding together with the Scots of Tennessee and Kentucky, who had won the Revolution. And if we boys played the War of 1812, we were another Scots hero, Andrew Jackson. He, too, was born in our beloved South Carolina. Our games were great, because we could play either as pirates in his ragtag forces or as the Scots of Tennessee and Kentucky, armed with their long rifles. We loved eviscerating the British at New Orleans. Did a boy need a greater hero than Andrew Jackson? Wasn't he that orphan who refused to clean the boots of a British officer during the Revolution and got a heroic scar across his face for his refusal? Didn't he lead us against the Indians? Didn't he beat the British at New Orleans? And hadn't he become President?

But in our childhood, we had so many other Scots we could admire. Our fathers, our mothers, and our school teachers made sure that we knew that the Scots were a glorious and profound people, making history in virtually every way. There was the Scot explorer who discovered the source of the Nile, James Bruce, or Lord Byron, Carolina Oliphant, and Robert Burns, poets of great renown, or the philosophers, Thomas Carlyle and David Hume, or the industrialist, David Dale, whose spinning mills consumed so much Southern cotton, or the inventor, Lord Kelvin, or the pirate, William Kidd (we boys were entranced with pirates and the glory of booty!), or the founder of our religion, John Knox, or road builder John McAdam, and so on.

So, all of us were brought up in a land which revered our ancestors and saw them as a mighty people. We had produced great warriors, scientists, inventors, writers, and poets. We were special.

At New Orleans, Andy Jackson had slain hundreds of British troops and had lost only a handful of his men. We knew we were better fighters than the British. The British infantry that fought at New Orleans were the same British infantry of Wellington's Army that had bested Napoleon. If we could beat the British, we could beat France's best, Napoleon. So if we could beat Napoleon, couldn't we beat some foreign immigrants that comprised the Yankee army?

In the beginning of the War, we were told, again and again, one Southerner can lick ten Yankees. Whence did this thought come? Why, from our own folklore! The North hadn't beaten the British in the American Revolution. The War had been won in the South. In the War of 1812, the Capital in Washington DC has been sacked, but the big city of New Orleans had been successfully defended. The difference? Kentucky long rifles in the hands of men who knew how to use them, Scots like Davey Crockett and Daniel Boone, and other men from Tennessee and Kentucky.

So were Robert, Douglas, and I so different today? We yelled our rebel yell with Scots pride, and charged the Yankees believing that our rebel yell would instill fear in the Federals and break their spirit. We were surely going to be able to whip 30 Yankees, weren't we?

*****

Robert MacDonald came up. "Doug, what are you guys doing?" He was ready to get into some mischief and wanted to know what our agenda was. Neither Douglas nor I had any energy to spare to do anything.

"Robbie, we ain't doing anything," Doug replied.

Robert sat down in the grass, and we all watched the last rays of sunlight fade away as the orange ball disappeared behind the trees. A couple of streaks of orange spread across the sky in a fan shape.

"I don't think I told you this," I began, "but after I lost Vicee's daguerreotype, some months later I picked up a Union soldier's daguerreotype."

"You did what?" Robbie looked at me as if I had pulled a fish that had gone bad from out of a newspaper. Doug hung back and said nothing. Although they were twins, and although they both had red hair, they didn't look alike. Douglas was shorter, more compact, and was the younger of the twins. Robert was taller, thinner, and more vivacious. He could not sit still for any length of time.

"It was a picture of his wife or sister, I don't know." I stopped. I thought about what I was going to say. I know this all sounded a little strange. I plunged ahead. I really didn't keep anything back from my oldest friends.

"I used to look at it and wonder: Who is she? What is she to the Union soldier? It was inscribed on the back: 'Your loving Bessie Adams.' There a letter from her, too, stuck in the back of the frame. I read it. I felt like I was spying on them, prying into something secret and private, something beautiful and rare."

Now, Doug was looking at me as if I were crazy, too.

"So after a while, I mailed it back to Bessie. I told her who I was, how I had found her picture, and how I thought that whoever had lost it would like her to have it again. I thought maybe Vicee's daguerreotype would somehow magically come back to me if I did this."

"And did it?" Both Douglas and Robert asked at the same time.

"No, it didn't. But I still think I did the right thing. Maybe I brought some civility back into the War."

CHAPTER 20:

MARCHING TO MARYLAND

Dear Mother! burst the tyrant's chain,
Maryland!
Virginia should not call in vain,
Maryland!
She meets her sisters on the plain-
"Sic semper!" 'tis the proud refrain
That baffles minions back again,
Maryland!
Arise in majesty again,
Maryland! My Maryland!
*-**Maryland, My Maryland!** Stanza VI*

April 1, 1865 7:00 PM

The best efforts of the Union Army of the Potomac had not borne fruit. We had decisively defeated them at Second Bull Run. Longstreet had dropped an axe upon the neck of the Union forces and had driven them back miles. It was only too bad that our cavalry had not been able to cut them off from the Stone Bridge across Bull Run before they had escaped. Our victory would have been total annihilation of the enemy, if they had sealed that Stone Bridge off.

But Second Manassas hadn't been a fluke. Bobby Lee, as we were starting to call him, had defeated Little Mac during the Seven Days. Beaver Dam had been a draw, but Little Mac had retreated. We beat them up at Gaines' Mill, which was a strong victory. Savage Station had to count as a victory, although it was incomplete. At Frayser's Farm, we had come within a whisker of that elusive total annihilation again. It was by the barest of margins that the Yankees had survived that one.

Malvern Hill, bloody Malvern Hill, was a disaster. But even after such a tremendous miscarriage on our part, General George McClellan retreated to the safety of James River at Harrison's Crossing. He sat there with his bigger, better supplied army huddled in terror against the James River banks, protected by his gunboats. The David had slain the Goliath. The Yankee hosts of 130,000 or so men had been pushed from some seven miles from Richmond to over thirty miles away from our Capital. In one week, the entire tenor of the war had changed. Lee's smaller army had defeated, manhandled, pushed back, and bullied McClellan's much larger army. And throughout, we had captured small arms, materials, supplies, uniforms, cannon, food stuffs, wagons, and horses that were left behind by a retreating, panic-stricken, demoralized Union Army. Then Lee left McClellan's Army behind, sure that Little Mac was too scared to do anything. He marched around the flank of another large Union Army led by General Pope. He wound up in Pope's rear, forcing Pope to attack Lee on ground of his own choosing. It was then, that Longstreet unleashed the dogs of war or a bear trap that was sprung in the form of a flank attack at Second Bull Run.

We were marching now, Vicee, past the site of our victory at Ball's Bluff a little over a year ago on our way to Leesburg. There, we splashed across the Potomac to enter Maryland. We were invading the North! Some of us went to White's Ford, while the rest of us went to Cheek's Ford. Men walked across the Potomac holding their powder, percussion caps, and muskets above their heads. Many stripped off their clothes. The crossing had the all the lark and frolic of an old waterhole on a hot summer day. The bands played 'Maryland, My Maryland' as these naked or near naked men crossed the river laughing and singing. We must have looked a sight! We, in our rag-a-muffin, tattered uniforms, scraggly beards, while some were sporting their birthday suits, forded the waters. An invasion of lice laden, scratchy men bent on bringing their scabs to the North. The horror that would befall the North was an invasion of lice!

Some of the men halted at the river bank and would go no farther. "We didn't sign up to invade no North," they said as they shook their heads. Others, footsore, weary after weeks of battle, having no food and no proper clothing, just sat down and fell asleep. The provost guard did nothing to force the men of either group to ford the river.

We thought, hoped, and prayed that throngs of men from the Old Line State would stand on the northern banks-the Maryland side-and greet us. Weren't they our brothers? Weren't we all below the Mason-Dixon Line? Surely, they would come and help us isolate the Capital of Washington?

But there was no one there waiting for us. Few Marylanders joined our ranks, although we had been assured that the men of Maryland would show up like the Minute Men of old and rally to save their State and the South.

Once across, we were greeted by men who spat at us or Marylanders, who flew the Stars and Stripes, not the Stars and Bars. They shouted obscenities at us. They refused to sell us food. They did not let us use their wells to drink water. Lee had forbidden our looting and pillaging. We were to pay for what we wanted. We were stunned at the reception. They were not our comrades; they were our enemy.

CHAPTER 21:

BLOOD RUNS RED IN THE ANTIETAM

"I am tired of the sickening sight of the battlefield with its mangled corpses & poor suffering wounded. Victory has no charms for men when purchased at such cost."
*-**General George B. McClellan***

April 1, 1865 7:45 PM

I never want to live again the fear, the horror, and the terror of quick marching into a cornfield as we did that early morning in September. Oh, so quickly we were thrust into the grip of fear! Its icy fingers encircle you like boney claws strangling the breath out of you. You have no choice: submit and slowly the life flows out of you as the air in your lungs turns stale and foul; resist and you go forward into the Valley of Death hoping that the Lord is with you, while the shot and shell explode above and around you.

And just moments before…we were behind the little, white Dunker Church. We had been told that we wouldn't be needed that day. The smell of breakfast wafted through the air. Sizzling bacon, Johnny cakes a' flipping in the pan, and coffee, real coffee in our tin cups awaited us. We had stacked our muskets. All thoughts were upon breakfast. Some of us were lounging back and thinking of getting some extra sleep. We weren't needed that day. The sun was just coming over the horizon, golden and round. Some of the trees were starting to change colors. For a moment I was marveling how fall came so early here in the north, in Maryland. There was a hint of fall chill in the air. It seemed as if we were in line for a perfect day.

Then the order came: "Boys, we got to hold the cornfield!"

We ran forward into the tall stalks of corn that were becoming brown, as our brothers in arms ran the other way, throwing down their muskets, screaming, "It's death to go forward! The whole Yankee nation is there!"

We strode across the furrowed ground where the hands of our fallen grasped at our pants legs trying to restrain us. We tripped over bodies and tumbled to the ground. The corn stalks were sharp, stiff, and hard being brown and dying. The stalks and the leaves of corn crunched underfoot, but this noise was wholly lost in the blast of cannon, the hiss of shells in flight, the explosions overhead, and the bullets zip-zipping near our heads like thousands of mosquitoes.

General John Bell Hood was with us. His faced was possessed by war, and he fairly gleamed, as if with white heat. His eyes were golden and blazing. "Onward men! Onward Texans! Forward! Into the gap!" The Texas Brigade followed their hero wherever he led.

Can we do it? Can we fill the gap? Can we stop them? Our hearts are racing. I feel the pounding. I can't breathe. The air is filled with smoke, dust, the dirt, and crumbled corn pulp. The air is strangely cold. Then I realize it is still very early morning. The sun is just rising.

At the booming of the cannon, there is a tearing sound ripping through the corn as thousands of canister balls shred both the corn and men to bits. Whole swaths of our line fall in a bloody mangle. The overwhelming sound now is of the screams. All around me are red splattered corn stalks still standing or blobs of blood on the groundstrewn with men's body parts, clothing, and crisscrossed stalks and leaves of destroyed corn.

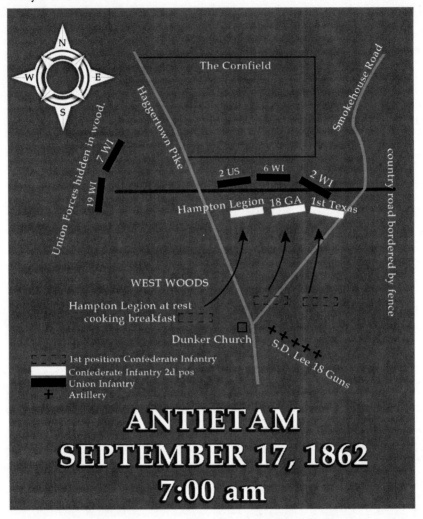

The white Church is to our left. We wheel towards our left. We raise our muskets and unleash a volley upon a line of Blue clad men who are standing maybe 30 or 40 feet from us. Our line is staggered as half of our men fall to the ground. The Texans and the South Carolinians of the Texas Brigade are intermixed such that no one can tell which unit is which or if there are still units at all. We jump the fence and volley again. The Blue line disappears into the grountd. Are they dead?

We are tripping over our dead, their dead, the fence rails on the ground. Can't see what's ahead until we collide with it-them. The Blue again. The blue, they fire.

The corn catches fire. A form runs through the cornstalks coming at me. I fire. The muzzle of my musket is almost against his stomach as he breaks through the yellow stalks. I look into the eyes of a blue-clad boy younger than me, and watch the horror of amazement and surprise register in his eyes as he grabs his stomach, and starts to put his intestines back inside of himself. The life drains from his eyes as he slumps to the ground. The dance of death continues as the drill routine of loading and firing takes over with mechanical precision.

The grime in my mouth of gun powder makes my tongue feel as if it is crackled and burning for water. I tear the paper of another cartridge with my teeth and feel the grit of powder. I ram another charge down my Enfield. I fire. I sense the men on either side of me. One has trouble with his gun. He rams down charge after charge but forgets to put a percussion cap on so his gun does not fire, until he finally remembers and puts a cap on and then his gun explodes from too much gun powder. He screams as his fingers are burnt. The other side is a Texan. He is picking out each target as if it were turkey. He is methodical and mechanical and he doesn't miss.

The Texans run forward. I surge with them. "For the Lone Star State!" I run when they run. The scream their hellish, ghoulish, throat-rattling yell. They scream as banshees. It is as eerie as the coyote; it is half wolf, half hound of hell. Our rebel yell rises over the field of battle!

There is another blue clad soldier in front of me. I club him with my musket. Someone calls retreat. Is it our side? I do not wait. I obey and retreat, as if the wind of a hurricane had blown me backwards.

The two sides part, as if Moses had struck his staff to the ground, and we soldiers were the waters of the Red Sea. We pull back. They pull back. Both sides are stumbling, tripping, falling, and limping out of the deadly corn.

"Days went by!" I cry. "Right? Days!" But it is 20 or 30 minutes. The sun is warmer now. It is over. I look around. I recognize no one. I see no one of the Hampton Legion. We had gone in with only 77 effectives. Am I the only survivor? Have I led my company to its death?

Then I see Hood. "Regroup! Reorganize!" He takes off his gloves and bats the dust from his jacket. "Men, we might have to go in again."

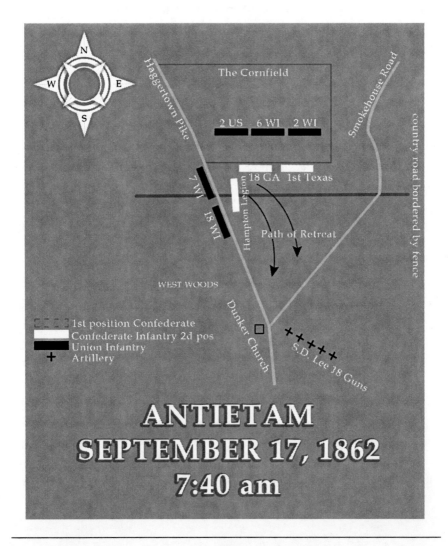

'Oh, my God!' My heart cries. 'Go in again? God, I cannot go in again.' Then someone cries, "Pullback!" That is the most wonderful, most beautiful word in the English language. It is the best word any man has ever heard uttered.

We are spent. But so is the enemy. The enemy fire seems to have moved to our right. The holocaust here is over.

I think I killed a man, maybe two. Then a friend, Robbie, and then another are clapping their hands on my back and congratulating me. "Corporal, what a fine shot you took. You got that Captain."

'What Captain?' I think. I ask myself. I don't remember shooting any Captain.

"You were a real hellion, swinging your musket like a club!" Robbie continues. "I bet you took down five of them!"

'Me? Five?' I don't remember anyone but the boy. I see his face, his eyes again in slow motion. That second when he realized he was shot, and he was dying. It is etched in my mind more strongly than any other memory in my life. I remember it better than my wedding day-I am sorry to say that to you, Vicee. So I guess, I never will. It is one of those things which will never get beyond these mental letters to you. I am sure you would never want to know that I recall every detail of that moment frozen in time, but I can't with any degree of equivalence remember our wedding...

CHAPTER 22:

THE BEST OF THE WAR

"The greatest mistake any man ever made is to suppose that the good things of the world are not worth the winning."
— **Anthony Trollope,** Barchester Towers

April 1, 1865 8:15 PM

"The best meal of the War? That's easy. When we captured General Pope's Supply Depot at Bristoe Station. While we were starving, those Yankees had every delight available in the world. Why we ate their oysters and champagne. We had every delicacy known to man!" McGowan settled back and smacked his lips. "It was so good sneaking up and around his flank and coming in on his rear. Why Old Jack drove us hard! 56 miles in 24 hours. We went over hill and dale, and around every small pathway in western Virginia. But we caught Pope with his pants down. Caught him bad. His pants were around his ankles and nearly off!"

We were playing a favorite parlor game at McGowan's headquarters. His staff was arrayed around the room in various states of luxuriating laziness. Legs were draped over the arms of chairs and sofas. Open bottles graced a table where a game of dominoes lay interrupted. Beside a candle stick, a china plate had been 'drafted' into the army and served as a cigar ash tray. I was sitting in a curve-backed chair off to one side of the fireplace. The white molding work of the room contrasted with the light green-almost mint-of the painted walls. The fireplace was a grey marble with broad white veins. Gun belts and sabre-belts hung from the mantel piece. A finely, no, intricately, carved brown box was filled with medium sized logs for the fireplace. Off to other side of the fireplace, there was an escritoire with a chair. The General's long frock coat with its cape hung loosely over the back of the chair.

It was Fitz's turn next. "My best meal?" He hemmed and hawed a moment. "I know. It was when I spent the night in a farmhouse after the Battle of…well, that does not really matter. Now does it? The lady of the house, she turned out the best bacon, eggs, hot gravy, and biscuits I've ever eaten."

McGowan guffawed. "Hell, that can't qualify for the best! Where's the special food?"

"Well, maybe it was the atmosphere!" Fitz shot back.

"The atmosphere?" McGowan leaned forward. "What'd ya mean?"

"Well, every time she leaned forward to serve me some food, she served me something special. I… I could see everything! Best damn meal in my mind!" McGowan roared with laughter. Then Fitz joined in. Soon, laughter erupted from every man in the room.

"Oh, so there was fresh milk?" The General inquired with a twinkle in his eye, which brought further gales of laughter.

It was my turn next. All I could say was that the best meal of the War was the one you served me when I went home last March. It wasn't funny, it wasn't the great food, and it wasn't bawdy. It was the best meal, because I was with you.

The conversation then turned to who was the best general. Several candidates were put forward and lively conversation ensued. But I noticed that as the staff members rated one general over another, General McGowan's visage became greatly saddened. "For me, it is all the good men we have lost. We have lost so many Generals."

"We lost a commander of an army in battle with Albert Sydney Johnston killed at Shiloh." Fitz interjected.

"Yes, he would have been a great leader had he lived." Captain Haskell sighed. He was the Assistant Adjutant. He was always with his brother, Lieutenant L.C. Haskell, who was an aide-de-camp to the General. The two men reminded me of my friends, Robbie and Doug MacDonald. Haskell was lively and animated; his brother quiet and thoughtful.

"But Stonewall was a better General. It was a shame dying like that at the height of his powers and success." Major Harry Hammond our Quartermaster spoke up. He always spoke highly of Stonewall, so his comment was expected.

We talked about Chancellorsville for a moment. General McGowan brightened up and said, "I think the greatest moment of the War was when Robert E. Lee rode Traveller along the Orange Turnpike with Chancellor's Tavern all aflame at Chancellorsville. The men of the Army of Northern Virginia parting like the Red Sea for Moses and cheering wildly for Lee after he defeated 'Fighting Joe Hooker.' This was perhaps our greatest day. It certainly was the greatest scene I can image. The triumphant general riding, as if in review of his victorious army, when it was clear that the tides of war should have favored his much stronger enemy. This was simply marvelous. It was really one of the greatest victories ever won by an Army. Little David had slain the giant Goliath." He stopped there. "But we lost Stonewall."

Still, the thoughts of dead men we had served under cast a dark pall over the conversation.

"Yes, we lost Stonewall then. Later, we lost Polk. Why one of the best division leaders we lost at Gettysburg was Dorsey Pender." Captain Haskell added.

"We lost Rodes and Ramseur and Cleburne, whom some called the Jackson of the West," I couldn't help but mention. "We also lost a South Carolinian, Brigadier-General Micah Jenkins, who was killed at Wilderness." I didn't think that Jenkins was a good general. I thought he was responsible for our loss at Wauhatchie, but he was a South Carolinian, and he had died for Our Cause, so that counted for something.

Then we started to talk about who was left. After a while, we talked about General Hill. "Powell is a fighter. He's a warrior's warrior. We'll be alright with him around." Hammond said.

Fitz said that shortly after Hill had lost his love to George McClellan, he was in love again. "This time it was with John Hunt Morgan's sister, Mrs. Kitty Morgan McClung. She was doll-like in appearance so that her nickname was 'Dolly'. She was vivacious, blue-eyed, with long, light brown hair. She even donated her wedding gown to make a flag for Hill's Light Division."

"John Hunt Morgan? You mean the cavalry General?" I couldn't see who asked, but I think it was Lieutenant C. G. Thompson, our brigade Ordnance Officer.

General McGowan interjected, "John Hunt Morgan was a direct descendant of Daniel Morgan, one of the heroes of the Revolution."

"Yeah," Fitz said. "We lost a great cavalryman, when we lost him last year at Greenville, Tennessee. Those Yankee cowards shot him in the back!"

For a moment, we were all lost in thought and sadness. The thought of the loss of John Hunt Morgan brought to mind the loss of Jeb Stuart. I couldn't keep it in. "Last summer was a bad season for our cavalry."

Around the room, several said, "Amen."

Fitz was the type of man who always got the last word, and often his last word was a bon mot. "Gentlemen, we have witnessed the death of the last cavaliers."

We were all quiet now and brooding.

Fitz asked if anyone had a cigar. When he was offered one, he said, "Powell Hill likes to smoke cigars. You know John Hunt Morgan was Powell Hill's best man."

Fitz lighted his cigar, and watched the smoke curl around the room. "Funny, Powell Hill never has owned a slave; however, he is an ardent supporter of states' rights."

The conversation returned to A. P. Hill. Hill had his detractors, who thought that his fight with Stonewall Jackson had impaired his ability to fight under that 'sainted General'. "That attack at Beaver Dam was premature," Major Harry Hammond said. "Jackson wasn't up so, it degenerated into a frontal assault and a slaughter." Some of us knew that Hammond had lost a younger brother in the attack. But when it came to Stonewall, Hammond always thought he could do no wrong.

"Yeah, but that flank attack on Burnside at Antietam could not have been more perfect." I defended Hill, not knowing why for sure. It seemed that most in the group felt that Hill had been a good General.

"Why, early, in the War, Hill drilled his troops until they appeared to be veterans. He believed in what he called 'forward spirit', the quality to be aggressive, hard-hitting men." General McGowan felt that he had to defend Hill. McGowan had served in Maxcy Gregg's brigade in Hill's Light Division. He had come to command Gregg's old brigade, after Gregg had been killed at Fredericksburg.

Right off the bat, in June of 1861, he was noted for his aggressive action of moving forward with his troops in accordance with Joe Johnston's order and taking Romney-New Creek. This action brought him to the attention of Johnston." McGowan continued.

The talk continued with one member of the staff after another contributing to the mosaic of A. P. Hill. "Hill possesses a chivalrous manner, fiery impetuosity." "His intellect is quick and retentive." "His manners are strangely fascinating and magnetic."

One man argued that Hill is the infantry counterpart to Jeb Stuart. "35 at war's start. Colonel to Major General in 90 days. An unquenchable thirst for battle. Nothing thrills him like the fierce joy of a victorious fight."

Everyone commented that in battle, he usually wears a red shirt with a black slouch hat and always has his sword drawn. None of us could understand why Jefferson Davis referred to him as 'Little Powell'. The man stood at least 5'9" tall. But all of us commented on his thinness, his gauntness. We worried about him because he had been so sick so often.

"But he is the figure of war. His red luxuriant beard and long curly hair flow in the wind like some Viking of old about to pillage a monastery."

"Why, he jokes with about everyone."

"Why do you think he does that?' Fitz asked.

McGowan answered, "He makes frequent rounds of camp and hospitals to improve the conditions of his men. Never seen a man so devoted to his men. That's what's inspires them. They adore him. He is so very kind to his subordinates. He has kind words for his couriers even during battle and times of stress. I think he often makes jokes to relieve the tension of war."

Fitz settled back, and we all knew that this meant Fitz was going to tell us another story.

CHAPTER 23:

DON'T GROW TOO FOND OF IT

"It is well that war is so terrible, or we would grow too fond of it."
*-****Robert E. Lee****, after the Battle of Fredericksburg*

April 1, 1865 9:00 PM

With the close of 1862, came another reorganization of the Army of Northern Virginia. I guess Robbie Lee had asked the Confederate Congress to allow him to make corps out of divisions, and to appoint corps commanders. But it went much further than that.

The Legion had suffered so many casualties at Antietam that we were reduced in size to two companies. We needed men. So as we lulled around the Culpepper Court House area of Virginia that fall, Congress acted, and so did Robert E. Lee.

On November 6, Congress passed a law allowing for the formation of Corps. On November 11, Lee issued Special Order No. 239. Thus, five major changes happened all at once. Not all of these changes were greeted with enthusiasm by the Legion.

First, the Hampton Legion was assigned to General George Pickett's division under General James Longstreet's First Corps.

Second, the Hampton Legion was brigaded with the 1st South Carolina Volunteers, the 2nd South Carolina Rifles, the 5th South Carolina Volunteers, the 6th South Carolina Volunteers, and the Palmetto Sharpshooters. Our commanding officer was South Carolina born and reared, Brigadier General Micah Jenkins. Thus, we were an all-South Carolina brigade. I had read in the papers, Vicee, that President Jefferson Davis had long wanted all the same state brigades. Still, we were disappointed that General Wade Hampton was not coming back to lead us. We learned that he would be leading Hampton's Legion Cavalry under Jeb Stuart.

Third, five companies composing the 4th South Carolina Battalion were reorganized into two companies which became Company I and K of the Legion to give us more men. The other companies, A through H, retained their structure from before, but were greatly reduced in manpower.

Fourth, we were now reorganized such that we had a further two years of service to perform for the Confederacy.

Fifth and finally, Martin Gary became our colonel as we were now classified as a regiment, although we retained the name "Legion".

And with the close of 1862, came another change of command of the Union Army of the Potomac and another campaign with the title: 'On to Richmond!' This time the commander was General Ambrose Burnside, and the place was Fredericksburg.

Burnside had really done a good job. I have to give him credit. He had managed to get to Fredericksburg by stealing a march on Bobby Lee. He had managed to do what no other Union commander had been able to do through the War. He got to a strategic position first with larger numbers. It was then that his campaign faltered. The pontoons which he had ordered from Washington to bridge the Rappahannock River weren't there.

What possessed him to do what he did next, one can only imagine. Our Confederate lines were along a high ridgeline behind the town of Fredericksburg. We dug in, we sighted artillery, and we stockpiled ammunition. In short we did everything we could to make the wide-open fields in front of most of our battle line killing fields. D. H. Hill said "A chicken could not cross that field, once we started to fire."

Fortunately, the Legion was given a support and a reserve role. We were placed behind the lines on Plank Road. We did not fire a shot, as rank upon rank of Union soldiers tried to climb Marye's Heights and attack our boys who were behind walls. Our men were so crowded together that we had several ranks of them behind the wall with one rank loading rifles, one rank ready to shot, and another rank firing.

One would think that a day shooting Yankees like Thanksgiving turkeys would be a good day, and in a way it was, but with maybe 15,000 of them dead, dying or wounded, lying on the cold, almost frozen ground in front of us, their screaming, moaning, begging – for - water pitiful cries, rent my heart. They remained there all night and all the next day. As time passed, the screaming, moaning and crying slowly died off. Then, when probably many of them were dead from lack of care and attention and the cold, the mercy of mercies happened, and the two sides allowed the blue clad bodies to be removed. Our losses were maybe 5,000, but, I still did not want to celebrate, like so many others did. All I could see was that we were approaching another Christmas, and that not much had changed. The Yankees still wanted to invade us, and we kept shooting them, and they kept shooting us. How long could this go one? How long could we stand this?

CHAPTER 24:

CHRISTMAS 1862

"With me is Right, before me is Duty, behind me is Home.
*-**Southern Volunteer**, 1861*

April 1, 1865 9:25 PM

We stayed in Camp near Fredericksburg from after the battle until February of 1863. Nothing could have been more gloomy and depressing. We spent a lot of our time burying the dead. With so many of our Confederate boys wounded, many of us worked in the hospitals to comfort them. I saw Sidney Cole there again, Vicee. He truly is an angel of mercy. He is not a man who is cut out for fighting, but surely is a man who is better suited to the care and comfort of the wounded and dying.

The Christmas was nothing like the first Christmas away from home. Last year, there had been some attempt to celebrate the birth of Our Savior. This year, we were too cold, too tired, too depressed, and too weary to do much. The Camp had those men who prayed, those chaplains who delivered sermons, but there was no spirit in it.

Even those men, who were prone to drinking, did not become boisterous, and did not frolic. Something has gone out of our men. The walls of Fredericksburg may have taken the lives of the Yankees, but it stole something else, something more precious, from us. We were now killers, and we all realized that we had enjoyed the killing. We had sinned, and we enjoyed the sinning. This was not something we could tell our sweethearts, who believed that we were fighting a holy war to keep our soil free of the heel of an invading tyrant. What we had done there was murder.

The Yankees didn't have a chance. In one sense, you had to admire them. They came, wave after wave, into the teeth of our musketry and the shot-gun like blasts of our canister fire from our cannon. They came knowing they would be rent apart most horribly, and yet they still came. That was heroic, but awfully foolish.

We all wondered now how long would this war go on? We had been reorganized in November for two more years. Could the Yankees throw men at us in wave after wave for two more years? Could we resist them for two more years?

What was it going to take to end this war? What was it going to take? Would it claim each and every man's life who sat here around a roaring campfire this Christmas day? Would every woman in the South be a widow? Would every child be without a father? A deep-seated thing was gnawing at our innards, and we did not speak its name out loud. We could not speak it, for to say it aloud was to raise it by incantation, and unleash it. Every man knew that once it was unleashed, there would be no end to its evil, much like Pandora opening the box.

"God, if You can hear me, please, I beg of You, end this war. Let all of us return to our wives and sweethearts. Let us return to our jobs and our farms and go in peace. Grant us the chance to live our lives and to raise our children. End all of this suffering, and bring all men to know You, and to believe in You. This I truly pray, in Your Son's Name, at the sound of which all men must kneel, Amen."

BOOK IV: THE WAR IS LOST IN A NIGHT-1863

CHAPTER 25:

A SIDE VISIT

"The view is wild, bleak, and desolate. The elements, which have been warring for the last fortnight, have called a truce and left a sea of mud."
– **George P. McClellan**, *155th Pennsylvania Infantry*

April 1, 1865 9:45 PM

I had been ordered to go to Hill's headquarters, so I did. It was about 3:00 PM this afternoon. But I hadn't been ordered to go there immediately, so I continued my personal mission to go to Tudor Hall. I wanted to see James Fitz James and the rest of the boys. I knew that I would have some time there away from the lines and the strain of being on the line. I could get warm there, learn some news to bring back to my men, and generally have a somewhat more pleasant day. Besides, I hadn't been there for a couple of days.

When we had first camped in this area, there were many woods surrounding Tudor Hall. Now, the winter had consumed the trees in countless fireplaces and campfires. We had not scavenged the planking from the building, but if we were much longer, then that, too, would be going to be sacrificed on the altar to Vulcan, as surely as the trees before had gone.

We had changed the landscape with our mighty shovels, picks, tin plates, and hands. From 8 in the morning till 4 in the afternoon, crews of men had worked, every day of the week, except Sundays, constructing our trench lines. The rule was clear. In front of the main trench, a ditch was dug, which was six feet in depth and eight feet in width. All of this earth was used to build the embankment fronting the main trench, which embankment was six feet in height. Our main trench was twelve feet on the base, and four feet of terreplein, that is a level area behind a parapet where our guns were sited. We made sure to build a neat revetment, which is a facing, with stone in some places, to keep the embankment in place. We had in many places a banquette tread, which is planking fitted in such a way as to make a walkway.

We topped our embankments with head logs, which were logs slightly higher than our heads with a slit below so we could fire out. We knew the head logs would save many a man from a head wound.

Outside of our trenches, we built abatis and other obstructions. Abatis are sharpened stakes attached to strong logs about the height of a man's chest.

We worked all winter. The Third Corps line was over eight miles long, and all of it had to be trenched. So when we were not working on the trenches, we were working to build our winter quarters.

The barrel is the most useful object one can image for building winter quarters. We used barrels for our chimneys. We used barrels as cisterns to catch rain water. We used barrels to create tables and chairs. I came to love barrels and I have such a fondness for them now.

But barrels, too, were an instrument of punishment. If man got out of line, he might have to wear a barrel, instead of clothes.

The work was hard for the ground was frozen. It took all our strength to fight our way through the frozen earth to create the miles of trenches and traverses, for every trench must have a traverse, which is …I'm not sure I should tell you everything about the construction of a trench.

Added to our work was the construction of a picket line trench. This was not as deeply dug or outfitted with traverses and so forth; it was to be a temporary shelter for the men, such as my company, who were to man this forward line such that when the enemy came, we would fire a few rounds at them and then scurry back to the main line. But our firing would alert the main line so that they could be ready for the onslaught. We were then the proverbial sentinels, charged with giving up our lives to warn the rest.

The ground had become so hard and our boys were now so weary for they had no real food to eat. We rarely, if ever, got meat to eat, and what we did receive was not fit to eat. A man's body needs meat to have and retain muscle. When we lost our meat, we lost our muscle. It evaporated away as readily as the trees went into the fireplaces and campfire to ward off the winter cold.

A couple of days ago, the Yankees attacked our picket lines in force. They ousted us from them. We ran back to our main lines expecting them to make a go at us. But they just stayed there. All that effort was solely to take our picket lines. What are they doing?

I ran up the steps to home and burst into the parlor expecting to see all of my friends. None were there. Where had they all gone? A whole different headquarters staff was there.

CHAPTER 26:

THE BOMBARDMENT

It seemed as if "the devils in hell were fighting in the air."
-Captain Michael Kelly, 2nd Connecticut Heavy Artillery

April 2, 1865 1:00 AM

Dear Vicee:

The mists have started to wrap around my feet. I pull my blanket around me more tightly. The night is dark. The moon was a little less than first quarter, and so she slinked off to slumber a little before midnight.

The Union artillery bombardment began at ten sharp. The shells were fired to pummel our main lines which are some 300 yards behind where I am. So, there was no reason for us on the picket line to fear it. So, I don't want you to worry about me, Vicee. I am alright. But now, with the moon down, I am a little afraid that they will lose their range and maybe fire a little short. This I won't tell you.

Still, what a way to spend a Saturday night! I'd much rather be there with you, maybe dancing before the fire, or chatting with friends around a warm fire. Or do anything before a warm, maybe even a hot, fire. Any fire actually would be alright. We can't have a fire tonight. It would silhouette us. For spring, this is cold. Damp. Cold. Very Damp.

I know in my heart that the Yankees are out there and they are massing to hit us once the bombardment ends. The day, the hour, the moment has come. Soon the hordes of Yankees will descend upon us like the Mongolian Horde under Genghis Khan. With their numbers, unlimited, fully armed, beautifully arrayed, completely outfitted in uniforms and boots (oh, my God, what I would give to have some new boots-I apologize to you, Vicee, that I have uttered the name of God in vain). They will soon be on their way here, and I fear that there is nothing we can do. They will be arrayed like the hosts of heavens, while we are barefoot, in rags, or threadbare clothes, or tatters for uniforms; we are thin, hungry, and near exhaustion. We, the few remaining, are all that's left to stand against them.

I know that somewhere out there a young boy from Ohio, New York, Delaware or somewhere up North, who is shaking in his boots afraid that he will be killed or, worse wounded, lose an arm, or worse yet, be shamed in front of his kinsfolk and townsmen because of fear, that cowardice inflicting fear, that renders him unable to do his duty. Maybe he wonders about me, here in the dark, the cold numbing dark, on the picket line, my heart pounding, my men worn out, hungry, barely clothed, our muskets in our hands, while we hope to get off one shot (I've told the men two, but who knows if they can even do that) before we run to our lines, but some 300 yards behind us.

We are too close to our lines. But what can we do? We were ousted from our first skirmish lines some half mile from our lines just a couple of days ago by the Yankee horde. We are so near our lines that I worry that there will not be enough time for our warning shots to be effective. Will we provide enough alarm? Will we wake the main lines in time? Will they have enough time to man the lines and hold back the blue horde piling upon us, rank upon rank, endlessly stretching back behind the Mason-Dixon Line, all the way back to New York, Boston, or Maine?

I damn the Maine boys. I wasn't there, Vicee, but Colonel Oakes said it was the Maine boys that broke his charge at Little Round Top at Gettysburg. It was the Vermont men who broke us at Culp's Hill.

But no matter who it was who stopped us, they stopped us. The dream of foreign intervention died once and for all then. Was it then the Confederacy died? Have we died?

The shelling goes on and on, Vicee. I see the orange blasts of light after their cannons fire. The fire silhouettes the Yankees as they stand on their lines. For just a moment, I can see blue clad men, with polished leather accoutrements, artillery implements in their hands surrounding their firing cannon. For just that same moment, the trees come out of the darkness for a second. There is day for a moment, and then it is black night.

"How long has it been Sgt. Bailey?" I ask the man in the dark about ten feet away, believing him to be the Sergeant.

"I'd say about two and a half hours, Lieutenant." A ghostly apparition answers through the mist and the dank of night. The fog wreaths us both and only occasionally, do I see anything more than a shadow of a form in the grey eddies and swirls.

They fire their cannon and we can see the flame leap from the mouths of their guns. Seconds later, the roar rumbles across the fields like distant thunder. Then the explosion rocks a spot on our line. Sometimes, a man screams the agony of... I should not be 'writing' this to you, Vicee. Oh, I know that I am not really 'writing' to you and that these words are like the air, ephemeral, wispy like the tendrils of a spider's web, mere gossamer-spun dreams that vanish as we shake our eyes awake at dawn's light.

Still, I wonder, I really wonder, Vicee, how my boys are faring a mere 300 yards behind us. A tree was just hit and a limb fell. I hope no one was under that tree. So far, we have had only one or two shells hit our picket line.

I must have fallen asleep for a minute or two, there, Vicee. I am sorry. I startled myself awake. It was only a minute or two, but I know

I shouldn't have, but today has been such a day of apprehension. We all feel it in our bones. I know I shouldn't have fallen asleep. How in God's name (I am sorry Vicee that I have again taken the Lord's name in vain) can one sleep in the middle of this holocaust? I am so tired, I can.

I turn to look at my men. There are so few of us. We are five yards apart. I walked through our main lines today. Why they are only manned as our skirmish lines would have been two or three years ago. Think shoulder to shoulder when we first started at the Peninsula or the Seven Days. We cannot reach out and even touch the man beside us. Now, our main line is maybe one man every ten or twelve feet.

I have heard the sounds of their marching all day. Their ranks are strong, all closed up, and ordered.

The Yankees have been probing west of us for the last few weeks and the last couple of days; I think we have been saved only due to the rain. Well, today, the rain stopped. Everything is drying out.

CHAPTER 27:
VOWS

"If a man makes a vow to the LORD, or takes an oath to bind himself with a binding obligation, he shall not violate his word; he shall do according to all that proceeds out of his mouth."
-Numbers 30:2

Marry on Monday for health
Tuesday to Wealth
Wednesday the Best day of all
Thursday for crosses
Friday for losses
And Saturday no luck at all.

April 2, 1865 1:15 AM

January 1863 was a momentous month for me, Vicee. First, on January 23, I turned twenty-three years of age. Then on January 26, I was elected 3rd Lieutenant. This was an affirmation not only of my popularity, but also, and more importantly, of my ability. The men trusted me and believed that I would do a good job. They had made it clear in the past that they were willing to vote out bad officers. Surely, the vote for Captain Spann was proof of that. Finally, however, the most important thing of all happened: I obtained a Furlough of Indulgence so that I could marry you.

I was stationed near Petersburg when the furlough came through. I was able to take a train from Petersburg south on the Weldon and Petersburg line. At Weldon, we did not have to change trains, because the track further south was the same gauge, and the Weldon railroad had trackage rights all the way to Wilmington. At Wilmington, I had to take a carriage from the city north of the Cape Fear River, over a bridge to the south side of Wilmington, where I could board the Wilmington and Manchester Railroad to Florence, South Carolina.

The greatest sight I have ever beheld, to that moment, was you waiting in the train station in Florence. You were a vision of loveliness. Seeing you was the moment that I realized that all I had gone through, all that I had done, was worth it, if it made you safe and gave us a chance at life together.

I threw my arms around you, and you cringed, for just a moment, I felt it, because you were worried what people would think of you greeting me in such a way when we were not married.

As I held you, a tear flowed from my eye. I could not believe that I was there with you, that the day was so bright for mid-winter, and that we were alive and could share this moment. It was as if the heavens themselves had opened, and we were in the bliss of the realms of our Lord and Savior. But after just a moment's hesitation, you threw yourself into that kiss as if we would never kiss again. We had not said a word, but we had spoken volumes.

My father then interrupted us. I hugged him, although I am not sure he knew why, but I loved him so much, and wanted him to know it. I was so grateful that you both were there waiting for me in the train depot.

*****

You talked the whole drive home. My father would not let me drive the carriage, but made me "rest, that's what you need, son," as he kept saying. I do not remember all of it. I recall how excited you were about your wedding dress. You kept asking how long my furlough was for. I told you I had to get back by early March. You could see that I was uncomfortable talking about anything that had to do with the War.

I tried several times to tell you about the War. "I have marched everywhere. I have been in so many states. But that's not it." I started again. "My feet are so sore from marching everywhere…" I stopped, because that was not it also. "I …I … have seen too much…"

I guessed then that you decided to divert my attention from the War by talking only about things which were happy and full of life. With that, you then turned back to your dress.

"I have decided that I am going to follow the example of Queen Victoria," you gushed. "I am going to wear white."

"I am sure that you will look lovely in any color," I replied as any male would have knowing nothing about fashions, colors, types of cloth or the massive attention that ladies pay to these details.

"Oh, James!" Your face turned a little sour at my lack of enthusiasm.

"Now, Vicee…" that was about all I could say.

"I am going to educate you, James, for your bride-to-be has given great thought to these matters, and your bride-to-be values these matters greatly." You fluttered your fan, and your eyes just hovered over the top edge of your fan. "Besides, I have looked at Godey's Lady's Book so many times, I can picture all the fashions in my mind's eye!"

"Well, then ma'am, I recognize that you outrank me in these matters, so I will obey my commanding officer." I saluted you as I said this, trying to play with you and yet acknowledge my willingness to submit to you on these matters. I almost asked what Godey's Lady's Book was, but then again thought about it, and realized this was probably the ladies' version of Hardee's Rifle and Light Infantry Tactics.

"I am making a gorgeous Victorian - style dupioni suit with much detail." You began your lesson.

I interrupted immediately. "I am afraid to say, that I do not know what dupioni is."

"Dupioni," Vicee said quite slowly, as if she were teaching a child, "is silk. It is quite luxurious. It is textured and has a brilliant luster."

"I am making a jacket which will have a lace yoke and satin buttons. I don't know if I want a ruffled neckline or not. What do you think?"

"Well, I don't like things that touch my neck and make me itch. So, if you're going to do it, I think you would want it small enough not to scrape your neck, but long enough such that it shows, because it would be such a nice detail."

You stared at me; your eyes wide open in surprise. "Why, James, that's actually quite a good analysis. You were listening."

I smiled weakly. I truly had been trying to follow along, but I didn't think my answer was anywhere as elegant as the thing you were talking about. I thought myself quite rough, as if I shouldn't be talking about such refined things.

You pulled your shawl around you more tightly as the winter day was becoming colder. "I see that you got my shawl back from Mrs. Wingate. I am glad that you did." That was about the extent of my contribution to the conversation.

After a long pause, you began to talk again about your dress. "The lace is a combination of Brussels and point Duchess," you said. "I know that Queen Victoria's dress of silk had Honiton lace, but I can't get that.

I am getting all of this material from Rebecca's wedding gown and my mother's, because it would cost a fortune, if we could import it through the blockade. We are just going to have to make do with what we have, because of *that* Yankee blockade." Your "*that*" before the words 'Yankee blockade' was about as close as you had ever gotten to cursing.

The sun was warm on this winter afternoon, besides I was back in South Carolina, and her climate was far fairer than Virginia's. The rhythm of the coach and clopping of the horses' hooves was helping to lull me asleep.

I heard words about wide cuffs faced with lace, and that your matching skirt would be full enough for a hoop, and having wide pleated hems, but they were not really registering. "I am wondering about a hat…James, are you listening?" Your question broke into my reverie.

"I…I…am… as best I can…" I was tired, and my voice conveyed my grand tiredness, a weariness that I did not know my soul carried, but was now overcoming me.

"Oh, I have gone on and on about women's stuff and there you are wanting to tell me about the War." You stopped and looked deeply in my eyes.

"No. I don't want to talk about the War." I hung my head. "I have had far too much War to want to talk about it."

We rode in silence then, and after a while, a short while, I fell asleep. I slept until we reached Timmonsville. Then, I do not know how, but I was placed in a bed, and I slept the rest of that day and most of the next.

*****

The Confederacy had carried over the tradition, derived from English Law, that a wedding must take place in the morning. The wedding was held in Vicee's Church, as was the custom. Vicee was a staunch Baptist.

My family had undergone a transformation from Catholic to Methodist and finally to Baptist. I did not know the minister or the church clerk, because I was from Stateburg, and we married in Timmonsville. Timmonsville, though, was becoming my home. My family had lived here briefly around the time of the 1850 census, but shortly thereafter my father had moved us to Stateburg.

As all of my friends were in the Confederate Army miles away, I had no one to be my ushers. You, Vicee, had thought of this and had dragooned my father, your father, and some men suggested by the minister. You made them favors, which are little white ribbon things with flowers, lace and some silver, which were then pinned to the shoulders of the ushers. Likewise, your bridesmaids had favors pinned to their sleeves. You had been very busy. You seemed to be responsible for every detail of the wedding, and yet you had done it all effortlessly.

We walked to the Church from your sister's house. We held hands and after a moment began swinging our arms. As we did, friends and neighbors strew our path with petals from flowers and some strew our path with the traditional orange blossoms, although I cannot say how they obtained them in the winter. We could hear the Church bells pealing. The sun was unusually bright this winter day, and there was a freshness in the air which whispered of spring on the hint of a breeze.

The guests filed into the church. My father was there, as was your sister, Mrs. Wingate, and so many that I did not know. Although usually, the Church ceremony was for the family, the War had changed that and now friends and family attended. I did not notice it then, but those who were still in mourning joined the other guests, but did so in such an unobtrusive manner so that their mourning would not in any way diminish our joy. Unfortunately, there were many in mourning. The War had hit our area hard. The Hampton Legion had suffered so many casualties, because we were the men called upon to do the hardest work or to handle the issue when no other unit could. We had suffered high casualty rates, not because Wade Hampton or Martin Whiterspoon Gary or any of our other leaders were bad at their job of command, but because this was the nature of War and especially of this War.

I took your hand in mine. Your glove was so soft. Your dress was stunning. Although you were beautifully attired, you were so demurely dressed. The Minister asked, "Do you take this woman to be your lawful wedded wife?" In that moment, I glimpsed our future. All that I had ever wanted was wrapped up in you, Vicee. "Do I?" Of course, I do, a thousand times I do.

Our wedding did not escape the War. Several men, who had served in the Confederate Army, provided us with an archway of swords as we left the Church. I would have liked not to have this reminder, but everyone told me that, as a Lieutenant in our 'Glorious Army', it was de rigueur to have such a patriotic display.

You, Vicee, were a marvel of lace, satin, and beauty. How you were able to make those old wedding dresses become such a vision was a wonder unto itself, I will never know. Nonetheless, I knew that I was marrying the most beautiful, most considerate, and most intelligent woman that had ever walked this earth. You were surrounded beforehand by your maids of honor. The colors of their different dresses made one think of a bouquet of flowers with you, Vicee, as the white rose in the center.

As we walked down the aisle to leave the Church, we observed tradition and did not look to the left or the right, but only glanced straight ahead. We knew that it was considered bad taste to acknowledge friends or acquaintances inside the Church. As we left the Church, our friends and relatives showered us with flower petals and orange blossoms.

We rode from the church in a carriage my father had made. I looked at you as we drove through a canopy of live oaks arching over the road, their branches bedecked with wistful, hanging Spanish Moss. The February day was kind to us as the weather held and was almost spring-like.

Our wedding had been the most beautiful ceremony celebrating our love and our new lives together as one. I smiled so broadly at you, for I felt so indebted to you for having made this occasion so momentous. I knew I could never love you as much as you loved me. I had been a soldier too long, and I was too besmirched by the evil of the world to be able to reach your perfection. The fact that you allowed me to inhabit your world was reward enough for me. I would be as good a husband as I could be for you and to you.

Our friends and family had all helped to bring food and beverages to our reception. The blockade made it difficult to obtain delicacies for our reception, but this did not really matter. You had baked a cake with little white ribbons streaming from it. Your bridesmaids were all aflutter about the 'cake pull'.

Being thoroughly unaware of what a cake pull was, I asked you, to which you replied, "Just wait. You'll see!"

The cake was placed on a table. Each of the bridesmaids selected a ribbon and began to pull on the ribbon.

"I want the one with the heart!" a bridesmaid called out.

Another, with a sly smile on her face eye said as she looked a handsome soldier, who blushed, "I want the ring!"

Your sister said, "I want the carriage!"

They all said together, "I don't want the thimble!"

"You leaned over to me and whispered, "The thimble means that the woman who gets it will be an old maid. I didn't put one in. Shush!"

One by one they pulled out the charms which had been attached to the ribbons. As the charms came out, you told me what they meant. The heart was everlasting love; the ring was the next woman to be engaged; and the carriage meant children.

You sister was thrilled to have gotten the carriage, although the other two bridesmaids got what the other had wanted. Still, everyone giggled and enjoyed the cake pull.

Our reception had no music or dancing, because we were Baptists.

*****

We spent that night in your sister's home. It was later. We were alone. Alone in our bedroom, we were ready to spend our first night together as man and wife. You asked me to remove your garter. I reached my hands up your legs, I had never done this before and was scared that I would somehow offend you or do it wrong. I found the garter and rolled it down your leg to your feet, when I saw it: it was in the design of the Stars and Bars. I gasped. You could see that I was taken aback.

"I'm sorry, James, darling…I thought, no…I didn't think…" You sobbed. I had made you cry on your wedding day. My heart was ready to break-the one thing I did not want to do, I had done.

I looked at the garter lying on the floor. I could see that you had gone to great trouble to sew it. I wondered where you had gotten all the colors of the cloth to make it. I then realized how much you had put into this simple little garter.

"No, Vicee…no…I love you. I understand…you wanted to honor me and my service…I love you, and I thank you."

*****

Spring had still not fully come when I had to return to my Company. I had to be back by March 2, 1863. I started to make arrangements, although I could see that every step I took to get ready hurt you deeply.

"I must go back."

"Why can't the others fight this War and leave you here with me?" you sobbed.

"Because I gave my word to them." I bent my head to the ground, because I already had enough to bear in leaving you and returning where I did not want to go.

"But you gave your word to me, too!" Your eyes flashed with a little anger.

"I will return to you, Vicee." My voice was as earnest and sincere as I could make it. Even then, I still truly believed I could control my destiny.

"Do you promise?" You turned your face to look up at me. Your eyes searched my soul.

"Yes." Then I had a thought. "Why don't you come with me on the train back to Petersburg? I could get a hotel room in Petersburg. I know a charming restaurant where we could eat, the Brickhouse Run. Nearby is the Farmer's Bank, which is an impressive red-brick building, built in 1817..."

"Do you know anything in Petersburg that's not related to bricks?" You smiled slyly at me.

"Well…" Then your joke hit me. "Still, Mrs. James A. McEachern, as a married woman in the company of your husband, it would be perfectly respectable for you to accompany him to Petersburg." I thought I had settled the matter.

"What would I do on the return trip? I would be alone." Your eyes conveyed your pain: you wanted to be with me longer, but you were afraid of being alone on the return trip.

"Maybe I could arrange for some of my men to get a furlough, and they could accompany you home."

*****

We journeyed together to Petersburg. Your sister, Mary, was kind enough to come with us. I am certain she hoped that she could spend some time with her husband. This meant however that you would have someone to travel with on the trip back home. We stayed in a small home not too far from where the Legion was camped. I knew it would not last, for I knew with spring would come the campaigning season, but I, too, wanted to push back the hands of time. I wanted to be in your embrace. I wanted to touch your face and kiss your lips. I wanted to make love to you and never again face the trials and tribulations of war. You stayed only a few days, and then, like the pink of dawn vanishes with the rise of the sun, you were gone.

I did not know it then, but I guess you did know that you were pregnant with our son.

*****

A lot had happened while I was away. Longstreet had tried and failed to besiege Suffolk. He had tried his hand at his defensive war tactic and, instead of defeating the Union forces that held this tidewater town, he spent months losing men.

CHAPTER 28:

WAUHATCHIE

"Our commanding officer could be of greater service elsewhere than at the head of the Army of Tennessee."
-**General James Longstreet** to President Jefferson David in the presence of Commanding General of the Army of Tennessee, Braxton Bragg, October 9, 1863

April 2, 1865 1:30 AM

Part I: Dissention at the Highest Level

I keep writing to you in my head, Vicee. I promised you that I would write, and I want to keep that promise even though there is no way that you will ever get these letters.

It is so dark now. This dark and the quiet remind me of the night of Wauhatchie. Wauhatchie: The word itself still terrifies me. The darkness of that night: the only light was the flash of muskets firing in the trees. Men were reduced by fear, first by the fear of not knowing where you were, second by the fear of not knowing where the enemy was, and third the fear that you were firing upon your own men. This fear made men truly quake in their boots. The horror of it was that you were running in the night while hoping that you were running right, so as not to run right into your enemy and your doom. Nothing I can say can encapsulate that night.

Added to this overwhelming fear was the crushing burden of knowing that this attack was crucial to winning the war. If we could hit the Yankees and drive them out of Lookout Valley, we would restore the siege of Chattanooga. There was a chance, slim albeit, but still a chance, that the Union forces in Chattanooga would be compelled to surrender. Even if they retreated back up to Nashville, that would be good. The western theatre could be won back. The relentless, ongoing, juggernaut of the tidal wave that was the Federal forces invading the South would have been turned back, beaten, and defeated! What Lee had failed to do at Gettysburg, would be done by Bragg in Tennessee! It was that dream that spurred us on that night, but it was also that dream that scared us so much that night: so much was riding on our success.

Why, oh why, did Longstreet not send in the whole corps? I heard Commanding General Braxton Bragg himself order James Longstreet, "For God's sake man! Use your whole corps, if need be, but oust those infernal Yankees from the Wauhatchie Valley." Bragg and Longstreet were perched upon Sunset Rock peering west from Lookout Mountain. The whole Valley was spread before them. They could easily see the small Union division holding the train station at Wauhatchie Junction.

Earlier in the day, we had watched the blue infantry spread across Lookout Valley below us. This was on October 28, 1863. They came up marching along the Nashville and Chattanooga Railroad. Most of them marched up to Brown's Ferry, but at least a division or so stopped at Wauhatchie Station and camped there. They were so impudent. They marched right up while Braxton Bragg and James Longstreet were having a conference on a shelf of Lookout Mountain, called Sunset Rock, overlooking the Valley. I was thrilled that I would be leading our company as 2nd Lieutenant. I had been elected 2nd Lieutenant that past January. The Hampton Legion was going to spearhead the attack on the enemy forces near Wauhatchie; we were not going to be a part of the blocking forces near Brown's Ferry. We would crush the Union forces at Wauhatchie. We would rout and disperse the enemy in the Wauhatchie Valley and reinstate the choking siege that threatened to destroy the Army of the Cumberland. Rosecrans and his men would starve and then surrender! So truly then, what Lee had failed to do at Gettysburg would be done by Bragg in Tennessee!

But all of this was not to be, for it was petty jealousy, greed for glory, and rank feuding that brought the South down! Oftentimes, two officers would feud and their bickering would impede an attack or allow the enemy to take a crucial position. Officers vying more against each other, than against the Yankees! Their bickering diverting them from fighting tooth and nail against that pernicious enemy, and their stupidity, their cupidity, and their absurdity cost the South the laurels of victory which should have been hers! Grant had no better assistants or handmaidens than the high command of the Confederacy, who plotted and planned treachery against Braxton Bragg at Chattanooga.

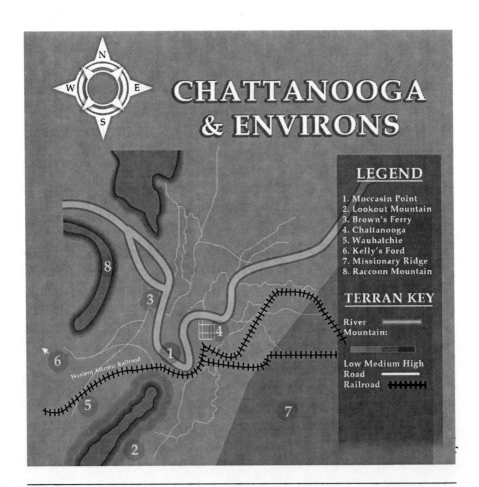

the high command, did their utmost to bring Bragg down (not that maybe Bragg didn't deserve it!) It was President Davis, who came from Richmond by rail, who kept Bragg in command over the strenuous objections of virtually every high ranking officer of the Army of Tennessee. This affirmation by Davis led Bragg to relieve members of his high command (whom he felt he could get rid of without repercussions!) that he deemed instrumental in forming and motivating the cabal: D.H. Hill and Buckner. He thought this would intimidate the others. Although Longstreet led the cabal and became its main spokesman, Bragg did not touch Longstreet, for Bragg feared what Davis would do. Even though it was an open secret that Longstreet had led the cabal to remove and replace Bragg with a new commanding general, with most betting that the new commanding general with whom Longstreet wanted to replace Bragg was Longstreet himself. Things would be thereafter frosty, to say the least, between Longstreet and Bragg. It seemed thereafter that Longstreet was openly insubordinate to Bragg.

Longstreet evolved a theory that he and his corps were not really a part of the Army of Tennessee, but was rather an independent command. Thus, Longstreet as an independent army commander could accept or reject Bragg's 'orders' as being mere 'suggestions' or 'recommendations'. Thus, when Bragg ordered Longstreet to post troops in the Wauhatchie Valley to guard against a Union invasion of the Valley, Longstreet ignored that order. That's why the Valley was open.

This intense situation unfolded while we, the men of the Hampton Legion, sat on top of Lookout Mountain. I had seen the Yankees enter the Valley on October 28th, 1863. You could see them for miles-may be even 30 miles-from our vantage point. They spread across the Valley like the plague took over Europe during the Middle Ages.

I ask again, Vicee, why, oh, why did Longstreet not take his whole corps down the mountain and destroy Union General Geary's force? I heard Bragg himself yell the order at Longstreet when they were perched on that outcropping ledge of Lookout Mountain known as Sunset Rock, because it afforded rare and beautiful views of the Valley in the late afternoon and early evening.

Bragg said it several times: "For God's sake man, use your whole damn corps if need be, but oust those infernal Yankees, that heathen blue filth, from the Wauhatchie Valley!" Bragg bellowed and bellowed like a bull moose.

Bragg wheeled on his heel after peering out from Sunset Rock and seeing the Union Army invading the Valley. He stared directly into the steel-blue eyes of Lee's favorite General. "Damn you! You must have been able to see **them** days away. Why didn't you take measures? Why didn't you take any steps to prevent this? Why didn't you inform me? Didn't I order you on October 25th to occupy that Valley? Didn't I?"

Longstreet tried in vain to interrupt Bragg. "General… General… Listen… General…"

Bragg drew in his breath. He balled his fist. "Why was there no opposition? The terrain between here and Bridgeport is a succession of ridges and valleys that run perpendicular to the enemy's line of march! It was highly defensible! But you sat on your high and mighty ass up here and did nothing. Nothing!"

Old Pete sputtered, hemmed, and hawed throughout Bragg's verbal assault for he had no good answer to his superior's questions.

"Why, in God's name," the profane General Bragg continued, "did you let them, in? Don't you know we had them besieged? We had cut them off from food, fodder, forage, and supplies? Do you know what you have done? You have lost the War!"

Longstreet tried to make an answer, "Well, General Bragg, I…I…I…I tried…I thought…" He sputtered to a halt.

"You did nothing! You could see them for miles to the south! At least 20 or 30 miles! What were you thinking? Were you just being perverse? You have wanted my command from the day you stepped off the train. Your charge at Chickamauga was just a fluke. There was no brilliance in it. Just as you ordered the charge, some Union general pulled his division out of the line! And it was right where you were going to charge! You weren't good; you were just damned lucky!" Bragg's face rumpled up with disdain.

"I resent the implications of your allegations…" Longstreet was angry now. His tall and lanky frame had straightened itself out to his full height of over six feet so now he towered over Bragg. The thought of a duel with Bragg crossed his mind.

Bragg started to wag his finger at Longstreet. "I gave you Command of the Left Wing of the Army at Chickamauga. I did that out of respect for Lee and his fine words about your abilities. I do not see how he ever could have praised you! You are an incompetent! I honored you without having seen your work. This is how you repay me? Did you let them invade, so you could get my command? Did you create this crisis for your own benefit? I think so!"

Longstreet was now so angry; his mind became filled with the vision of Bragg at his feet, dead, after a duel. Longstreet was from South Carolina. He had his pride and his honor to uphold. His right hand went to his holster. He hesitated for a second. 'What would Louise do if I were killed? Could she stand the pain of another loss after the deaths of our three children only a year ago January…' He stopped his hand. The fiery heat of his anger still burned. His mouth contorted and his jaw hardened.

Bragg fired more orders. "Get on with it. Take your corps and destroy them! Get it done and get it done today!" His tone was completely dismissive and condescending.

Longstreet stood there dumbstruck. His loathing of the irascible figure of a man in front of him made his blood boil. He still had not fully settled in his mind whether he would just kill Bragg there and then, when Bragg began yelling again.

"Well, General, say 'yes, sir' and get it done!" Bragg rushed by his subordinate, nearly knocking him down, as strode away from the ledge and vaulted on his horse. His aide handed him the reins. Bragg turned to Longstreet and saluted, but his eyes were averted with disgust.

Longstreet now became the model soldier, "Yes, sir. Right away, sir." He saluted back.

Part II: Dissention at the Legion Level

But, Vicee, maybe the crisis wasn't caused only by Bragg and Longstreet feuding. Bragg had played a bigger role in the whole shebang unwinding than his diatribe against Longstreet may have indicated. Braxton Bragg had a fine cavalry leader in Fighting Joe Wheeler. Joe was the rare New Englander who fought for the South. Although he had been born near Augusta, Georgia, a fact that he made sure everyone knew, he had been raised by relatives in Connecticut, a fact that he tried to make sure no one knew. He was a West Pointer, which Bragg liked, and from early in the war, when Bragg was commander of Ft. Barrancas near Pensacola, Wheeler had reported to Bragg. At Shiloh, Wheeler had fought extremely well under Bragg. In fact, Braxton Bragg had formed as much of a friendship with Wheeler as with any other man in his life, although no one would say that Wheeler was an intimate of Bragg.

Bragg had thought that he had the Union so well sealed up in Chattanooga that he could allow Wheeler to raid the Union supply line far north of Chattanooga. Bragg had not thought of putting any cavalry to his west, so there was no trip line to tell him if the Union was moving forces from the west, which they were, to relieve Chattanooga.

In addition, Bragg had had a dispute with Nathan Bedford Forrest, who was one of the best cavalry officers in the South. Forrest was so convinced that Bragg was incompetent, he had vowed never to fight under him again. He had then taken his much needed cavalry and had gone off to fight Yankees elsewhere. We were, therefore, bereft of cavalry- we had no eyes and ears out there patrolling for Yankees.

We also had our own feud much closer to home that played an important role in the whole mess.

Our troubles began innocently.

Brig. Gen. Evander McIvor Law now commanded Hood's division of which Hampton's Legion was now a part. This had come about after General John Bell Hood had been seriously wounded. We were proud of our service under John Bell Hood. We had fought beside his Texas Brigade since quite early in the war. We were proud that, under Hood, we had given Robert E. Lee his first victory at Gaines' Mill. Hood had been seriously wounded at Gettysburg, which left him with a useless left arm. Now, in our victory at Chickamauga, Hood had lost his right leg. We did not know then if he would ever serve again. Meanwhile, Brig. Gen. Micah Jenkins coveted command of Hood's division. He thought that his commission was dated a few days earlier than Law's and so he thought he should command.

It's not that any of us thought that General Micah Jenkins was not brave. It was something else, for we had all heard the story of how when he was twelve years old, he impaled a very large fishhook through his wrist.

The surgeon came, and when he was ready to remove the barb, he said to his young patient, "This is going to hurt. Here, son, take a gulp of this whiskey, it will help with the pain."

The young Jenkins was reported to have responded, "Oh, no, sir, I cannot. I have promised my mother that I would never drink intoxicating liquor."

The young Jenkins did not take any chloroform or other drugs to dull the pain. The surgeon did his work, during which Jenkins fainted from the pain.

We all thought this story told us two things about our General. One, he was true to a promise to his mother, and two, he was brave.

Still, there was something that the men sensed that made them leery of the General. They just didn't trust him. We called him the Prince of Edisto, which showed we didn't think of him as being one of us. He always seemed to be trying to be perfect, in conduct, in appearance, and in almost everything. At the Citadel, he spent his entire academic career trying to be the first soldier in both deportment and in military science. His English teacher at the Citadel had said that his first impression of Micah Jenkins was formed by Jenkin's first words to the teacher. "It was, as I remember, the day he enrolled that he stated to me, as we stood together near the sally port of The Citadel, which he intended to be first in his class."

His ambition was so great that nothing would get in the way of him being number one. One time, when the town boys and the cadets engaged in what can only be called a skirmish, the school thereafter confined the cadets to school and awarded all of them a large number of demerits. Jenkins felt that the number of demerits threatened his chances of being number one in his class, because he believed he could never work them off. Jenkins was willing to accept confinement, he said, but not the demerits. Although it could not later be proved, rumors swirled that Micah, who was one of the few pay students (that is a student who not only could afford the $200 per year tuition, but also actually paid it!), had his father, Captain John Jenkins, intervene discreetly in the matter. Captain John, as he was known, was a tall man of over six feet, two inches. He had served in the State Legislature, as had his brother, Colonel Joseph Evans Jenkins. The Jenkins family had great wealth, aristocratic homes in Charleston, summer homes on Edingsville Beach, plantations on Edisto Island, an army of servants and slaves, and untold connections throughout the state. After much review, the administration removed all the punishments and rescinded all the demerits. When Jenkins graduated, he was asked to read his valedictory address due to his ranking first in his class in both academically and as a soldier.

But coupled with this character flaw of trying to be perfect was a greater one: Jenkins was quick to take offense, if he thought someone had wronged him. The package of his personality traits had a bow tying it all up: he was bulled - headed. His family had tried to get him to enter the military or law after his graduation from the Citadel. He wanted to be a teacher. The Jenkins family felt that teaching was below him and the family socially. He tried being a lawyer for a few months, while he hatched a plan to buy some land and buildings in Yorkville, so that he could start a military academy and teach. His reasoning, apparently, was that his family could not object if his teaching was at a military academy. This was the start of the Kings Mountain Military Academy.

So, coming back to Jenkins, Law, and how it affected Hampton's Legion, when Law requested permission for a furlough, so that he could visit Hood in a hospital in Georgia, Jenkins saw his opening.

When Law left on October 24, 1863, Micah Jenkins was left in charge of the division. One could say that the source of the trouble between Law and Jenkins lay with Longstreet. At one time or another, Longstreet had promised both Law and Jenkins command of Hood's division, if ever the command of Hood's division became available.

But the seeds of the dispute between Law and Jenkins were there long before Longstreet muddled into it. The two men despised each other. Both were young. Jenkins, from Edisto Island, was born just a few months before Law, who hailed from our own Darlington, Vicee. Jenkins was always a sartorial splendor, with hair and mustache groomed

North of the city, across the wide Tennessee River is Moccasin Point which is the very end of Moccasin Peninsula, which formed when the Tennessee River doubled back on itself from the southwest of the city to the northwest, creating a thin neck between two lengths of the River. On the western bank of the furthest west loop of the river is Brown's Ferry. This point, if controlled by the Union, would allow supplies to be ferried across the River, then across Moccasin Peninsula, and then by ferry into the city.

We held Brown's Ferry. This point prevented the enemy from ferrying supplies across and was the stranglehold on the city. We also thought we held the Wauhatchie Valley to the west of Lookout Mountain and Brown's Ferry.

Bragg had ordered Longstreet on several occasions to send forces into the Wauhatchie Valley to guard Brown's Ferry and otherwise seal the Valley off from Union forces coming from the southwest. Longstreet resisted these orders-why? I don't know-as being 'suggestions'. Finally, Longstreet acted.

Longstreet, for reasons no one can fathom, had issued an order directly to Law, before his departure, to deploy his forces such that two small regiments of his five regiments were in the Wauhatchie Valley, mainly near Brown's Ferry. Why Longstreet by-passed the chain of command can only be answered by the fact that Law was now his favorite, and Jenkins was not. There were no other forces near Wauhatchie or anywhere else in the Valley watching for the possibility of Union forces coming from the southwest from Bridgeport, Alabama.

Law dutifully moved the two regiments as Longstreet ordered. But when he got to the Valley, which suddenly got bigger than it appeared from the mountain, Law, on his own initiative, brought down his other three regiments.

Then, when Law went on his furlough to visit the wounded Hood, Jenkins, who stated that he would follow the letter of Longstreet's order (but who was probably just being peevish), pulled back Law's other three regiments.

So, as I said, Vicee, Jenkins changed the dispositions. He removed, all but two of the regiments from the Wauhatchie Valley, leaving one to guard Brown's Ferry, the other to guard the Valley. Brown's Ferry, that incredibly valuable real estate, was guarded by a mere couple of hundred men.

Lest you think that the danger from the southwest was not recognized or widely known, I would include with this letter, if I still had them, the clippings from the newspapers, the Daily Courier, from Charleston and the Republican from Savannah. I think it was correspondents, Felix de Fontaine and P. A. Alexander, who wrote that the only way the Yankees could approach was from the southwest through the Wauhatchie Valley.

General McGowan told me that victorious Roman generals would come back to Rome heavily laden with gold, silver, and jewelry, slaves marching before them. When the Senate granted the victorious general a triumph, the general would ride a golden chariot dressed as Jupiter Best and Greatest, face reddened with copper, waving at the crowds, while a slave stood by and whispered in the general's ear, "Don't forget you are mortal!" Somehow in these journalists, I could see and hear the slaves of Rome whispering in the ear of Longstreet in his chariot, celebrating his victory at Chickamauga, their incantations of "Beware the Attack from Bridgeport!" and Longstreet blithely not heeding their warnings!

The Yankees were far more vigilant and far more industrious. Recognizing that Rosecrans' Army was slowly starving to death, Grant decided to open up a supply line. His brilliant plan was three-pronged. The first prong involved floating forces from Chattanooga down river on rafts to Brown's Ferry. Now, knowing that Grant had done something similar before at Vicksburg should have alerted Bragg to that possibility. On the night of October 27, 1863, Grant had some four thousand men float silently past our forces on the northern tip of Lookout Mountain. They came ashore at Brown's Ferry and brushed aside our pitiful handful of a force there. Meanwhile, another 8,000 men marched across Moccasin Peninsula, with pontoon bridging materials. At a point opposite Brown's Ferry, once they knew Brown's Ferry had been taken, under the cover of night, they laid across the river a pontoon bridge. By morning, some 12,000 Yankees held Brown's Ferry.

The last prong was to have Hooker, with his corps, which had come on train from the eastern theatre move into the Wauhatchie Valley from Bridgeport, Alabama, just as the Roman slave newspapermen had warned. On cue, Hooker and his corps linked up with the forces at Brown's Ferry, except for Geary's men who formed a small camp around Wauhatchie Station. They had been last in the line of march of Hooker's corps. I guess they stopped, because it was the end of the day, and it looked like a good place to camp.

Part III: Night is No Time to Fight

At around sunset, about 1,600 Yankees went into camp near the Station at Wauhatchie. This was our chance.

The plan called for one part of our force to come down the mountain, cross the bridge, and then move north on the road to sweep towards the Yankees at Brown's Ferry. This portion would straddle the road and prevent the Yankees at Brown's Ferry from reinforcing the lonely outpost at Wauhatchie Station. This portion consisted of Law's Division reinforced by the Texas Brigade.

The second portion would come down off the mountain, cross the same bridge behind Law's men, and then once at the road, would turn south and surround the Yankees at Wauhatchie Station. We were in the second portion, the so-called South Carolina Brigade. Again, we were the ones that everyone turned to when there was a real job to be done. We were under Colonel John Bratton. I felt a certain empathy with the Colonel. He had been wounded at Seven Pines leading South Carolinians, much as I had been wounded. He had it worse though, for he was captured and spent a couple of months in a Yankee prison before being exchanged. The men had real admiration for the man, because he had enlisted as a private at the beginning of the War. As a both a practicing surgeon, having attended and graduated from South Carolina College in Columbia, and a successful planter, he could have easily secured a commission as an officer. It was through his bravery and his skill that he earned promotion. Colonel Bratton was not a particularly good looking man for he had high cheek bones and eyes that were a little too close together, but he was the right type of man in battle, because he cared for his men and did not lose them needlessly.

The Federal camp at Wauhatchie Station was about four miles from Brown's Ferry. The lynch pin of the plan was this distance. If we would keep the Union forces separated, we would destroy the force at Wauhatchie Station.

Things went wrong right from the very beginning. For reasons, not at all clear to us, during the afternoon, the Legion marched to the top of Lookout Mountain by a road that was far to the south. Once, we got there, orders came for us to march down the mountain again and return to where we had started. Where we had started was on the far side of the mountain from where we were to go later that evening.

But that was not the only thing. Jenkins, who was the overall commander of this night, left out Anderson's brigade, which would have added a couple more thousand men to the attack. He also left out at least 7 companies (some said it was 14, Vicee!) of the South Carolina Brigade. So we went in grossly undermanned in an attack that was supposed to include all of Longstreet's Corps!

Just after dark, our movement started. We crossed over the mountain. We descended down the western side of the mountain. As we did so, the just passed full moon rose higher and higher towards the zenith, such that by the time we got to the bridge over Wauhatchie Creek, the moon was almost over head. There was no romance in seeing that moon. The officers who had laid out the plan wanted its brightness to help us to see to fight, but we, in the ranks, knew that the better we could see, the better our enemy could see. It was a mixed blessing. So most of us thought that its silver light was our enemy. We wanted it to be as dark as possible so that the Yankees did not see us coming. The plain of Wauhatchie was aglow with bright moonlight. One could read a newspaper, it was so brilliant.

The night was cold. Being late October atop a mountain, the wind tore through our threadbare uniforms. Many of my men did not have brogans; some had brogans that did not have soles. Only a few, a lucky few, had shoes with soles. Our gun barrels felt particularly frigid to the touch. Our exertion in climbing down the mountain helped us to warm up.

We reached the foot of the mountain and headed west towards the creek. The bridge could handle only so many of us at a time. I wondered, Vicee, what would happen if disaster befell us and we had to retreat across the bridge in disorder?

We advanced south. The plain that we found ourselves in was fairly level. There were no trees, just tall broom grass that crunched under foot as we marched. We soon struck the pickets of Union General John Geary. Our line erupted in fire against their pickets who returned our fire and then melted back toward their main lines. Thus, informed of our presence, General Geary threw his men into a line of battle that resembled a capital letter 'L'. Geary had his men in front of his artillery and his wagon train. Geary's men were both New Yorkers and Pennsylvanians-veterans who had been hardened in battle.

I have learned that the Germans have a word for what we experienced that night, 'Totentanz,' the Dance of Death. The battle in the moonlight was beautiful in a strange and exciting way. The muskets firing were ripping across the open plain like little fireflies, orange streaks in silver light against a background of green and brown waving tall broom grass. An artist would have marveled at the light. Soon, a brighter orange erupted from the Union lines; four cannon began belching forth fire, flames, grey smoke rings that lighted up for a few seconds, followed by a resounding boom. Bodies were going down in our lines and theirs, falling in grotesque forms of twisted motion that no live man could ever have attained in life without the greatest pain. Screams punctuated the pops of the musket fire and were drowned by the overwhelming claps of the cannonade. Light changed colors with each man-made explosion. Statues were created out of men. It was all the arts: music by explosion, sculpture by death, painting by dazzling moonlight and cannon fire.

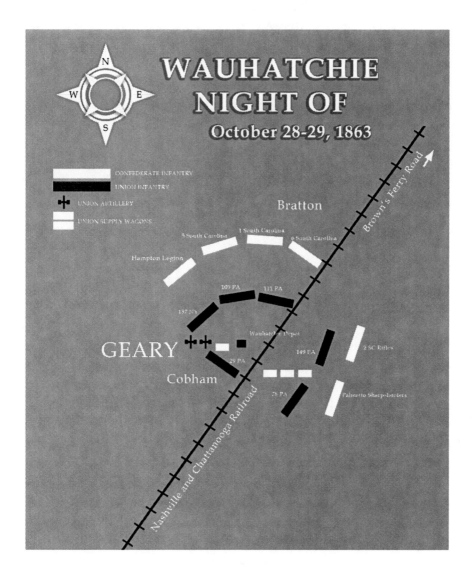

We started to spread further and further to our left and to our right, trying to find the ends of their flanks in hopes that we could wrap around them and thus defeat them. Their cannon were taking a fearful toll. Our line now formed an arc. We were on the far western side of the arc, with the 5th South Carolina, followed by the 1st, the 6th, and 2nd South Carolina regiments spanning from us to our eastern most regiment, the Palmetto Sharpshooters. The more we tried to get around them Yankees, the more hunkered down they became. Geary had his men fighting Indian-style. They were drawn in almost a box with the artillery and the wagons in the middle.

We managed to get in among the wagons, and then the worst nature of our men took hold. A number of our men dropped out of the fight and began to loot the wagons, looking for food, or anything else of interest, such as liquor.

I rallied my company. "Men we have got to silence those guns!" I pointed my rifle at the battery.

Doug was there by my side. "Why don't we flank them and then let loose a volley?"

I like his plan better than mine which was to charge the guns. "Men, double-quick to our right about 50 yards. Get astride of them guns and then, on my order, loose a volley!"

Now, I would like to say that by the textbook we double-quicked, but in reality, we ran. We got to where we had flanked the guns. I could see the cannoneers turning the tails of their guns to fire upon us. I knew that any moment we would be christened by canister and ripped to pieces. One of their officers, a lieutenant, appeared to be the bravest of them all. He stood calmly and coolly, ordering his men. "Wheel those cannons! Put your backs in it. Move men, move!" A sergeant came up to him, "Get down, Lieutenant Geary! They'll kill you!"

I had not a moment to spare. It was this lieutenant or that one who was going to survive this night. I cried out, "Up men! Fire! Now!" I know, Vicee, that this is not a correct order, but my men knew what they were doing. A rank of them stood and fired and then a second later, our second rank fired. The guns were silenced. No canister rained down upon us. I could see all of the officers of the battery were on the ground. We had killed or wounded all of them. Around them, it appears that maybe thirty or thirty-five of the horses were down, with maybe 10 or so still standing.

We started to bayonet the horses of the artillery and the mules of the wagon train. The poor animals started to stampede. In their flight from our fury, many of the Union boys were trampled under hoof.

Now, the fact that we were missing so many companies of the South Carolina Brigade started to tell on us. We just didn't seem to have enough men to stay inside the Union defensive box. Geary's men started to drive us out.

I then saw something which made my heart break. Across the camp, the Union General came running. He was surrounded by his staff. He knelt down by the shattered battery of cannon and grasped a dead body in his arms-it was the brave lieutenant. The form lay limp in his arms, limbs dangling as the General stood up. I could hear his scream.

I started to level my Enfield musket. I had the general in my sights. Then I thought of my father. What if he were kneeling over me while I lay dying? How would I feel if a Yankee slew him in that moment of grief?

Just then, a courier rode up shouting an order: "Retreat!" Colonel Gary could not believe his ears. He pulled the courier off of his horse. He hauled him to a campfire to make sure that he was not drunk or otherwise 'demoralized'.

"Who are you?" Gary yelled at the horseman.

"I am Corporal John Benning, courier to General Jenkins. I have been ordered to ride to you and to order you to fall back, sir."

Gary was disgusted. He spat a chaw of tobacco to the ground and yelled, "Retreat! Fall back!"

I hadn't pulled the trigger. I couldn't pull the trigger.

We pulled back just as we were on the verge of victory. We pulled back through the plain that we had fought so hard to win.

"Lieutenant," Robbie was being formal, "why are we pulling back?"

"I don't know. I heard the order and I obey."

"But we were winning…" The anguish in his voice was great and clear.

I, too, wanted to know why we were retreating, but I had a job to do.

"Captain, do you know what's going on?" I whispered.

Captain William Bowers Councill looked at me. "I don't know. Let's get the men out of here. Safely." He had taken command of the company last January 29th. He was always looking out for the welfare of his troops. He had been a doctor. He had shown such care and concern for the men during the measles and mumps epidemics.

We pulled back to the bridge across the creek. Because we were one of the last companies to come up, we were delegated the 'honor' of being the rear guard for the bridgehead. We looked across the creek and saw that our reserves were still there on the other side.

"Tough night," called out a member of the Legion to the reserves on the other side.

"Wouldn't know. We weren't put in the fray. Sat here all night," came the wistful answer from the reserve troops.

"God damn! God damn him, Jenkins! God damn Longstreet! God damn Bragg! God damn them all!" roared Captain Councill. I had never seen him so angry. "We're out there fighting for our lives and coming within a whisker's breadth of victory. All we needed were a few more men. And God damn it, they're sitting right here all night playing poker, smoking, and having a social in the moonlight!" He spat on the ground.

"Captain," I took him by the shoulder. "Do you really want to be saying them things?"

"No, I don't Lieutenant, but by God, I will say them. God damn them! This whole attack was botched from beginning to end, and good men, my men, were killed and wounded out there tonight. They don't give a damn."

Now I am a God-fearing man, but I will admit, Vicee, that I have, on an occasion, cursed, but I have never heard so many damns and God damns in any such tirade.

The Legion took a lot of losses that night. Twelve of us died near the wagons, another six died within a few days. Some sixty-five were wounded, but most hurtful of all, some twenty of our men were prisoners.

CHAPTER 29:

WAUHATCHIE REVISITED

CHATTANOOGA, Sunday, Nov. 1, 1863.
Gen. GEARY's (Second) division, Twelfth army corps, under command of Maj. Gen, HOOKER, fought the battle of Wauhatchie, Tenn., in Lookout Creek Valley, early on the morning of the 29th of October, 1863. Three brigades of HOOD'S division, LONGSTREET'S corps, sought to surprise and capture Gen. GEARY'S advance, which was holding the intersection of the Wauhatchie and Brown's Ferry Road with the Kelly's Ferry Road .- New York Times

April 2, 1865 2:00 AM

Camp Near Chattanooga Lines
Oct 31st, 1863

My Dear Vicee:

I received your letter of the 22nd that arrived this afternoon. I am glad to hear that you was well & all the rest-at-home, but I thought you would have been safe at your Sister's. I sent one letter to you at Darlington, but I didn't get a response so I hardly know where to mail this letter, but I will send it to Timmonsville. I suppose Sister has not received your letter, as she would have sent for you had she read it. But she may have neglected it. But I suppose your second letter will make it to her. But we both maybe mistaken. I have not read any letters in answer to those yet-But I will write to her again soon for, perhaps, she has not received mine. But-I hope this will find you wife well and safe.

General Jenkins brigade has had a showing at the Yanks at last. The Legion fought well. For a while we thought our Company would have the good luck to miss the Fight. We was detained on Picket, just before the Legion started off to go into the Fight. But we did not know for certain that they was agoing to fight. Then we got our orders. We got sent in. About 8 hours after we left, we all got into it in good fashion. It was about 2 o'clock at night when we commenced fighting. We fought hard for over two hours. So many of us were killed and wounded in every company that was into the fight. I think there was seven companies out of ten in the fight. 185 were killed, wounded and missing. We had to leave behind all of some of our wounded and all of our dead. We lost some good men. I don't think there will be much of a chance for a fight here unless the Yanks attack us.

But it was bad management in our Generals for letting past us on the mountain on this side of the River. And I am afraid that it will cause Bragg to fall back before the Yanks because winter is coming.

I think I will know what we will do by the time I write again. I am anxious to get something to Eat for I want a change. We have nothing good to Eat, but Corn Meal and awful poor beef and bad yams.

Well Dear I love you. I had good news with this night. Well Dear I miss you. Give my Love to all. J.A. McEachern

(NB Then written up and down the page the letter continues. This handwriting obscures the text written left to right as well as up and down.)

I send you all my money to pay for things and will send you some more as soon as I can get it from the Quarter Master. I am fighting a relaxed man who does not understand that I need to send it on to you. But my anniversary Bill is coming so I should get more soon. Love to you, James

CHAPTER 30:

ANOTHER SIEGE

In war even the easiest things are difficult.
*-**Clausewitz**, On War*

April 2, 1865 2:15 AM

We were walking (to say we were marching would be a vast overstatement, because we were not an army, but a rabble in rags). We left Missionary Ridge outside of Chattanooga. We were going northeast. None of us knew why we were going, only that we were going. Some speculated that we were returning to Virginia via the mountain passes. Some said we were turning to meet Burnside who was near Knoxville, so that he could not assail Bragg's rear, while Bragg continued the siege of Chattanooga. I had no opinion. I just wanted to get away from the damned mountains, the cold, the lack of rations, and the whole state of Tennessee.

Whatever we were doing, things weren't going right. A couple of days ago, we were sitting near a dilapidated train depot. Then, we were called to assembly. Colonel Gary had stood in front of us and told us, "Men, we're supposed to be meeting some trains to take us where we are going. It seems that they're not on time." We all laughed at his joke. "And it seems they're not coming for a while." He paused a moment, and shifted on his feet. "I don't know how to tell you this, but we're going to march there or at least some of the way there."

A man called out, "Begging your pardon, sir, but 'where' is there? I mean no offense, but we'd like to know, sir."

"Well, that I can't tell you, 'cause I don't know. I just know I got to get your rascally souls there." The men laughed again. Colonel Gary had a way with the men, which kept them calm and trusting in him.

So, we started off on foot. We skirted both sides of the railroad. I guess the thinking was that when the trains did come, Vicee, they would come along the tracks, and we'd just hop in, and away we'd go. Somewhere, after a couple of days, some trains did show up.

We boarded them. We thought our troubles were over now, but, in truth, they had just begun.

The locomotives that pulled the trains were too weak to take the grades of the mountains. So periodically, we had to unload from the boxcars, march alongside the train, and then jump back on board down the road. This was very hard on the men, because the grades were usually so narrow, so rocky, and so steep, that the men, with all their equipment, often fell and hurt themselves.

Well, we had gotten used to this routine, when the engineers announced that they hadn't brought enough wood to fuel the boilers. "Everyone will have to get out and wait for us to come back," they ordered.

Colonel Gary would have none of that. He pointed his pistol at one of the engineers. "We've had enough of this. Damn you to hell! You didn't bring enough fuel? Hell, we will dismantle the boxcars, we'll strip the fences from along the track siding, and we'll take the planks of any barn or shed we see. You ain't going to drive away and leave me men here!"

After eight grueling days, the men had made the trip to Sweetwater, Tennessee, where they disembarked from the trains. Now, Sweetwater was only 60 miles away from where we started so, we made about 7 miles a day by boarding the trains. None of us had had any food now for at least the last three days.

At Sweetwater, we had been promised that rations, blankets, and other supplies would be waiting for us. Nothing was there. We all started to curse the commissary department. I am sorry to say that I might have been the loudest of them, Vicee.

It was now November 12, 1863. Winter had definitely come to the mountains. We were suffering greatly from a lack of everything.

Now, we were asked to do herculean labors. Longstreet had learned that General Ambrose Burnside (yes, the same Union General of Fredericksburg) was racing back to Knoxville and his entrenchments there. If we could beat Burnside to Campbell's Station, we could cut him off from Knoxville and fight him in the open.

As part of Jenkins' division, we were ordered to march at double-quick time to Campbell's Station. McLaws' division was ordered to Campbell's Station by a different and shorter route, the Kingston Road. But for reasons that none of us could fathom, Longstreet had neglected to order McLaws' men to double-quick. In addition, Longstreet had ordered our cavalry under General Joseph Wheeler to Maryville, where it didn't help at all in holding the important crossroads of Campbell's Station. So, McLaws, not knowing the importance of his mission, engaged in a dilatory march, which enabled the Federals to beat him by only fifteen minutes to the crucial junction.

Longstreet tried to blame the debacle upon the muddy, bad roads, but no one really believed him. For hadn't Burnside, his men, and his immense wagon trains marched over the selfsame roads?

It was about this time that the men lost all faith in Longstreet. Too many of us remembered the botched attack at Seven Pines, where Longstreet marched down the wrong road. Doug said, "I don't think he can read a map!" Others of us blamed him for what happened at Chattanooga. As leader of the cabal, he had undercut his commanding general and had caused great dissension among generals and the ranks. Some of those generals had lost their commands because of him. Now, none of us really liked General Bragg, but the siege at Chattanooga had been going pretty well until Longstreet blundered and let the Yankees into the Wauhatchie Valley. Others pointed to Gettysburg, "Had Longstreet been too slow on his march on July 2nd?" asked Robbie. I tried to keep the men in line, but they were grumbling now, because of the cold winter weather, the lack of food, the lack of blankets, and the hard marches. When things get bad for the men, they blame their commanders. Now, things were very bad, so we blamed Longstreet for everything without mercy.

Soldiers can be very superstitious. Although what had happened at Campbell's Station was but a skirmish, it had larger ramifications. Jenkins men were very shaken by an incident that had happened that day. The 5th South Carolina was in line of battle, ready to be thrown into the fray, when a shell from a Union cannon hit a man almost exactly at the center of the 5th's line. This was most unfortunate for virtually everyone in the 5th saw what happened next. The shell ripped off the arm of Private Robert McKnight. The severed arm flew, tumbled through the air, and struck Private Lorraine Swann. The arm struck his head and killed him instantly. His blood and brains splattered all over Lieutenant J. D. McConnell's coat. The regiment collectively gasped at the horror in the front rank.

Something happened to the men that day at the minor skirmish. So, too, something had happened to Longstreet. The men's grumbling got to him. He seemed not to know what to do. His lack of confidence was felt by the men. The men of Longstreet's corps, who had been the victors time and time again in the east, now saw themselves as defeated, hungry, tired men, without a future and without hope in the west. The same men who had nicknamed General James Longstreet, "the Bull of the Woods", after his stunning attack, which had led to victory at Chickamauga, were now calling him by a new moniker, "Peter the Slow".

Next day, we caught up with part of Burnside's wagon train and captured hundreds of wagons filled food, tools, supplies, a pontoon bridge, and other war material, including wonderful, warm blankets, thank God! We explored the entrenchments of Knoxville and found no weaknesses. So we settled down for another siege, the third for Longstreet. This was true, even though Burnside's forces outnumbered us in both infantry and cavalry.

During this siege, it seemed that Longstreet decided on one plan one day and then changed his mind the next. He ordered Porter Alexander to ferry his artillery across the Holston River and then to haul it up a steep hill, known as Cherokee Heights, to bombard the Union lines at Knoxville, with Fort Stanley as the focal point. After a day and half of hard, heavy work, Alexander found the range of 2,400 yards to be too much, something that could have been ascertained by a good reconnaissance. So, Longstreet then ordered the artillery back. "I have never been so disgusted in all my life," Colonel Porter Alexander declared to anyone who would listen. "Fortunately it was down Hill this time," Alexander wrote.

The next day, Bragg's chief engineer, General Leadbetter, arrived. Longstreet and Leadbetter surveyed the Union lines all that day and most of the next. At first, the plan was to attack Mabry's Hill. Then, after consultation with Longstreet's lieutenants, including Bushrod Johnson and Archibald Grace, the point of attack was changed back to Fort Stanley.

Once again, Alexander was ordered to ferry his artillery across the Holston River, haul it up Cherokee Heights, and to prepare to bombard Fort Stanley. Colonel Alexander was now livid. "There was never a more complete fiasco than the attempt to find a favorable point for attack," he yelled at his subordinates, who were embarrassed at his unusual tirade and afraid for their commander's position, if Longstreet heard the Colonel's words.

We were ordered with the rest of Jenkins' men to be ready at dawn to assault Fort Stanley. The plan was that, under the cover of Alexander's guns, we would charge the Union picket lines. Then, after Alexander bombarded the fort for some time, we would charge the fort in column and carry it.

The day of the attack, fog and rain prevented Alexander from supporting the infantry assault. So Longstreet delayed the attack from dawn to mid-afternoon. McLaws, as Longstreet's most senior division commander, felt that the attack should be delayed to the next day.

Now, with more time on his hands, Longstreet began to re-think his attack. If idle hands are the devil's workshop, and idle lips are his mouthpiece, then an idle mind is the devil's playground. Longstreet asked himself if a preliminary bombardment would alert the Yankees to the impending attack and answered himself in the affirmative. 'I will order McLaws to seize the Federal rifles pits predawn. I'll have him place sharpshooters in the rifle pits to harass the Yankees when he and Jenkins charge. I'll have them attack in two separate columns from two different directions." He sat down and wrote orders to Alexander that would silence his guns both before and during the attack.

Later, when Alexander received his new orders, he stormed around his tent. "This plan's features are crazy enough to have been devised in Bedlam! The fool! After days of conserving ammunition to support this attack and after having hauled cannon hither and yon, my guns are merely signal blasts to start the show!"

Porter Alexander was not the only one who was disturbed by the features of the plan that night. General Lafayette McLaws had received intelligence that the ditch around the fort was ten or more feet deep. He wrote to General Longstreet that he had received reports of the greater depth of the ditch, and asked if his men could carry ladders to scale the walls of the forts and fascines to bridge the ditch.

Longstreet perceived in McLaws' letter a lack of confidence in the plan. Answering the element of the lack of confidence in the plan, Longstreet wrote a letter back to McLaws. "Please urge your officers the importance of making the assault with a determination to succeed. If the assault is made in that spirit, I shall feel no doubt of its success." He then addressed the depth of ditch by remarking how he had seen a Yankee soldier walking along in the ditch, which appeared to him to be no more than two or three feet deep.

McLaws respond to Longstreet with a second letter. He wrote, "There are rumors that Bragg has been defeated at Chattanooga and has retreated. If these rumors are true, then what can be gained by attacking Burnside at Knoxville? And therefore I advise that the assault not be made, but that we relinquish the siege of Knoxville at once & put our force in motion towards Virginia."

Longstreet was getting annoyed with McLaws and with what Longstreet perceived were McLaws' doubts in the plan. He wrote back to McLaws again with the intention of silencing him. "Your letter is received. I am not at all confident that Genl. Bragg has had a serious battle at Chattanooga, but there is a report that he has fallen back to Tunnel Hill. Under this report, I am entirely confident that our only safety is in making this assault…It is a great mistake to suppose that there is any safety for us in going to Virginia if Genl. Bragg has been defeated, for we leave him at the mercy of his victors."

While this exchange was going on, I went to Colonel Gary. "Colonel, the men would like to be issued ladders such that we can place them alongside the walls of Fort Stanley when we assault tomorrow morning. Those walls look pretty steep, and the men don't think they can do it without ladders."

Colonel Gary then went to General Jenkins. General Jenkins had been thinking the same thing, and he had become apprehensive about the lack of ladders. Jenkins decided to visit McLaws to discuss the situation with him.

When Jenkins reached McLaws headquarters, he received a reception he did not expect. McLaws, still smarting over the rebuffs he had received from Longstreet, said, "I do not know anything about such things, and we should trust to luck to get us around or over obstacles."

With that, Jenkins stormed out of McLaws' Headquarters. He bumped into Colonel Alexander. "Do you think you could come with me to discuss the attack plan with General Longstreet?" Jenkins asked Alexander.

"I am unusually tired this evening. I had to ferry my artillery around all over Hell-and-Gone, but I will be glad to relay to the commanding general my approval of your plan to bring ladders and fascines."

Jenkins then decided to write a letter to Longstreet, proposing to bring ladders and fascines. He felt that the fascines, that is bundles of sticks, were important to fill in the ditches, so the men could walk over the mud and not be impeded by the slopes of the ditches.

Longstreet responded to Jenkins, whom he thought was talking of defeat, by writing, "If we go in with the idea of defeat, then we shall fail. Let me urge you not to entertain such feelings for a moment. Do not let anyone fail or anything."

At midnight, two of McLaws' brigades stormed across the open field in front of the picket line near Fort Stanley. Quickly, they seized the Union rifle pits. Though they had moved very fast, it was not quickly enough. For the Yankees fired a volley and then fled the picket line. Nonetheless, Fort Stanley was alerted to the impending peril.

The attack at 4:00 am came as no surprise to the prepared, waiting Federal troops in Fort Stanley. Porter Alexander's cannon fired the signal to start the charge. The Confederates surged forward in the gloom that still dark night. Rank after rank fell - some actually broke a leg or an ankle - on the telegraph wire the Union forces had strung just a foot off the ground as an obstacle. When Longstreet's boys had recovered, they plunged into the ditch. The ditch was well over ten feet deep. What Longstreet had seen was a Yankee soldier walking on a plank boardwalk, which the Federal forces had pulled back into the fort.

The rain of the last couple of days had frozen overnight. The walls of the fort were slick and icy. They were impossible to scale. Yankees were taking pot shots at the swarms of Rebel soldiers in the ditch. In panic, Confederates tried to boost one man on the shoulders of another to reach the top of the parapet, but to no avail. Then, the Yankees threw lighted artillery shells over the walls and into the ditch, blowing massive holes in the crowded Confederates, who were penned in with no hope of escape. All the Confederates in the depths of the ditch merely churned the floor into mud, which further prevented the Confederates from getting up and over the walls of the fort. A few Rebel color bearers managed to get up the wall and planted their flags there to rally the troops. But all of these brave men were shot down. A couple of brave men used their bayonets as mountain picks to climb up the wall, but they, too, were shot down. Thirty minutes of carnage, thirty minutes of death and destruction, thirty minutes of Hell and Damnation, the Confederates endured and then they could endure no more.

Alexander, seeing the attack collapse into abject failure, and against Longstreet's orders, started to fire his guns to give cover as the Rebels began their disorderly retreat. This was the one respite the Rebels had that day.

As I retreated, Doug and Robert were beside me. "It was doomed to failure from the beginning," Doug screamed. "The walls were one continual slope, without any place to stand upon or to get a foot hold to climb up on!"

Robbie cried, "If we ever got into the ditch, then we were like rats in a cage trap."

I agreed. "We were in a close huddle and couldn't get out!"

*****

Within a few hours of the failure of the assault upon Fort Stanley, Longstreet received a telegram from President Jefferson Davis advising Longstreet of the complete defeat of Bragg before Chattanooga and ordering Longstreet to rejoin Bragg in northern Georgia. The Knoxville campaign was over; Longstreet's siege had failed.

BOOK V: WE ENDURE BEYOND ENDURANCE-1864

CHAPTER 31:
SILENCE

"Silence is a great peacemaker."
-Henry Wadsworth Longfellow, Table-Talk

April 2, 1865 2:30 AM

It has stopped, Vicee. The infernal artillery bombardment has stopped. Three hours long. Three unbelievably long hours. The eerie silence that has followed is unnerving. Vicee, I do not know what is happening, but I feel in my bones that this is it. I can feel the damned Yankees moving around out there. I can't hear them. But I feel them, sneaking around, crawling on the ground silently, getting ready to do evil and harm to us. They are creeping up. I know it for sure. I know it in my bones.

What do I do? Do I go and tell someone? And if I do go and tell someone, who do I tell and what do I tell them? If I tell them the Yankees are coming, they will ask, "What did you see? What did you hear?" I'll have to say that I heard nothing and I saw nothing. Then they will look at me and shake their heads. I'll be a damned fool. They'll say, "He's just scared." Then they will look at me and inwardly say to themselves, "That's too bad. He used to be such a good officer. Now, he's yellow."

Maybe it's the dark, Vicee. The night is dark now. The moon set some time ago. The blinding orange and yellow flashes of the Union cannon are gone. There is nothing to illuminate the plain-or is it a marsh?-that lies between us and the enemy.

It is well after 2:00am. I am here in a trench. The bottom of which is a basin in which rainwater collects. My feet are cold and wet. My hands are cold. I can't see anything. Maybe my imagination is getting away with me. But I know something is happening. Or it is about to happen. Yet, I am helpless to prevent it.

One of men is walking up to me. "Hell of a night, heh, Lieutenant?" Doug asks in the dark. I cannot see his mouth moving. I can almost imagine that the words are whirling out of the mist and the depths of the night. But somehow I see enough of a form of a man, and I know the sound of his voice to know who it is.

"Yes, I don't know what to make of it," I reply.

"Well, neither do I. Something's gonna happen." There it is. He feels it too. Doug spits a chaw of tobacco on the Yankee side of our trench. "It's too damned quiet out there. I wish I could smoke."

I answer, "I don't think you should do that. I think any light could be seen by the Johnnies easily." I hold my musket more tightly as if that could help me to command me my men better.

We are standing in the water-filled trench, lounging our bodies while holding our muskets over the wall of our trench peering into the evil that is this night. The night's cold is permeating our bodies. We exercise our eyes to strain to see something out there, anywhere out there. There is the bare shadows of the trees along the Yankee line a mile or so away. The gloomy night's ink prevents our sight from picking up anything.

*****

A shot goes off somewhere in front of us.

Our line erupts in fire. I can't see anything.

"Can anyone see anything?" Captain Carson calls out.

The firing keeps going.

I yell much louder, "Did anyone see anything?"

"Nope."

"I didn't."

"Not a thing."

Voices call out all along our line.

"Cease firing," Captain Carson yells.

I repeat the order, "Cease firing."

We listen. All is quiet. We listen some more. If they are out there, they are quiet. Calm, silence, and dark is restored. We listen carefully as time ticks by.

*****

"How's yer wife?" Doug asks as he clicks his nails on the wood stock of his gun in a rhythmic, repetitive, serial way, one finger nail after another.

"Stop that."

"What?"

"That damned clicking. It's making me hear your nails and nothing but." I settle back a moment. I hadn't realized how weary I was.

"Vicee…well, Vicee," I start up. "I ain't heard from her in long while. I guess pen and ink and paper are as scarce there as they are here." I stop. The thought that it might be worse for her back home had caught me off guard and deeply hurt me. I wanted nothing to be bad for her. I started wondering why I had gone off and left her. Wasn't I supposed to protect her, my wife? Was it really about state's rights? Was this really my war? Was this merely a way to keep rich men rich and protect their slaves and their way of life? I made carriages, so maybe it wasn't so bad for the rich to be rich, for otherwise, for whom would I build carriages?

As I started to think of carriages, I saw my father standing there beside me chastising me missing a spot as I painted the carriage he had built with his two hands. I was rocked by the thought: Would there even be a market for carriages after the war?

I must have said that out loud for Robbie brought me out of my reverie, "What'd you mean 'after tha War?'"

"I don't really know."

"Oh, come on, Lieutenant. What'd you mean?"

"There are times, when even I don't know what I am thinking. Are we finished? Do we have it in ourselves to hold this line and stopped them damn Yankees? Sometimes I ain't got no more in me to give. I can't seem to find the hatred to kill Yankees no more. Then there are times, when I could lift my sword and cut a swath through them like some ancient judge of Israel visiting divine judgment upon them. I need to do as much for the South as I can-I rail against Sheridan and all he has done to ravage the Shenandoah, burning farms, busting up saw mills and grist mills. Why'd he have to burn out them poor farmers? Poor people who ain't have nothing and not doing anything to anyone but raising some hogs, growing some corn and wheat, scratching a living from the soil. Why'd they have to do that?"

"Lieutenant," Doug rested his head on the side of our trench, "I don't got no understanding of that. Why don't the Yankees stand up and fire at us, and we can fire at them, and the one's who got's someone standing last wins! Why'd they have to go after womenfolk and children? That ain't right!"

We are sitting here now, Vicee. Just thinking and watching. The night is enveloping us in the cold. The silence is enveloping us in its unease and restlessness. But for thoughts of you, I have no reason to go on.

CHAPTER 32:

I JINE THE CAVALRY

*We're the boys that rode around McClellan,
Rode around McClellan, Rode around McClellan!
We're the boys that rode around McClellan,
Bully boys, hey! Bully boys, ho!
Chorus:
If you want to have a good time, jine the cavalry!
Jine the cavalry! Jine the cavalry!
If you want to catch the Devil, if you want to have fun,
If you want to smell Hell, jine the cavalry!
-Jine the Cavalry*

April 2, 1865 2:45 AM

You know, Vicee, that I had always wanted to be in the cavalry. I had also long wanted to reunite the Legion after its division into infantry and cavalry. It is strange to recall how these wishes actually came about.

The long simmering rivalry of Jenkins and Law boiled over in the early part of 1864. Longstreet's corps was in utter chaos. The long standing question of who would lead Hood's old division led Longstreet to arrest both General Jerome Robertson and McIvor Law. We all knew that the charges were trumped up. They were merely a fairly transparent way to clear the path such that Jenkins could command. Jenkins was a Longstreet favorite and now was the time for favorites to rule, or so Longstreet thought. At the same time that Longstreet removed Evander McIvor Law, he also removed Lafayette McLaws from command of his division and replaced him with another favorite, General Joseph B. Kershaw. So, it was the ongoing jealousy of Jenkins for Law that sent us on the fork in the road that none of us knew was even there.

The War Department saw through what Longstreet was doing. So on February 12, 1864 orders were issued for General Charles W. Field to assume command of Hood's Division. Longstreet, as irascible as ever, sought to circumvent that plan. He granted a furlough to Jenkins and put General Simon B. Buckner in command. Everyone saw this for what it was: a ploy to bide some time until Jenkins returned from his furlough. Then, Longstreet would reinstate him in command of Hood's Division.

The powers that be did not react well to this stratagem. Adjutant General Samuel Cooper, one of the oldest generals in the Civil War, having been born in 1796, and also the highest ranking officer in the Confederate Army (he outranked Bobby Lee, Beauregard, and Joe Johnston!) and who reported directly to the President, sent a peremptory order in the name of the President ordering Longstreet to execute the prior order placing General Charles W. Field in command of Hood's Division.

But the entire ruckus had focused attention upon the Hampton Legion, for both of the combatants, Jenkins and Law, had a long association with the Legion. Cooper had an aide by the name of Major Samuel W. Melton. Melton was a South Carolinian. Across his desk had come a request from Wade Hampton in Virginia for more recruits to bolster his depleted cavalry ranks. Melton floated an idea to Cooper in a memorandum on March 14, 1864, which read:

"Colonel Gary has been in more battles, perhaps, than any other officer of his grade in the service. He is a thoroughbred fighter, cool and deliberate, with great good sense, and that rare quality which enables him to make his men feel confident and firm under him. We need such a man to meet sudden advances upon the capital with his band of trained veterans-men who have often fought as infantry alone can fight."

Cooper decided that a need he had in Virginia had met with a means to fulfill that need as well as settling some other issues concurrently. Forthwith, the Hampton Legion Infantry was ordered to march to Greenville, South Carolina from Tennessee. There, we were given twenty days of furlough, which the men greeted with great enthusiasm, for many of us had not been home since the start of the War. This was prelude to a much different role for us.

I was sure when I heard that Wade Hampton needed new cavalry replacements because of the great loses he had suffered that some of the Legion would rejoin him as cavalry. I never thought that the entire Legion Infantry would become mounted infantry, carrying our Enfield muskets.

I was especially proud of my rifle. It was a Pattern 1853 Enfield. It weighed nearly ten pounds and was about 55 inches in length. Its barrel had originally been a smoothbore, but had been replaced by a rifled barrel. It had an adjustable step-ladder type of sight, which we usually left set at 100 yards, although the weapon was accurate up to 400 yards. We had been told that the British Army had been trained to hit a target at 650 yards, but we never had enough ammunition to practice at that range. I loved the royal crown engraving which was just behind the hammer. The wood of the stock and butt was stained cherry.

It was a lovely rifle, but it was far too long and heavy for a cavalry piece, but I had no choice but to carry it. I paired it with an 1851 Model Navy Colt six shooter revolver. Thus, we had to fight as dismounted infantry. We would ride to the battle line. Then, we would dismount and fight as infantry. There was one problem. Like cavalry, every fourth member of our mounted infantry had to be designated a horse holder, such that this fourth man held the reigns to four horses while the other three of us fought. That fourth man had a real challenge to hold the reins of four stupid scared, angry horses while explosions were going on all around him. He had to stand and be a target. Even though the horses were behind the lines, they couldn't be too far behind the lines or else we lost any chance to be mobile when it was necessary.

The infantry laughed at us, for we were mounted. They jeered us with the age old jibe, "Did you ever see a dead cavalryman?" There was something that inspired infantry to be jealous of the mounted man and to, therefore, insult him as he went by-transportation by horse was seen as less manly.

The cavalry laughed at us, for we were merely infantry on horses, and not cavalry. We were not seen as having the same élan or dash as the regular cavalry.

So, we had to suffer the slings and arrows of an outrageous fortune. We were neither fish nor fowl, and, being neither, all despised us. Gone were my dreams of riding upon the back of a noble steed in a charge that would break the enemy line.

When we marched out of Bull's Gap on March 22, 1864, we had to go over the mountains through Broad Valley to Ashville, North Carolina. From then, we marched south to Greenville. The calendar said spring, but the weather said winter. The sky was grey and threatened snow. The temperature seemed to keep plummeting. The next day, snow did fall and it kept falling throughout the night and the next day. While six to eight inches of snow lay in the Valley, higher up in the mountains, the snow really piled up. It was March 30th before we got to Greenville.

We marched into town a bunch of ragamuffins beneath an arched wreath the ladies had strung across Main Street reading, "Welcome Ye Brave Heroes." Our band was blaring. We doffed our hats to the cheering throng mainly made up of women and children.

Now, one of the most unfortunate policies of the Confederacy reared its ugly head for we who were new cavalrymen. The Confederacy did not provide mounts to their cavalry. Each man had to procure his own mount at his own expense. Riding into Greenville, we were greeted by advertisements in the newspapers offering horses for between $1,000 and $2,000. This was an astronomical sum for the Privates in our Legion who did not make even $15 a month.

"Why were horses in such demand?" I asked a horse trader named Jim. He didn't offer a last name. His rugged and dirty clothing, surrounded by a smell of animals and tobacco, spoke of a man not used to being sociable. But you had to admire his business sense. He was there on Main Street as the troops came in with a brace of horses ready to sell.

"Well, I reckon, 'cause there ain't none of them to be had." Jim spit a chaw of tobacco on the ground in front of me, which I decided not to take as an insult.

"I understand that. But why is it?" I asked naively.

"Well, the best horse regions are Kentuck and Tennessee. They ain't in the Confederacy no more. And yer Carolinas, they don't have no horses. Most animals that haul and pull around's here are mules, what's some call a brevet horse, ha, hah, and stupid oxen. Now, do you have the money 'er not?"

I turned away. I did not have $1,500 for an animal that had clearly seen better days. I wished him luck, but on the other hand, I did not want my men to spend good money for bad horses.

I was wondering what I was going to do, when I saw what looked like a familiar buckboard coming up the street.

"Father," I cried. "You are here?"

"Yes, son. How are you?"

"You are a sight for sore eyes." I hugged him. Tears flowed down my cheeks. I had not seen my Father since the last March when I was on furlough due to my being wounded.

"I've come to take you home."

I mounted the buckboard, and we made for Timmonsville, where Vicee was staying.

My earliest memories are of my father, Daniel, being industrious. He was always working on a carriage for a client or working on our home, repairing this, fixing that, upgrading here, and rebuilding there. He was always in motion. He was so handy with his tools. I wanted to be like him and be able to create something out of wood. He was like Michelangelo looking at a piece of wood and seeing the piece of art that lay within it. I wanted to do the things that he did. I remember him looking a piece of wood from all angles. He would note the whirls and the swirls of the grain of the wood. He would see the knots and the wide, white spaces between the lines.

One day, I took a plank in my hands. I turned it over and over and spent a great deal of time looking at it. Finally, I proclaimed to him, "I can see the grain."

He laughed. "Yes," he said, "I, too, see the grain, but I see in the wood which piece of the carriage this plank ought to be. This plank can only be one certain part, for it grew all of its life to become, to be, to have its destiny fulfilled as a step, or as a back rest, or as a seat, or as a side of a beautiful, ornate carriage. It is that certain part and no other."

It took me years to understand the artistry, the true artistry, which he saw in making a carriage. Where I saw an assemblage of parts to construct a whole, he saw beauty with light glistening off of polished and varnished wood. He knew everything there was to know about every type of wood, such as whether it could be honed, or whether it was durable, or which woods could be shaped by steam, how much effort each wood would require to be perfectly sanded, or whether a wood would take a certain stain or paint.

I worked as his apprentice. I sanded, I painted, and I hauled boards. I did all the menial jobs one does to help a master create a masterpiece. I was at a master's feet, but it took me years to realize that my father was a master.

What I would give now to stand next to him and sand a board. Then, Vicee, it hit me: I might never see him again. I might not ever be graced with the honor, the privilege, the pleasure of being with him, of working with him, and of learning from him. My eyes started to tear.

Oh, my God! What if, Vicee, I never see you again in this life? Am I fated to be only with you again when we are reunited in heaven? Is that the Lord's plan? I can hardly control myself now. To lose you, is to lose everything. You have been my love since I first saw you, when you were 13. You were my Beatrice-the vision to Dante, which filled his life with grace and meaning. I know you will not know what I think now (I wish I could say 'write', but alas these lines thought now may fade before ever being committed to paper), but Dante was a poet who wrote of God, of Heaven, of Hell-and when he saw his love, he knew God had truly blessed him, as I was truly blessed when you first entered my life. This happens only once a century or maybe a millennium. And it happened to me, when I first saw you.

Who were my childhood friends? Where was my school? What did it look like? Which subjects interested me and which subjects did I dislike?

Is this what people mean when they say your whole life flashes before your eyes at the moment of your death? I am engaged in reflection hour upon hour of every aspect of my life and it is certainly not a moment flashing. It is slow, agonizing and painful realization that any moment I let slip by where I did not tell you that I loved you, that I did not show you my love, that I did not do something to convey how much you truly mean to me was a waste of the most precious commodity in the universe. I realize now I have been a fool.

CHAPTER 33:

AT HOME WITH VICEE

"I am afraid that you will scarcely recognize me. I am a veteran, not merely by name, but also by looks."
-Union 15th Corps soldier

April 2, 1865 3:00 AM

My father and I drove straight home. I am sure that he could sense how desperately I wanted to see you. Yes, I wanted to see him and my step-mother, Caroline, and all my brothers and sisters, but it was you, most of all, that I wanted to see.

I cannot believe it. I am in Darlington with you my wife. I hold you in my arms. I want you so much. I have not held you now for so long. I can't help it. My eyes tear over. Your eyes tear over. I have lived for this moment. I have dreamed of this moment. I have fantasized about this moment. It is happening and yet it does not seem real. Have I thought so much about this moment that the reality of it can't match the dream of it? Or do I not believe that I am really here.

I look at you. I stroke your raven long hair. You have let it down for me to admire. Your brown eyes are deep and inviting. I see the beautiful lace around your neck and the locket I gave you. You are dressed in a deep blue dress that highlights your white, fair skin. I notice now how thin you are. I realize that you are not eating enough. Is the food scare here too? What deprivations have you suffered? I don't want to ask and break the fragile egg-shell quality of this moment, which I know would shatter into a million pieces, and all the king's horses and all the king's men would not suffice to set it aright again.

I look into your eyes. I see the future. I see our lives together after this storm has passed. I see children playing. I hear their voices laughing. I see us together on the porch swinging in the summer's night's breeze holding hands. I see us growing old together. Oh, God! Please let this vision happen, I pray.

Thinking of you and thinking of home, has made me think that I would tell you, Vicee, of my life in a nutshell. You never knew my mother; you only knew my step-mother, Caroline. My father married my mother, who was named Margaret, on January 14, 1839. The saddest thing is that I do not know what my mother's maiden name was, or who her father or her mother was. I know so very little about the woman who gave birth to me. She was simply known to me as "Mother." Father once said that he thought that Margaret was born in 1813, which would have made her 27 when I was born. Other than that, I only know that she came from Marlboro, South Carolina.

My memories of her are more like sensations than memories. I remember her being soft and comforting. I could cry in the night. She would come, and the world would be better. I think I have a memory of her mending my clothes. She was there, silent, but always protecting and comforting. What I do remember is that she was a happy woman. She sang all the time. She was always humming and carrying a tune. "The Lord likes a happy heart," she would say. She recited poetry from memory. Beautiful words poured forth from her, my mother, whirling about the room as if they were grey smoke curling in the breeze. She was a good story-teller. She told me a story each night before bed.

I was born on January 23, 1840. I was followed by my sister, Helen Amanda, who was born on March 16, 1842. Mandy and I were close playmates as children. She had flaming red hair which she inherited from our father, as did I. She was right handed, whereas I was left handed. She always seemed to be able to do fine tasks better than I could. My old clothes went to her, when I out-grew them.

Margaret was a frugal woman and saved those hand-me-downs for her third child, Gilbert, who was born in 1850. The shame of it is that I do not recall the day of his birth. Father went all to pieces that day, for while we were thrilled with the birth of another son, Margaret died giving him life. So we never really celebrated his birthday.

Because Gilbert died a few weeks after he was born, my father felt that his birth was "a waste, because he killed the only women I ever loved." Father told me later that he became despondent over the death of Margaret. He felt that he could not cope with two children and continue to work the business.

There was a 'widow' lady nearby by the name of Caroline E. Lewis. She had been married to Daniel McCallum. I don't remember a thing about him. Caroline was such a part of my childhood, because I was ten when Father married her. She became my mother, even though she was my step–mother. It was years later that I learned that she had been married to Daniel McCallum on November 29, 1849, but that he had not died-they had grown apart quickly in their marriage and agreed to end their marriage. Caroline was three years older than Daniel, and said he was too much of a child for her to handle. He started to drink, and she could not abide by a man who drank. She married my father in 1850, after my mother died, but I don't remember the month or the day.

Caroline was a different type of woman from my mother. She was very practical. Yes, she was frugal, but she had none of the artistic flair my mother had. She did not believe in poetry or music. She was very religious and made sure that we read our Bible every day. She was a staunch Baptist, and we went to Church every Sunday, no matter the weather, even if we were ill, no matter nothing. She kept the 'books' of my father's carriage-making business and we started to prosper, because she made sure to collect every penny that was owed to my father.

My father was very much the master craftsman and artist when it came to building a carriage, but he was not much of a business man. It was Caroline who instilled in him the discipline to negotiate the price beforehand and to collect the price afterwards.

After Caroline came, I was apprenticed to my father. I learned every facet of the carriage business, because my father wanted to build a company that would employ his children and provide for them after he was gone. I spent my years as a teenager working side by side with my father.

Amanda worked with us. She followed Caroline around and was learning the numbers side of the business, how to draw up a bill, how to pay bills, how to keep accounts. It was a true tragedy when she died on July 17, 1860. She caught a fever that summer, and, within days, she was gone. I was devastated, because she had been my playmate and friend. She was just 18 years old.

Father and Caroline wanted to build a family together, because father had come from such a large family, and Caroline had not. The loftily-named Robert Barnwell Rhett was born June 30, 1851. Bobby was a child who was always so very happy; he just bubbled with fun and excitement. He, too, caught a fever during the summer and died on August 18, 1862.

Caroline had two still births after Bobby, babies she called Margaret and Angus. It seemed as if we were always steeped in tragedy and anguish. "Dogged doubt to threaten our faith," Caroline said. "God sends us only that which we can bear. With faith and prayer we can get through anything," Caroline intoned these words so often that it became our family chant.

Sister Margaret Viola was born on October 24, 1856 in Timmonsville. Caroline went there to visit some friends, the Traxlers, and to undergo her confinement there, thinking that she had lost her two children, because she had not rested enough near their births. Viola had a great sense of humor and loved to play pranks. The usual target of her mischief was Amanda, who always let Viola get away with everything.

Then Caroline gave birth to another girl in 1858, whom she named Elizabeth Florence, because she delivered her in Florence, South Carolina, at the home of another set of friends, the Harrisons. Florence was five when she died in the summer of 1863. The coming of each summer was dreaded by us, for it seemed that disease came up out of the swamps and swallowed some young children and also the oldsters.

I greeted the birth of William Walter, who followed Florence, with some mixed feelings. His birthdate of November 1, 1860 was just too close to the death of my beloved sister, Amanda. To have lost Amanda in July, it seemed too soon to welcome a new member to our family. But, Vicee, this was God's plan to call Amanda to Him and to give us William. I really did not get to know William before this War came. Maybe, when this War ends, I will get to know my little brother. Will I, though, be able to look at him and not think of Amanda?

*****

We were in bed. The moonlight shone in through the window. The lace curtains were just parted so the sliver of silver passed through the space. The light reflected off of your nipple which gently rose and fell with your sleeping breath. I watched you sleep in awe that such a magnificent creature such as you could be mine. Your beauty was like that of a Grecian goddess, resting from her labors of bringing spring and light to the world.

Somehow in my soul I knew that, for once, I was in the right place at the right time. The stars had aligned perfectly. It was a mystical union of place, person, time, and soul.

Somehow, I knew also that you would be pregnant and would bear me a son. I was as sure of it as I have ever been of anything. I felt so strongly that I was in unison with God and that His blessings would flow upon us.

We had made love. I was amazed that your desire seemed as strong as mine. I had been brought up to believe that women endured the sexual act for the benefit of their husbands. I was thrilled that you could respond so much to me and I to you. It was a sacred act, but so filled with passion and tenderness. How can a man not worship his wife? I know that you are the better one of the two of us.

My musings must have awakened you for you turned to me, and I saw your smile in the faint fading moonlight, as night was turning into dawn. You put your finger to your mouth to hush me from talking. Then you pulled me close to you, and we started another rhythmic communion of our souls. The pink of the dawning day flooded our room.

"I love you," we whispered to one another as we gasped.

*****

Another night a thunderstorm had come up. The wind whipped the rains which felt in torrents.

I turned to you in the half light of our bedroom. "I want a child," I whispered.

"So do I." I could not see your face clearly, but the light just gleamed off of your teeth so I knew you were smiling.

The rhythm of the rain began to be matched by the rhythm of our bodies. The waxing and waning of the rain and the wind made us luxuriate in one another.

We had reached that moment of sweet surrender and bliss, when the hairs on the small of my neck and back began to stand up. Then came a crackle followed by a booming noise. The smell of acrid smoke filled the air. Totally frightened, we both jumped up in the bed. It took us several seconds to realize that a bolt of lightning had struck our bedroom. We went from the most sensuous love to fear to laughter in a matter of seconds.

"Why, James, I knew you wanted a child. But I didn't know you could make fireworks, too!"

*****

"I am named after Queen Victoria. You should pay me the respect my name deserves and demands. Kneel down before me. I may knight you, or I may not. It is my right to decide who might be the Knights of my Garter!" I had never heard you be so playful and so risqué. I started thinking that marriage might be fun after all. You held out a garter and nodded your head to indicate that I was to tie it where it was supposed to go.

I was all thumbs, never having tied a garter before and certainly not ever having been that close to where a garter was supposed to be tied.

"Jamie, what am I going to do with you?" You laughed. "How are you ever going to be a good carriage maker, if you can't even tie a simple little garter?" Your smile was infectious, playful, coy, and tantalizing. You were giving me a message that was obvious even to me.

"But it's mid-day?" I asked quite stupidly.

"Yes! And how often are you here even at night to get the job done? You want a child don't you?" You thumped your fingers impatiently on the banister leading upstairs to our bedroom. Now, you were being down right explicit.

I got your meaning. "Not often enough. Not often enough," I repeated as I took off my shirt.

I wish I could have told Fitz and the rest of them at McGowan's headquarters this story, because this was the best afternoon of the War for me. But I would never share it with them, for it was so intimate. I wanted nothing to sully you in anyway, Vicee.

CHAPTER 34:

A GIFT

"We have all been home on a 30 day furlough, and were received by our friends and kindred with a great deal of enthusiasm and joy. We enjoyed ourselves gayly. On the 27th of April we left Sidney on the 2 o'clock train, and it was somewhat a difficult matter for us to part with our friends, and especially those of our own fireside: yet so strong is the love we have for our country, its rights and institutions, that we forsake all the endearments of home to strike a blow in her defense. Hope the friends will not forget us in their prayers at a throne of grace, or remit the interest they have in their country."
-**Confederate Soldier** *in the Legion writing about his furlough*

April 2, 1865 3:15 AM

The time home was a time to recruit not only horses, but also men to fill our ranks. Some were new recruits. Some were what we called "exchanges." A man who had a horse, but was in another unit would replace a man in our unit who could not muster up a horse, whether by inability to pay for one, or by inability to find one. I was beginning to be afraid that I would be one of those "exchanges," because I could not find a horse at a reasonable price. I did not have $1,000.00.

The day of the grand party being hosted by the Ladies of Columbia was set for April 22, 1865. We all were supposed to return to Columbia in time for the party, and then the next day, we would be on our way back to Virginia.

As that day approached, I became more and more restive. I wanted to remain with my friends and my Company, but it was looking like that was not going to happen. I spent a lot of time visiting the farms around Darlington looking for a suitable horse. Many of the horses I saw were just not up to the task of being a mount for mounted infantry. They were simply too tired and too worn out. I really didn't know how they could even be of any use to the farmer. Nonetheless, each farmer zealously guarded his animal.

It was the day before I was to leave for Columbia. The grand fete of the Ladies was to be held on the grounds of the State Asylum for the Insane (I could write volumes about the irony of members of the Hampton Legion Infantry assembling at an insane asylum to attend a party before going off to War once again mounted on horses, knowing what they knew!)

My father knocked at our door. (Thank goodness we were not playing Knights of the Garter then!)

I went to the door and there was my father with two horses. His two horses. That he needed for his carriage business.

"Son, here, you need these. I don't."

Tears welled up in my eyes. "But Father, without them you can't deliver carriages. Won't this hurt your business?"

"Son, there is not much carriage business now-a-days. There won't be any carriage business, if we lose this War. Nobody will have anything, if we lose. The rich planters will lose their slaves and then there will be no one with money to buy any carriages. You take them." He handed the reigns to me.

"You take them, and maybe there will be a carriage business again in the future." Now his eyes were welling up with tears.

We stood there father and son crying our eyes out. I am not sure whether we were crying because we would be separated again, or whether because we both feared this would be the last time we would see each other, or whether because we were crying because we both knew the South was dying.

CHAPTER 35:

THE HORSE MARCH

I can make a General in five minutes but a good horse is hard to replace.
-Abraham Lincoln

April 2, 1865 3:27 AM

Our bittersweet respite from the War came to an end far too quickly. Men had gone all over South Carolina, although some, like Mully Logan (or should I say Lt. Colonel Thomas Muldrop Logan), who was originally with Company A, the Washington Light Volunteers, and later of the staff of the Legion, went to Virginia on a personal mission. First, I should say that Mully was a brave man. He was severely wounded at Gaines' Mill (and would be later wounded again, and again, quite severely at Riddell's Shop, through both shoulders!). He used this time to go acourting of a Miss Kate Virginia Cox of Chesterfield County. Her father was a former Speaker of the Virginia House of Burgesses. Although they were not engaged by the time he to returned to the Legion's fold, he arrived at an 'understanding with her' that was conditioned upon her father making inquiries into the character and background of the Lt. Colonel.

We gathered at Columbia with our horses. The majority of the men had found mounts, but there were some who did not. Those who did not have mounts could transfer to a non-mounted unit, provided there was a man in such unit who was willing and able to provide mounts for himself.

We gathered at the grounds of the State Asylum for the Insane in the State Capital. The ladies of Columbia had decided that a party with barbecue would be the best way to honor the Legion. Now, one would have thought that the grounds of an Insane Asylum would be an ironic or certainly incongruous place to hold such an event. In reality, the grounds were the perfect place, because they were shaded by large live oaks and its nearness to the city provided ready means to get everything to hold such an event. Originally, the Hampton Legion was the only unit, which was going to so honored, but as the event was being planned, the ladies learned that First and Second South Carolina Cavalry were also undergoing the same process as we were, and they were going to be leaving only days after us, so they were included in the festivities.

We were shocked when the barbecue was attended by thousands of guest from all over Columbia.

The men of the Legion that gathered at Columbia for our fete at the Insane Asylum were a different lot from those who had gone home on furlough. First, there were some 106 new enlistments. Of this number, a few, but not many, were conscripts. We didn't think they would last long. Our experience was that drafted men tended to disappear with the first battle, either through wounding (some were intentional), death, or more often by slipping away under the cover of the din of battle.

Next, we had some men who transferred to the Legion from other units. This added seventeen new faces. But they were welcome for they were men who had fought before and we knew they would not run.

Finally, there were some rather compulsory transfers. Two cavalry companies, which had been attached to the 20th South Carolina Infantry, were going to be disbanded. These two companies were given the 'choice' of transferring to the Legion or facing conscription. The Fourth

South Carolina Cavalry had a large number of privates from Company B assigned to the Legion under similar duress.

Nonetheless, the Legion left South Carolina with now 940 men on its muster rolls, of which about 800 were effectives.

We were supposed to leave the next day, but as things happen in the Confederate Army, all was not ready. We had not been provided saddles, harnesses, and other equipment. We were still in Columbia, when on May 5, 1864, Robert E. Lee sent an urgent request to Adjutant General Cooper that the Army of Northern Virginia needed troopers. As there were no trains available for the horses, they had to march overland. One man in four was detailed to ride one horse, and lead three others. The rest of us were to board trains. The first train though did not come until the 9th of May. The second detachment did not leave until 9 days later. So, we arrived back in Virginia in dribs and drabs. But our horses were still miles behind us.

The horses were following originally the railroad line of the new Piedmont Railroad. Once, it became clear that line would not have any rolling stock available anytime soon; the horses were diverted to the Raleigh and Weldon line. Somewhere between Greensboro and Durham, North Carolina, this rail line was abandoned and the horses were taken overland to Clarksville, Virginia, and, thence, to Richmond.

It was early June by the time we were reunited with our horses. It was, however, that the Hampton Legion was not the same force it had been before. We were really raw recruits again. Many of us had not even ridden in a parade, let alone a military maneuver. Further, our horses were exhausted from their travels. Many were fully blown, and were now worthless as mounts. Other horses had died along the way. So men, now, had to find replacement mounts or be transferred out of the Legion. The men, themselves, were exhausted from their travels. Finally, we still did not have full equipment to be an effective mounted unit.

When we reached Virginia, the Legion had a pall cast over it, though. We learned that General Micah Jenkins had died of his wounds incurred in the same volley that had seriously wounded General James Longstreet during the Wilderness Battle. How could one fathom that fate could play such a cruel and tragic trick? We could not get over the amazing coincidence that right near where Stonewall Jackson had been mistakenly shot and killed by his own men just a year before, the same fate befell Longstreet and Jenkins to be shot by their own men. We were spooked by these events. No matter what we thought of these two men, they were our officers under whom we had fought, and we were upset at their loss from our cause.

But also when we reached Virginia, Grant was on the move. Robert E. Lee turned to one of his favorite troops to stop Grant: The Hampton Legion. The place where we had to stop Grant was Riddell's Shop. This would be a baptism by fire for us.

CHAPTER 36:
RIDDELL'S SHOP

I have not witnessed a more gallant affair with our cavalry this campaign than the one of yesterday. The line as at present held by the cavalry is very bad for them, on account of the scarcity of water... If we drive them from Riddell's Shop they will only swing back toward Willis Church, whilst they might move more rapidly by a cross-road and strike the Charles City road in my rear. I would suggest that a demonstration be made on the Charles City road, whilst a real attack is made on the Long Bridge road, below Riddell's Shop, by Butler, and one on my right by the infantry. We could converge toward the shop, and I think the enemy would be forced back...I am, very respectfully, yours,
WADE HAMPTON,
Major-General

April 2, 1865 3:43 AM

June 3, 1864 was a glorious day for the Confederacy, if you can call the death and wounding of 10,000 or more Union soldiers glorious. Grant had thrown maybe 20,000, or 30,000 or some said 50,000 men against our lines at Old Cold Harbor. Our defensive lines were just too strong, and, though wave upon wave of blue crested upon our earthworks, none of the waves broke our lines. The ground in front of us was drenched with Yankee blood.

There was a time when I would have rejoiced in such bloodshed, but the loss of 10,000 Yankees did little to console the loss of 4,000 Confederates. The way I saw it, it was the loss of 14,000 men, good men, men who had wives, and were loved by them, men who had children, who would now forever lament the loss of their fathers, men who were uncles, or brothers or friends. I know I should have lauded Lee's great victory in battle on the open field. For those of us who went through the siege of Petersburg, little did we know that this would be the last victory Lee would ever have on the open field. I didn't feel it in my heart. Some were cheering, but I was just damned tired. I am sorry, Vicee; I have sworn an oath again. But Vicee I was just sick looking out over that battlefield. I saw the mangled bodies, the fingers separated from hands, the heads blown off bodies. I saw the bloated bellies of horses swelling up with the death gas. It is hard to be proud when all you see is carnage, death, pain, and suffering. The waste. The utter and complete waste. I was getting sick of the waste. I just wanted it all to stop. Wasn't there a better way to resolve this question of whether the States or the Federal Government controlled the nation?

Grant's men, they stayed in their trenches from June 3 until June 12, 1864. Maybe they were too horrified by what had happened in just a half an hour, too shocked, or too stunned to stir. They moved on the 12th. Again, they marched south and east. They were trying to get around us again, to outflank us, and somehow get across the James River, then somehow take Petersburg, and, thus, slice Richmond off from the rest of the Confederacy, and win the war.

Grant was trying to march via the roads which crossed the Chickahominy River at Bottom's Bride, Long Bridge, and Jones' Bridge. Now, all of these bridges had been destroyed by us a long time ago. Grant had brought with him pontoons so he could lay down his own bridge anywhere.

Once across the Chickahominy, Grant would pass by the puzzle of roads that led to Malvern Hill and Harrison's Landing. The road that travelled this distance was the Bottom's Bridge Road. It went through White Oak Swamp and through a country-cross roads village, where six roads intersected, including the Quaker Road to Malvern Hill and Charles Road to Richmond. Thus, a tiny country crossroad became the most important and valuable piece of terrain in the world at that moment.

This crossroad was the site of a blacksmith shop which was owned and operated by a man named Riddell. Over the years, this was a place where the farmers could bring their horses and mules to be shod with shoes, and farm implements could be repaired. It became a meeting place where men could rest, maybe smoke a pipe, chew some tobacco, and pull a tug or two upon a jug that came out when the women weren't around. So, into this bucolic place, war would intrude and rampage without consideration of the sensibilities of simple men who only wanted to farm, live their lives, and enjoy God's green earth.

It was so strange that we were marching over and fighting over the same battle fields that Lee and McClellan had fought over during the Seven Days Battles in June of 1862. The difference in the two years was confounding, amazing, shocking, disquieting, and disconcerting. Had so much happened in those two years? Had so many hundreds of thousands of men died only to be back virtually back at the beginning of the War? I have been in so many battles in so many different states. I have marched from here to there and back again. It is only a few of us that fought both in west and in the east. Was it a privilege? Hell no. Sorry again, Vicee, about my swearing. I am sure that, if I counted it all up, maybe 200 different men have been in Company G, the Claremont Rifles of Hampton's Legion since the beginning of the War. We started with 80, way back when the ladies of Stateburg gave us our flag, but then some men died of disease, some were wounded, some were killed, and some deserted us. We got reinforcements and transfers, and the process began again.

I could not, as others did, draw strength from this occurrence that we were fighting again on the old battlefields outside of Richmond that we had fought over some two years before. "Lee pulled off a miracle then. He'll damn well do it again!" I heard this refrain time and time again in these words and others echoing them. If Lee had pulled off a miracle then, it was by God's grace. If he was going to do it again, I was well sure that God would not grant such a boon to men who cursed and took his name in vain: me included.

I was on the back of my horse as was the rest of the Legion under General Gary. My poor animal was as worn out as I was. I know that some men name their horses with heroic names, like Prince or Hero; I could only think of what the horse represented to me, Friend.

We were there with another small brigade of cavalry under Rufus Barringer. He was about 20 years my senior. He was from North Carolina, and had attended, and graduated from University of North Carolina at Chapel Hill. He had studied law and then had become partners with his brother in the practice of law. He was not a handsome man. His bald pate was always shiny. His full beard and mustache evoked the reaction that you wanted to move them to the top of his head. His first wife had died before the war of typhoid fever, but the fever spared his two children. His first wife was Eugenia Morrison. She had two sisters, one of whom married Thomas Jonathan Jackson, and the other married D. H. Hill. Barringer's second wife died just last year. His face was always creased with what looked like deep sadness and grief. He was a quiet man who liked to be left alone.

Grant's plan was executed on June 13, 1864. During the night, General James H. Wilson pushed aside our pickets. He led some cavalry, as well as two divisions of infantry that simply overwhelmed all opposition in their rapid sprint across the Chickahominy River.

General James H. Wilson had been promoted to Brigadier General by Grant just days before. He had been an engineer, but now Grant had moved him to lead some of his cavalry. He was a smart and an ambitious man. He wore a van dyke beard, and, although his hairline was receding, it only emphasized the striking and sharp features of his face. He was a West Point graduate, 6th in his class, who knew how to do his job.

Just before noon, the Yankees pulled up at the small crossroad. We were posted on both side of Long Bridge Road - all 2,000 or so of us. The Union force, exceeding some 6,000 men, stretched far and wide, way over-lapping our lines.

My company, which I was leading for the first time, was mounted. We went into battle by counting off by fours. This meant that in each quartet, one man held the reigns of the four horses, while the other three fought dismounted. I was one of the three. The order was to fix bayonets. I also checked my Navy Colt .36 revolver. The fighting took place on either side of the Long Bridge Road, east of Riddell's Shop, and also on the Charles City Road, northwest of the little crossroads. All of this area densely wooded. There was thick, almost impenetrable underbrush. Only a few small farm clearings broke the woods and underbrush.

Somehow, we resisted the first federal advance. Then, Wilson took his time and dressed his lines. He ordered his men to flank Gary's force on both flanks while the rest of his men, by sheer dint of weight, would press forward. It was as if we were on the anvil. The forces in front of us held us, while the wings beat us as if they were two hammers wielded by strong, muscular smithies. We fell back stubbornly, losing men and horses with each pace. Gary directed us up the Charles City Road towards Richmond. We were Richmond's shield, and the Yankees were Viking raiders beating us with their war hammers, battle axes, and swords.

For four long hours, we fought. Every man was exhausted; we were running low on ammunition. As we were completely out of breath, so, too, our horses were blown. Our arms ached from pulling our horses. Our fingers were strained from firing our pistols, muskets, and slashing with our swords. We could not hold on much longer. We were on the verge of being overwhelmed, because we were thoroughly exhausted.

Gary was there, exhorting us and driving us on. I give him great credit for no man wanted to disappoint that brave leader. Barringer fought like a devil. I made a mental note that I never wanted to face him in court after the War.

Then, when our last ounce of will was draining away, Powell Hill and his boys approached the crossroads and fought Wilson to a standstill. We had bought Lee time, and Lee had used it to throw his warrior in a red flannel shirt into the fray. We mounted to retreat out of the way of the infantry. As I rounded my feet into the stirrups, I was shot, or rather a spent bullet hit my head, and knocked me from the saddle. I blacked out and fell to the ground.

I do not know what else happened that afternoon. I only know that, by late evening, I was in a Yankee camp, sprawled upon a hospital bed. I started to get up, only to have my head be flooded by waves of pain and nausea. I threw up and collapsed back upon the bed. I held my eyes tightly closed, trying to drive the pain away. I gritted my teeth, but nothing seemed to help.

A Union doctor was standing over me bed. "I'd give you some laudanum, if you want it." He held some reddish-brown powder in the palm of his hand. "You ain't hurt too bad. You should recover completely, but you took quite a bump to the head. A day or two and you'll be fine." He pushed the hand closer to me. I sat up on the bed and was almost knocked over by the pain and the nausea. He cupped my head with his other hand and helped me to take some of the powder into my mouth. The stuff was the most bitter, vile thing I have ever ingested. He gave me some coffee, real coffee - not phony Confederate coffee made of chicory-water, to wash it down. I was asleep in a few moments.

By morning, I could sit up, but was still suffering from the most profound headache I had ever had. I had had some migraines in my life, but this was so much worse that I thank God that my migraines were so mild.

I also realized that I had been captured. It broke my spirit to think that I had been captured and would sit out the rest of the War. I wondered what you would think of me, Vicee. I wondered whether you would learn that I was captured, or whether you would think that I was wounded or killed. I was contemplating my new situation when the doctor who had taken care of me earlier returned.

"I have a son. He is a Lieutenant, just like you. He was in the fight at Riddell's Shop, just like you. He was captured, just like you." He looked at the ground as he said this. His face could not have been more mournful or dejected. He then looked up at me. "Are you a man of your word? Do you fear God? Would you keep your oath?" His voice was pleading, not insulting in tone.

"I am a man who believes in God. My Vicee, my wife, is a devout Southern Baptist. She takes me to Church and insists that I worship as she does. If I were to break my word, I would have not only the angels of heaven casting me into Hell, but also my wife would be there to help throw me in."

I tried to smile as I said this. I believed it, but I didn't know if he believed it. I also didn't know why he was asking me this.

He looked deeply into my eyes. "Are you telling me the truth?" His eyes clouded up, and a tear formed in his eye, and then the tear fell from his eye cutting a pink-white path across his cheek as it cleared the grime, dirt, and soot that blackened his cheek.

"Yes, sir. I am." I tried to make my voice sound as sincere as my heart knew my words were.

"I've got a proposition then for you. I've got all the papers here to do what I'm going to tell you. All I need is your word that you will do as you have promised." He hesitated a moment, and I didn't try to fill the void.

He started again. "Swear that if I let you go with on parole, you will do everything you can to get my son paroled, and sent back to me. Your life, for my son's life. Each of you would be swapped one for the other. An even exchange of one officer of the same rank for the other.

I know that this isn't done anymore between our two nations...I mean armies...but I've... I've got the paperwork here. If you swear then..." He stopped there, his eyes flooding with tears and his voice quivering.

"I'm a father, too." I said. "I give you a father's oath, because I would want my son sent back, if I were in your position. I swear. I swear I will do it."

He handed me the paperwork, which now was laden with tear stains. He took my hand and walked me to the edge of the camp. We walked through the guards and out into the space between two armies. He shook my hand, and I shook his. We stared at one another, and then I walked south towards the Confederate Army of Northern Virginia. I clutched my parole.

*****

It was days later, when I found the doctor's son. I explained the deal of my parole to Wade Hampton.

"This is unprecedented." He read the documents. He looked up at me, and then back at papers.

"I gave my word as a southern gentleman, an officer, and as a father." I said softly.

He looked at me. "How long have you been with the Legion, son?"

"Since July 15, 1861, sir! Begging the General's pardon, I met the general though before the war."

"What's that?" Hampton stared over the top of the documents to look more closely at me.

"In Columbia, sir. I brought you your new carriage, a landau, and you paid me, sir. It was the night you joined the Minute Men, I think."

He looked more intensely at me. Several moments went by. "Yes, I remember you. You were the boy who was trying to find Mr. Preston!"

"Yes, thank you for remembering me, sir."

"Well, I was impressed with your honesty then, and I will grant your request now. Go and release this lieutenant, and send him back on his way to his father. I will prepare the proper papers."

"Thank you, General, sir."

"No, thank you, Lieutenant."

*****

I was doing the endless paperwork of the Company later. I was tallying the number of killed, wounded, and missing. The Legion had taken about a 100 losses at Riddell's Shop. Although a lot of casualties were in the 7th South Carolina, my Company had suffered, too. I thought about the men who were gone. They had been friends, some of whom I had known since childhood. They were sons, fathers, brothers, uncles, and cousins. Their deaths ripped holes in the fabric of their families. Wives, sweethearts, mothers, and sisters would be grieving, perhaps, forever, for the men who did not come home again. "In peace, sons bury their fathers, in war, fathers bury their sons," I muttered, although it brought no relief to voice these melancholy thoughts. The thread of these men's lives was cut short, and their future, their destiny left unfulfilled. They would not father any more children, and the children, they left behind, would grow up without playing with their fathers again, without their guidance, without learning at their knees. The weight of this knowledge, the burden of it, broke my heart, and I burst out crying, Vicee. Tears flowed down my face only like the time I fell as a boy and broke my leg. "All those men…and for what?" I found myself asking. "For what?"

BOOK VI: BREAKTHROUGH-THE WAR ENDS-1865

CHAPTER 37:

1865 DAWNS

"The end seems to be surely and swiftly approaching."
*-**Robert Kean**, Clerk to Confederate Assistant Secretary of War, John Archibald Campbell*

April 2, 1865 4:01 AM

I was born on January 23, 1840. I always felt that there was a mystical connection between my birthday and the change of the year and the decades. For with each New Year, soon after it was the New Year, I was a year older. When the decade changed, I changed decades.

Further, I was truly a child of Janus. I started each New Year looking both forwards and backwards. I reflected on what had happened in the past year and what would happen in the New Year. I was somehow intertwined with time. From my earliest years, I felt this connection, this electricity, this thread tying me to things, events, and places beyond my ken. For this reason, I have a sense, an awareness of time that I know is greater than the normal man's. I feel deeply that the sands of time are running out in my life, faster than most men's lives. What am I to do? What is my destiny? Why do I feel time more strongly than others?

Now it was January 23, 1865. The winter continued to ravage us at Tudor Hall. We did not have the ravages of mumps or measles, but men were dying due to colds, coughs, and fevers. As I had done before, I nursed men-my men. I coughed and I coughed, but I knew my cough was from my wound and not from disease. I wished that our winter cabins were warmer, that we had more and better blankets, and that we had better food. I felt unable to fulfill my duty to my men, because I could not find any way to help their plight.

My birthday. I was now twenty-five years old. I had received a letter from you, Vicee, that our son had been born and that you were well. I wanted more than anything else that you would be well. I do not want to lose you in childbirth. My family had lost too many good women to childbirth. I did not want to rage against the wind like my father about my son having stolen the life of my wife. Your letter was proof that my fears had not been justified. You told me that within days you were up and round. My brave strong, wife. I cannot tell you how much it means to me to know that you are alive and that we have a son.

You told me that you named him George Carson. Neither of these names is traditional within my family. Scots always name the son for the grandfather and, thus, alternate between usually only two names. But I know it is unwise to chastise you. You are there, and you are confronting these things without me. Your choice and your decision are wise enough. Maybe we should break the shackles of the past, and carve a new path through the wilderness. Maybe the new names, George and Carson (did you name our son after my Captain?), will write a new era in the saga of our family, a better saga.

I am twenty-five, but I feel fifty. I have not confided in you that my wound still hurts and makes it hard for me to breathe. I don't think I ever full recovered from being shot through the lung. I was able to get back in the ranks within three weeks, but it still hits me at times that I can't breathe. I felt I was needed. It was Lee's first offensive, and, thus, I reported back and fought throughout the Seven Days. I think I should have waited longer to come back, but then again, I don't know if any amount of time would have allowed me to heal. I cough all the time.

I remember parting from you that last April. An infantryman leaves his wife, with whom he desperately desires to stay, to join a party at an Insane Asylum, before he goes off to war as a mounted man, leading men who barely know how to ride a horse-what am I doing?

"You will come back to me. You will survive. You will live for me and our child. We will rebuild our lives. We will rebuild our home. Swear it!" You looked so stern.

"Yes, I swear." I replied mechanically.

"No, swear it like you really mean it. As if your life depended upon it. Swear it to me as a blood oath!" The sharpness in your voice surprised me.

"You will swear this to me, James Augustus McEachern. You will swear it to me, and then you will keep your oath. You will come back to me, and we will live together our lives with our child after this awful war is over. I do not care about your vow to the Confederate Army. The Confederacy will not survive, but we will." You put out your hand, and took my hand in yours. It was as if by holding my hand in yours, you could hold back the moment, and prevent time from marching forward. You would still my beating heart, and encapsulate this moment forever in a sheath of love and promise. This moment would never die, because it would continue on forever, like no moment that had ever come before it.

Last April after my furlough, I saw you in my mind's eye like this. You were a magnificent Amazon warrior. The gauzy light of dawn was breaking. Your naked form was just barely visible in the pale light. The passion in your voice was so striking and so plaintive. I wanted to love you again then and there, although we had spent this night, our last night together on my furlough making love time and again.

You held my hand again then. "You have not forgotten your vow?"

"No, I have not." My voice trembled a bit.

"You cannot have any doubts. If you doubt, you will die. You must not waver. You must keep true to your vow." Your raven black hair swept across the sheets and pillows in billows of perfectly aligned waves of beauty. Your eyes drilled themselves into mine, as if to possess me, and, thus, prevent me from ever coming to harm. "I pray for you each day. Do you pray each day, James?"

"I do not, I am sorry to say."

"Then start now, with me. Pray that Almighty God keeps you in his hands, and never lets anything of harm come your way."

We held hands. Each of us silently prayed. Then you said aloud: "Our Father, who art in heaven…"

*****

I have grown old with this Confederacy. I was a boy when I joined that January of 1861. The ladies were all atwitter, laughing, singing, cajoling the boys to join. I don't remember you telling me to join. I remember that you held back. I now know why. You were so wise then. Wiser than of the rest of us. We all got caught up in the swirl of events. It seemed so gay then, so exciting, so thrilling. Now, I know that War is an illusion. It is the antithesis of life, beauty, and all that is sacred. I am left now with only my duty to be done, until the War is done.

CHAPTER 38:

THE WORLD TURNED UPSIDE DOWN

Grant's "move seriously threatens our position and diminishes our ability to maintain our present line."
*-**Robert E. Lee** to Jefferson Davis*

April 2, 1865 4:12 AM

They say that March goes out like a lamb. Well, that was not the case with the March of 1865 in northern Virginia. It went out with a ferocity that reminded us of the bitter winter we had endured.

Nor, were we looking forward to April. It was not just the weather, although the dull grey of endless winter clouds, spewing cold raw rain, were more than unpleasant. There was a feeling in the air. It was undefinable. It was electric. But it did nothing to revive us. All the energy had flowed out of us and flowed into the Yankees a mile and a half away.

No one spoke to one another. There was no greeting when you met someone for the first time in the morning. There was barely any civility around the fire trying to get warm, trying to get dry. We were spent, tired, depleted, wasted, burnt out, and ready to crawl up into a hole and just stay there no matter what. Floods could have risen over the banks of rivers, great forest fires could have burned, the earth could have rent itself beneath our feet, the fiercest of windstorms could have shattered all buildings, snapped trucks of trees, and leveled mountains, and we would have not noticed.

What is left of Company G of the Hampton Legion is quite small, Vicee. There is but a handful of us. Most nights, there are only 17 or so of us on picket duty. A few of us are ill. A few of us are recovering from wounds. A few of us are just so worn out from lack of food, lack of sleep, and lack of any decent clothing, that we cannot serve, and a few of us have deserted. So we are a remnant.

I have stayed here even though General McGowan and his South Carolinians have moved southwest to fight with Pickett, because I have no orders to leave, or to rejoin my unit. I don't even know where the Legion is. Last I heard, they were maybe somewhere to the east of us. But what I heard was a long time ago.

Let me tell you where I am. I have mentioned Tudor Hall and the environs here where our winter camp of log cabins stand. Out in front of us, about a mile away is the Union main line. It is studded with forts. I can see at least three of them which I think are named from east to west, Fort Fisher, Fort Welch, and Fort Gregg. These are no castles, and they are not made of stone. They are dirt forts reinforced with wood. Ft. Fisher is fairly formidable, but the other two are certainly lesser in size and wall thickness. Do they really think we have the power to attack any of these forts? I guess they do, because of Lee's desperate attempt to take Fort Stedman.

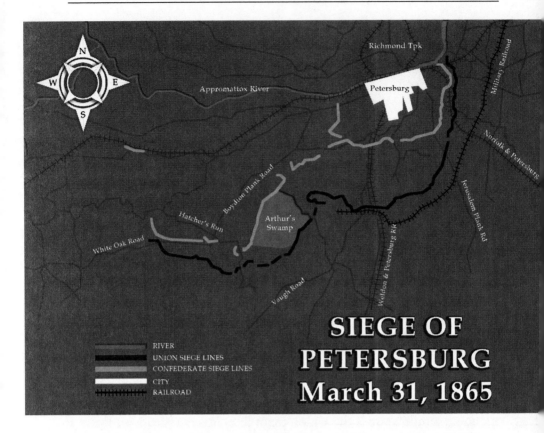

General Lee had General Gordon devise a plan to take Fort Stedman, thinking that the taking of this fort would force the Yankees to bring back some troops from the west that were being used to stretch our lines further and further west. Fort Stedman was directly east of Petersburg on and dominating the Jordan Plank Road, just below where the Petersburg and City Point Railroad enters Petersburg. Threatening this point was a direct arrow at where the Union Army of the Potomac was anchored on the Appomattox River. If Fort Stedman could be taken, the whole Union line would unravel and would have to retreat back from Petersburg. Lee had picked the crucial point of attack.

Our position is at a crisis at this time. There is only one railroad in and out of Petersburg, the South Side Railroad line, and just before this train track is the Boydton Plank Road, which is virtually the only road. Everything of supply that we needed and all the food feeding the people of Richmond and Petersburg comes over these two thoroughfares of communication.

Lee's lines are stretched from slightly northwest of Richmond in an arc running along the old defensive lines from the Seven Days battles some three years ago. They parallel in the north the Chickahominy River, then sharply turn south west of the old battlefields of Deep Bottom, Bermuda One Hundred, and Malvern Hill, till our lines hit the north side of Petersburg. There they continue in an arc around that city. Then below Petersburg, we make a sharp turn to the west-almost due west for miles beyond Petersburg. Our lines are over 30 miles long and are manned by maybe 30,000 men. With each foot further west that Grant's men take, our line is one more foot we have to man until we are stretched further and further: we are bound to snap somewhere and soon.

So far, our lines have held. We are strong, as long as the Yankees attacked us frontally. Our trenches are deep, they are well-laid out. Each palisade has been built with log-head logs such that our men can stand in the ditch of the trench and fire through a slit of wood which protects their heads. We have cannon at various places and have stacked up rounds of canister to spray as giant shot guns, if the Yankees get in close. Beyond our trenches are rows upon rows of abatis. Abatis are sharpened wood obstacles. Essentially, you cut down a tree. Then you take the tree and cut off the weak branches, but keep the stronger ones. You take off all the leaves and you sharpen the ends of all the strong branches such that the log appears to be multiple wheels of spikes. The spikes are long enough to make it very difficult for troops to get around them and hopefully many Yankees will lose their lives by being run through. We know that they will send pioneers with axes to cut and hack their way through our abatis. This will take time during which we can shoot at them and cut them down. So far, our lines have held. But now, with battles going further and further west, Lee is bleeding off troops from the line to meet these new threats.

General Gordon is commanding the Second Corps and is a good choice to lead this attack. He staunched the bloody attack at Spotsylvania and, thus, knows more than just about anyone else about how to defend entrenchments. He has thought long and hard about attacking the Yankee entrenchments, and his discussions with Lee have led to a sound plan of attack. The plan has evolved from conversations Lee and Gordon held on March 1, 1865.

"What would you do, General," Lee asked in a tired and haggard voice, "if you led the Army of Northern Virginia?"

General Gordon, who was a slight, perhaps, gaunt looking man, settled back and thought. He stroked his small goatee and bushy mustache which hid the cadaverous quality of his skull. His excessively high forehead exaggerated the skeletal look to his face. His thin waist and his sway back completed the impression of a man who was literally on his last legs. However, the man had a good mind and was a brilliant lawyer.

"Well, General," Gordon started his oral argument, "I have three possible recommendations. I make these in decreasing order of my preference, sir." His mind dealt in hierarchies and logical steps. "First, I would offer peace terms to General Grant. I think there is nothing that this Army can accomplish that will alter the outcome of this War."

Lee frowned at this suggestion and began to interject. Gordon raised his hand and continued. "My second course of action would be to retreat from Petersburg and Richmond, link up with General Joe Johnston in North Carolina. If we could effectuate such a linkage and defeat and demolish General Sherman, then maybe we can turn and deal with General Grant."

Lee began to demur again, when Gordon outlined his third suggestion. "Third and finally, we could hit Grant here at some salient, crucial place and break out of this siege. We must end this siege on our own terms, and we must end it fast, else our Army will deteriorate and be unable to take the offensive and win. We barely have it within us at this moment to fight and win."

General Robert E. Lee stood looking at General Gordon for a moment. "Are you finished, sir?"

"Yes, sir, I am." Gordon stroked his goatee again.

"General, I appreciate your candor. I do not think that we can offer terms of peace to General Grant, however much we might wish to do so. The concluding of peace is solely within the province of the Government. If, President Jefferson wants to make overtures of peace, then, he will do so through the appointed bodies of his Cabinet. It is not for us to presume to the power of the people which is vested in the Government and take that for ourselves. I am the leader of his military forces, and he is the leader of the nation. As Commander, I must take my orders from my Commander-in-Chief."

"But General, there comes a time in the course of events that compels us to do that which is right for our nation, even though we are but the military authority." General Gordon was up on his feet and making his final argument to the jury, although none was assembled.

"General Gordon, we will confine ourselves solely to the military situation and leave the political situation to the elected Government and its elected leader!" Lee's voice increased more and more in volume, as he spoke that last sentence.

General Gordon could see that he would not be able to convince his commander of the wisdom of the first route. He switched gears and started to talk of the military situation. "Well, then, sir, I would heartily argue that we stealthfully withdraw from the trenches before Petersburg, and steal a march on General Grant. If done with proper planning, we could be upon General Sherman, united with General Johnston and the Army of the Tennessee. We could then destroy that Union Army. If that could be done before Grant is able to intervene, then thus reinforced, and, thus, emboldened with victory, we could smash General Grant."

Lee looked at Gordon as if the man had just told him the most outrageous lie. "Sir, do you really, truly think that this Army is able to pick up so quietly that the Army of the Potomac would not notice that we are gone? And how do we get there to North Carolina? We do not have the transport. Our horses are shot, we do not have fodder for our horses and mules, our men are starving and their uniforms are threadbare? Can we ask them to withstand further privations?"

"Sir, whether we stay or we go, our fodder problem is the same-we do not have any. Maybe there will be better grass further south in areas that have not been so ravaged?" Gordon crossed the room of the parlor of Edge Hill. He looked out of the window. The grey sky of winter hung close to the earth and kept it wrapped in winter's cold grip.

*****

On March 6, 1865, Lee recalled General Gordon to his headquarters at Edge Hill. Lee told him, "There seems to be but one thing that we can do—fight. To stand still is death. It could only be death if we fought and failed."

"General, I think it is better to fight here, where we are. You are right. We must fight and fight now. As soon as we can, we must fight, while we still have the chance." Lee walked over to General Gordon. He put his arm around his Gordon's shoulder.

Lee looked off in the distance. "If we merely hold these lines, sooner or later, Grant could, no, will, cut the railroad. Richmond will then starve. If we move to protect the Railroad, then we have to leave our trenches. We will be fighting in the open; we will be able to maneuver; although our lack of manpower there will be telling. Stay and we will be fighting Grant's type of battle. Maybe in the open we will be fighting our type of battle. We must hit Grant hard. Scare him. Force him to contract his lines. Force him to reinforce his lines. Then, maybe we have a chance. Maybe we can join General Johnston. Maybe something else will show up. But, this is our only hope."

"John, you have given me good service in the past. I cannot forget what you did at Spotsylvania. Look at the enemy's entrenchments. Pick the weakest spot that will do him the most harm. Come back to me with a proposed plan and we will look at it together." Lee shook Gordon's hand excessively and strode off.

*****

March 25, 1865 was another gloomy day. Gordon timed his attack to go at dawn. General Lee had been generous. He had given Gordon half the army for the attack. Gordon had made a careful study. Fort Stedman was one of the weakest points in the Union line. It was badly constructed and poorly sited. It looked like the ideal target. Just a mile or so behind Fort Stedman, the Union Army's military railroad ran out to the supply depot at City Point. This was the supply for the entire left-the western portion-of Grant's Army. If the military railroad could be taken, maybe Grant's entire western half would have to retreat.

Out of the morning gloom, out of the mist, just before the sun rose, Gordon's men hit Fort Stedman. The Yankee picket lines were overrun quickly. Then, almost as quickly, the Fort itself fell. Gordon's men spread out and took the Union trenches to the north and south of the Fort. For several hundred yards now, Gordon's men were victors. Grey clad men now turned to the east, the military railroad, and the Union rear. Victory was in sight! Glory was theirs, if they could take it.

From somewhere and somehow, Union artillery was pulled out of line and rushed to the scene. Next, the boys in grey were being pummeled by shot and shell. Then, fresh troops, lots of fresh troops in blue, counter-attacked. They hit the trench lines both north and south of the Fort. They overwhelmed the Confederate defenders in the Fort. They bullied the boys in grey back across the Union picket lines. By mid-morning, Lee ordered the retreat. Some 4,000 Confederates did not return from the fight. Lee's last chance, Lee's last gamble had failed.

"The most frightening thing about this attack," General Gordon reported to General Lee, "is that in the Union rear, while our attack was going on, General Grant was there with President Lincoln holding a review of the troops. They were seemingly not in the least concerned and appeared as if nothing had happened. Our attack was so inconsequential to them, they didn't even react!" General Gordon turned away from General Lee. Sobbing uncontrollably with tears flooding his eyes, he choked, "They didn't even react! I attacked them with half of our Army, and they didn't react!"

CHAPTER 39:

THE DANCE BEGINS

Whereas ye know not what shall be on the morrow. For what is your life? It is even a vapour, that appeareth for a little time, and then vanisheth away.
-James 4:14

The Night of April 1, April 2, 1865

A.P. Hill rested a moment. He smoked a cigar. The fresh taste of the tobacco enlivened him somewhat. He had come to rue the day that he had stopped in New York City on the way back to West Point. He had been warned not to visit the establishments on Mercer Street, but as an 18 year old rambunctious male, he had gone anyway. The fact that he had caught gonorrhea at first made him feel that much more that he was a man. His colleagues at school told him so. But as August faded into September, and then October into November, the pain keep on increasing in his body, and finally he was so debilitated that he had to leave the Point on a two-week medical furlough. He was so very weak that his family sent a slave to care for him and help him get on the train home. Then the furlough was extended for a month, then another and another until it was June of the next year, before he would return to the Point and start classes. Then and there, he had begun to pay for his breach of discipline. A Board had determined that he was so far behind academically that he was unfit to continue with his class-his chemistry was deficient. He had to repeat the year. He was crestfallen. He lost all of his friends. He was utterly embarrassed.

Now, nearly twenty years later, the illness still wracked his body. The pain was overwhelming. The fevers, the inability to urinate, the weakness that beset his body had robbed him time and time again of the things he wanted to enjoy in life or the work he had to do. 'Years of pain and suffering for one night's pleasure. My life's a morality play,' he sighed.

He wanted to go back to his cottage and sleep, but even though his wife, Dolly, awaited him, with their daughter, Netty, he knew there would be little comfort there. It was not because his wife did not do everything she could think of to help him, to provide him with solace. She was an angel of mercy who ministered to him. No, there was no comfort to be had, for his body would never ever forgive him for what he had so foolishly done to it.

He stubbed out his cigar. 'How I love cigars,' he thought. "Should I light another one?'

He continued his lonely vigil. He wanted to go home. All of sudden he was feeling the weight of his ancestry. Had he let his family down? The weight of his family heritage burdened him. His family was one of the first to come to Virginia in the 1600's. His was one of the first families of Virginia, yet he felt anything but first now. He wanted to return to his family homestead at Culpepper. It was so invitingly named "Stranger's Rest." "I am a stranger now to my own family, my wife and my four daughters".

He wondered what his paternal grandfather, Henry, who had served with Lighthorse Harry Lee in the Revolution, and his maternal great-grandfather, Ambrose Powell, a famed Indian fighter, adventurer, and a surveyor, who settled the Virginia-Kentucky border line, would have thought of him for waging war against the nation they had built.

He thought that his fever might have spiked, for now he could see himself playing with this childhood friend and playmate, James L. Kemper. He was now a boy again. His mother was reading to him. He couldn't hear it for sure, but thought that it was Shakespeare or the Bible He loved it when his mother read to him. "I love books because of my mother," he muttered.

He recalled being a teenager reading every book he could get his hands on about the exploits of Napoleon. He was studying again at the nearby Bleak Hill Academy, the name of which seemed to be an echo of Charles Dicken's novel. "I love novels." Then he thought, "Have I become thoroughly addled in my brain. I am speaking drivel." Thoughts of old Professor Sims filled his mind. He could see him continually spouting Latin mottoes. "Old Sims loved Latin mottoes and drilled them into 'his boys' day and night," Hill mused.

When Hill was 15, he had a religious awakening, which was to shape the rest of his life. He went to his mother, one of whose names was Baptist, and told her of a wonderful evangelist named Ireland. Ireland was so inspiring that Hill and his entire family converted to the 'New Light' Baptist movement, which led to the family eschewing cards, dancing, theatre, and alcohol.

"Why did I choose to join the military then, if I loved the Word of God so?" He remembered how much his decision to go to West Point had hurt his mother. His father, over the strong objections of his mother, did everything he could to obtain an appointment to West Point for his son.

"But If I had not gone to West Point, I would not have met my best friend." Swirling images of George Brinton McClellan, who was his roommate in 1842, filled his head. McClellan was slender, even, perhaps, a diminutive man. Both McClellan and Hill were younger than their classmates, with McClellan being 15 and Hill being 16. He soon became friends with Cadmus Wilcox and George Pickett. Although Thomas J. Jackson was in his class, they were not friends. Hill recalled the first time he saw the strange and gawky youth from the mountains of Virginia. Jackson had a look that said I am not interested in friends or frivolity-I am here to work.

"Then I became ill. I sinned at Mercer Street, and I have paid for it forever after."

He had the sensation that he was falling from his horse. He knew he was quite sick and that his fever was raging. He knew that he was delirious, but he had no power to resist. He grabbed the reigns even tighter as the next wave of the fever passed through his body.

His vision was of Henry Heth. "Heth and I were in my last year at West Point." He saw again the night when Harry Heth concocted a plan to right what they felt was a grave injustice when the Army Officers at the Point did not invite, as was the custom, the Cadet Captain, and the Adjutant to attend a banquet to celebrate Washington's Birthday. "Although, I held neither of these posts, my sense of justice was so violated, I agreed to hold a meeting in my room which was attend by Harry Heth and eight other cadets." Heth proposed to the assembled group, whom he named the 'Vindicators', that they would gather at the officers' mess with garment bags to loot the officers' food lockers. At the designated hour, the cadets gathered and broke into the mess. There, they gathered a wide variety of delicacies, including oranges, nuts, apples, wines, and cigars. Heth and another cadet waited for the serving man carrying the main course for the banquet to appear. When he did, the other cadet, struck the serving man behind the ear causing him to lose balance. Heth quickly grabbed the turkey, and all the cadets ran off. Heth reminisced, "Never were ten boys happier, never did a turkey before or since, have the flavor of this turkey," while the wine had "a bouquet flavor superior to old Madeira." Thereafter, they always called this caper, 'The Great Food Theft.'

Had he been sleeping? Had sleep finally come to him? Had hours gone by? He lighted another cigar. The little orange nub glowed in the night and although it gave off little heat, he imagined it to be as welcome as a campfire.

For about a half an hour, he stood there, clinging to the neck of his horse. His mind seemed to clear as the night got more misty and colder. His breathing was more even, and he seemed more awake. Somehow now, he had a better grasp on himself. He still knew that he could not go back to Netty. He decided that he would ride to General Lee's Headquarters and see if there was anything useful he could do there. If not, then, at least he done all that he could do this evening.

CHAPTER 40:

COWPENS REVISITED

Tomorrow will be "a day of carnage & blood between the contending armies around Richmond."
-Union Brigadier General

April 2, 1865 4:18 am

Captain Elisha Scott Carson, Jr. told me to get the company ready to fight. Like me, he was certain that the Yankees would come tonight. "They'll come at dawn. They'll come through the mist, once it is bright enough to see a few feet in front on one's self."

I looked at him. He was now the highest ranking officer of our Company. He had been with us from the first. He was still two years younger than I am, but he looks so old now. He is gaunt and haggard. But he was a steady man. He assumed command of our Company on April 1, 1864. Since then he had amassed a fine record. He had organized our successful rearguard action at Second Deep Bottom on August 14th-18th, 1864. He had always been one promotion ahead of me during the War. When I became Corporal, he became Sergeant. When I became Sergeant in April of 1862, he had become Lieutenant. But we had always been an effective team. I had long ago gotten over being just behind him in command, because it was clear that he deserved the command. Now, it was just the two of us left to ride herd over the Company.

"Have the men stay and fire at least two shots. Tell them to retreat up Arthur's Swamp and fill in the line there. Got it?" I can't really see his face, but by now, I know the look he has upon it. He is grim and determined. He started out as a boy, even though he graduated from King's Mountain Military Academy, but now he is a hard man.

"Captain, thinking on your Military Academy, being named after the great Victory in the Revolution, where my granddaddy fought, reminded me of General Morgan the night before Cowpens. My granddaddy said General Morgan joked with each man, asked about their families, and instructed them to fire two shots and fall back. I'd like to try my hand at that."

*****

"One more night of glory! That's what I am asking! That's all I am asking, men." I am talking in the dark not knowing exactly where my men are, but knowing they are out there, somewhere. "It's the last chance we have to salvage this thing, this life, this world, we call the Confederacy!"

Robert MacDonald answers back from some 50 or more feet down the picket trench. "By first light, I'd expect. We'd see'd them then!"

"Yes, I reckon so," I reply to the darkness, the great void of blackness that has swallowed up my men. I am really replying to where I think he is in that inky night. Is my voice being swallowed up by the great void?

I hear voices grunting in agreement. I know the men by their voices, but I wish that I could see their faces as well. It would comfort me to see them. I can read so much more when I can see a man's face. Like Robbie MacDonald has a tell-a telltale sign-when he is lying. I watched him play poker. (No, Vicee, I have not broken my promise to you. I don't gamble.) When he is bluffing, he always rubs the corner of his left eye with his left hand. Is he rubbing his eye now?

Doug speaks next. "Do you really think they'll come?" His question floats in the air and hangs there pregnant with expectation.

No one wants to answer that question. To answer it would give credence to it. It would make it real. So, we all sort of ignore it, till he asks it again. "Do you really think they'll come?"

I wait a moment. I am not sure how I should answer him. Should I tell him the truth? That they're coming and there's so many more of them acoming that we'll be brushed away as so many flies are swept off the back of the horse when a bucket of water is thrown on her back on a hot summer's day?

"No, boys, they'll not be acoming tonight," I hear myself saying before I have even formed the words in my head. I hear myself saying that knowing that I am lying and not knowing why.

Then I continue, as if I am in control of myself, "But if they come, I want you to let off two controlled shots. I want one more night of glory. I don't want anybody to be brave. We fire, and we fall back. We fire again, and then we retreat to the main line. Follow Arthur's Swamp. Two shots! That's all we have to do." Just like Danny Morgan told his men at Cowpens, I am telling my men now. I am inspired now, Vicee.

I walk down the line to the south. I stumble over my own men in the darkness.

"Is that you, Douglas?" I ask blindly.

"No, I'm Randall McDaniel, sir."

"Right. Give 'em two shots, if they come. Then, upon my order, fall back along the line of Arthur's Swamp. Use the Swamp to guide you." I pause a second. "How's yer sister, Jill?"

"She is still the best quilter in Timmonsville, she is."

I look at his face, if he is eighteen, I am a hundred, but I never ask.

I go down the line. "Is that you, Douglas?"

"Yes, sir. Douglas Angus MacFarlane, sir."

"Well, Angus, yer mom makes the best, the best peach pie, I've ever tasted."

"That she does, sir." MacFarlane answers.

"The MacFarlanes come from Argyll, don't they?" I asked, knowing the answer.

"Right they do!" MacFarlane replies crisply.

"My ancestors Colin and Kathleen erected a cross in 1514 on Argyll. Our Clans go way back."

"Yes, sir."

"Give 'em two shots, if they come. Then, upon my order, fall back along the line of Arthur's Swamp. I want to see you after this…"

I turn to the darkness. "I want all of you to know that I expect you to fire twice and then fall back. But I don't want any man to die or get wounded here tonight. No heroics."

I go down the trench line stumbling over man after man until there's no one left to stumble over, Vicee. I can't find the flank where my men end and then next boys begin. Are they not out there? I go north and I continue talking with each man until I know my command is ready.

The night is dark, and it swallows up our fears, because no one can see that look on our faces in the black of this night.

Captain Elisha Scott Carson greets me when I return. "Everything ready?"

"Yes, sir," I reply automatically. "Do you really think they're acoming?"

"Yep, I do."

CHAPTER 41:

LEE TO THE REAR!

And Hazael said, Why weepeth my lord? And he answered, Because I know the evil that thou wilt do unto the children of Israel: their strong holds wilt thou set on fire, and their young men wilt thou slay with the sword, and wilt dash their children, and rip up their women with child.
-2 Kings 8:12

April 2, 1865 4:37 am

The fighting at Five Forks had gone on all day April 1st. Now, this night had been rent by a violent bombardment. Hell had broken forth in flame, fire, fury, and sound. Now, it was quiet. I started to go through in my mind what more I could do. I felt the Yankees were going to attack at any moment. Or was this only my nerves talking? Aren't the Yankees about a mile and a quarter away in their Forts Welch, Gregg, and Fisher? Wouldn't we hear them as they formed their battle lines and marched across that distance? I comforted myself with these thoughts. I rested my head for a second on the front of our trench. My eyes may have drifted closed. Then I heard it. Was that a twig breaking?

Then, I heard thousands of feet running towards us. The dawn was just breaking, but we were still mired in mist. The grey, gloom of night still wrapped herself around us.

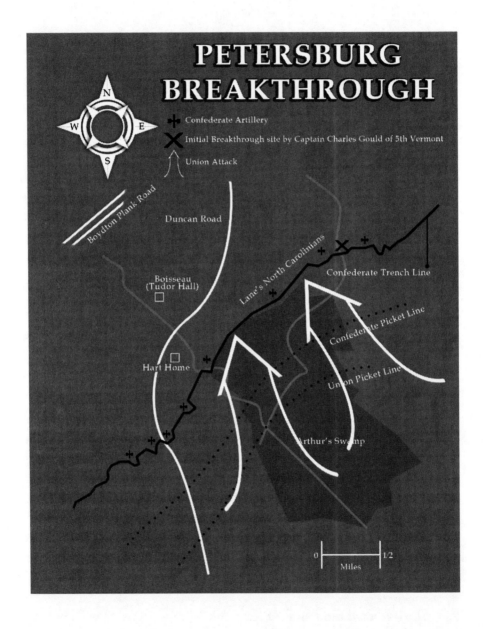

"Wake up! They're coming! The Yankees are attacking!"

Into the night, Hell had loosed all of her ghouls and demons.

Within seconds, they covered the ground to our trenches. We fired a volley. I could see that we were going to be overwhelmed, flattened, and swept away. We could not hold our picket-line trench.

"Retreat!" I yelled at the top of my lungs. No Cowpens today. No second volley. To say we retreated to the main trenches is a lie. We ran scared, our legs barely carrying us in front of the vast swell rising in the ocean of blue behind us. 300 yards melted away in a second!

Within moments, we had retreated, well, fled, all the way back to our main lines at Arthur's Swamp. We skirted the abatis, running its zigzag pattern we knew so well. We jumped in the main trench, while steeling ourselves to the bloody task at hand. We raised rifled muskets. We fired a volley, belching forth our hot stream of lead. They came over our walls. We met them with the cold steel of our bayonets, but still the fury of the Yankees came on. Like a tidal wave, it washed up and over Arthur's Swamp, to which we had fallen back.

Unlike the rest of the line, Arthur's Swamp, being a nasty little swamp, was not as well defended with abatis, trenches, and cannon. We believed that the natural defenses would be enough. Now, I could see that this theory had been wrong-dead wrong.

Up the beach, the wave, the storm, and the fury came, inexorable, unstoppable, and indefensible, sweeping away all before it. I saw a brave Yankee Captain jump the wall of our trench. He was virtually alone, but then moments later his men followed him over our ramparts. So many of our men fired at him, I could not believe that he would be able to go on, yet, still, he came blazing forward. He raised his sword. This act seemed a summons to his men to exert themselves more to hoist themselves over our trench walls. Then someone bayoneted him. He fell back and then, my God, he got up again, and came forward! It was the most marvelous thing I have ever seen. Had it not been so very damning for us, I would have cheered his courage. I would have clapped for his nerve. But, as it was, he was a symbol that they, the Union, would not be denied. And, by God, they were not denied. Doug MacDonald at my side, as he always seemed to be, saw the blue Captain aiming for me, so he hurtled his body focusing all of his energy into his musket's bayonet, which pierced the Yankee Captain. As he did so, a Yankee Sergeant yelled, "They've killed Captain Gould!" The Sergeant fired his musket, and Doug went down. Doug was dead. I could see his glassy eyes. Robert MacDonald rushed the Sergeant, "My God! You've kilt my brother!" A wall of blue volleyed, and Robert MacDonald fell to the ground, his body riddled with holes.

Now, the blue wave was flooding over our trench walls. Blue was everywhere. Grey seemed to be falling under the weight of the blue surge. I was now on the rampart of the back wall, only a few of my boys were with me. Our backs were to the west, and I guess the darkness of night was still behind us, for we could easily see the forms of the Union soldiers against the dawning pink-grey sky.

I had only a few moments to order the men back to the log cabins behind the trench-line. They had been our winter quarters. There was no time to stop and get our possessions, our little things from home, our Bibles, our wives knitting, our extra socks. All that would have made our lives just that little tiny bit better, within seconds, was behind Union lines and was cut off from our lives. Those cabins had been our homes for months, and now they belonged to a foreign and hostile land.

Off to our south, I could see the hallowed white planks of Tudor Hall. For a brief second, a flood of memories of the good times I had spent there with General McGowan and his staff flashed through my mind. It was like a dream that speeds up before one's eyes in the last seconds before awakening.

I rallied my men. "Let's give them a volley!" Just a few ragged shots were fired. Did it even stop one blue figure?

Then I cried, "Let's pull back to the Boydton Plank Road!" It was only about a half mile to our rear. That precious road we had defended all these months. Without it, the food stuffs, the ammunition, the blankets, and the necessities that keep an army in the field would not get through to our boys. Our line had to be re-established there, or we had lost the siege of Petersburg. Without the Road, we lost everything.

We were mixed in with Lane's North Carolinians. The Union Corps that hit us was punching through our lines. I could see that the left part facing us was trying to turn north, while their right was trying to turn south. They were going to blast a hole through our lines, and then roll up the newly created flanks in both directions. They were exploiting their breech, and there appeared to be nothing that we could about it. I had no time to think of my friends, my best friends, Douglas and Robert MacDonald, lying dead back there in our trenches. I had my men, my company, to think of, and to save.

I didn't see General Lane at first. I had been told that he had been such an inspiration at Gettysburg leading the way at Pickett's Charge. He had been wounded then with his horse being shot out from under him. Later, General James Lane had been wounded in the groin at Cold Harbor, just a few months ago. He was a scholarly man, who, after having graduated from VMI, was offered professorships at both VMI and North Carolina Military Institute before the War. Still, he was a brave man and a leader whose troops loved him.

Then coming out of the smoke of the fray, Lane appeared like a god of war, sword in hand directing his battered men. "General, where do you want my company from the Hampton Legion?"

"Hampton's Legion? You're far from home. Join my left flank. They're swinging us back like a barn door. Need to hold the left."

He disappeared into the smoke and haze.

"On me, men!" I gestured to some grey scurrying forms. I couldn't see faces. I ran for Lane's left. It was already across the Boydton Plank Road. Lane's line was bent back like some lazy capital letter 'L'. It was clear that without a great deal more men the end of the 'L' to the north would be outflanked and turned back on itself such that the 'L' would become a 'U'.

"Form on me!" As I was forming my company, I saw Sargent George W. Tucker riding to the east.

"Tucker! Tucker," I shouted to get his attention. It was odd that Tucker was leading one horse, while riding another.

His dirty grimy face was tracked with tears that formed little white rivulets down his cheeks. I suddenly realized why Tucker was leading a horse. "The General's dead! The General's dead!" Tucker sobbed.

"Tucker, Hill's dead?" I said dumbfounded.

"Oh, my God! Yes, Hill is dead." He snorted some tears back and wiped his nose on his sleeve. "I've got to tell Lee."

Angus MacFarlane stared at me in disbelief. My men were clearly shaken. Hill was one of those legendary men. Anyone, who had served under him, knew that the diminutive soldier loved his men and did all he could to take care of them. He was fearless in battle always wearing his red battle shirt and smoking a cigar.

"God no! Not him!" Angus screamed.

"Sir, maybe you had better come with me to the General Lee's headquarters. Lee might need some good men to ride throughout the army with what's going on…" Tucker gestured towards the blue flood that showed no signs of cresting. It was clear that my few men could do little to nothing to staunch the flow. "He might need some couriers… Weren't yer men cavalry?"

To think that we had been cavalry was both a compliment and an insult. We had been mounted infantry for a few months throughout which our bad horses and bad fodder had really destroyed whatever chance we had of being effective. But Tucker meant well, and his thought made sense.

"Where should we report?" I wasn't really sure where Lee's headquarters were.

"He's at William Turnbull's House, called Edge Hill. It's northwest of here, about a mile and half. Longstreet should be with him. They were together when General Hill and I rode out a while ago." With that, Tucker rode off, and we followed him as best we could.

The bulk of the Union VI Corps turned southwest and pushed our boys in Heth's division to the southwest, and some others were pushing what was left of Lane and Thomas to the northeast. It was clear that our Army was being divided into smaller pieces.

I drove the men. Although we were tired, I had them go at double quick - pace for as long as they could to get to Lee.

"We've gotta get to Lee." I shouted time and again.

It was now about 5:30 am. We were moving up the Boydton Plank Road and coming up on Edge Hill. I could see that blue soldiers were just to the south of that grand house, less than a half mile away. Edge Hill was squarely in their path. I could see Tucker was there with a group of horsemen. We raced to beat the Yankees.

I burst into the Headquarters. I could see Lee was barking orders to the telegraphic team. Dispatches were flying to President Jefferson Davis, to General Ewell, and to Secretary of War John C. Breckenridge. As I came up, panting from the run, I heard Lee dictating his message to the Secretary of War. "I advise that preparation be made for leaving Richmond tonight. I will advise you later, according to circumstances."

Tucker ducked his head inside the Headquarters. "General, we've gotta leave. Them Yankees look awfully ugly." Lee looked at Tucker. Reminded of the loss of General A. P. Hill, a tear welled up in Lee's eye. "Hill is at rest now and we, who are left, are the ones to suffer." Lee's voice was hoarse and raspy.

Lee moved outdoors, but still continued to dictate dispatches. Still his keen eye was searching the terrain for information about the enemy and how best to stop them.

Just then a Union Battery at the edge of the trees across the pasture began shelling the Headquarters. The first shell fell around the grounds of the home, but the third one directly hit the Headquarters, vaporizing it into dust, timbers, splinters, and throwing up a cloud of debris and dust. What was left of the house burst into flames. Dust and debris coated Lee and the rest of the staff.

"Dismantle the telegraph, and leave here as soon as is possible," Lee said calmly. "Lieutenant," he said as he looked at me with sad eyes, "I need you to go to Richmond. You must impress upon President Davis the profound gravity of our situation. I can no longer vouchsafe the Capital. The Government must leave today, tonight at the latest. It should make for Danville."

He turned away from me. Lee had formulated his plan for defense of the headquarters. "Bring up those two sections of guns, and hit those people back!" Lee shouted over the rising din of battle. Federal troops were now running across the field and up the hill towards Edge Hill. Lee went beside the six cannon and began issuing the orders for the various steps to load and fire. The first wave of Yankees took some canister and then faded back. On again a few minutes later came a second wave. "Double canister, on my order, fire!" Lee yelled, obviously relishing his role as artillery commander.

He looked over at me. "Well, what are you doing there? Get going Lieutenant, I have given you an order." He motioned to a staff member to hand me the reins of his horse.

"But my men…?"

"They'll be fine here with me. When I am finished with them, I will detail them back to Hampton's Legion. After you have met with the President, I want you to report back to the Legion also. And thank you, Lieutenant." Lee slapped the side of the horse.

The explosion rang out before I could get on the horse. A shell had exploded within feet of Lee. A horse near him had been gravely, perhaps, mortally wounded. Lee stared at the thrashing beast as it expired. His face had a cold and distant expression as the final throes of death were punctuated with a splaying of hooves.

I jumped on the horse given to me and wheeled north on the Boydton Plank Road. As I rode off, I turned back to see the Turnbull House in flames. Lee had ordered off all the others, while he and the gun crews got off one last round of cannon fire. I could only see in my mind's eye the stark juxtaposition between the scene now and one which occurred less than 2 years ago. Lee furiously ordering desperate cannon fire as staff and other officers, and my battered small company of the Legion were running off to the northwest to avoid the flood of blue charging up the hill crested by Edge Hill burning furiously.

Had it been only 23 months ago almost to the day, that Lee, regal in pose and poise, rode his horse, Traveller, through the cheering throngs of the Army of Northern Virginia, while the dancing bright orange and yellow light cast by the burning hulk of the remains of Chancellors Tavern along the Orange Plank Road at Chancellorsville, Virginia flickered on Lee's face? Then, it was the crest of the High Tide of the Confederacy. The miracle had happened. This was one of the greatest victories in history. Fighting Joe Hooker had been 'suppressed' and beaten. Confederate artillery from Hazel Grove had hit one of the white columns of the Chancellor House, and either the shell or a bit of wood of the column had knocked Hooker unconscious. His Army of the Potomac of some 133,000 had been bested by Lee's Army of Northern Virginia of less than 35,000. Lee's flank attack led by Stonewall Jackson had destroyed the Union 11th Corps. But then, as now, Lee had lost a key lieutenant. Lee had said, "Jackson has lost his left arm, but I have lost my right one."

So within fewer than two years, Lee had gone from the very heights of the pantheon of the gods of war to now a lowly artillery officer, desperately facing off an unstoppable charge of Union infantry. The incongruity of the thought almost knocked me off my horse. But I had a job to do, a singularly important job to do. I turned north towards Richmond and didn't look back again.

CHAPTER 42:

FIRE STRIKES AGAIN

"John answered them all, saying, 'I baptize you with water, but He who is mightier than I is coming, the strap of whose sandals I am not worthy to untie. He will baptize you with the Holy Spirit and fire.'"
- Luke 3:16

April 2, 1865 7:45 AM

I rode off not knowing that Lee was organizing a last stand defense. There were not enough men to hold Forts Gregg and Whitworth. The Army of Northern Virginia had been broken by the multiple attacks of Grant's men and was now in at least five pieces. Lee's task was simple in concept, but extremely hard in practice: unite the five pieces and become an effective fighting force again. Lee had no choice: "Order the men at Forts Gregg and Whitworth to hold their positions at all hazards until I can get the Army ready to slip away to the west." There it was: a death sentence, a suicide sentence. The few would hold and fight and die, so the many could flee and survive.

There the legend would be born. The rebel response by the men of the Forts, when they were called upon by the Federals to surrender, was "See you in Hell first." Fort Gregg became the Confederate Alamo.

I continued to ride to Richmond, unaware, in some senses thankfully, of what was happening to the Army of Northern Virginia at Petersburg. I only knew that I had a message that had to be delivered to the President of the Confederacy from General Lee. The miles ticked by. Although my horse was clearly blown, I made as much speed as I could over the course of the twenty or so miles I had to ride.

By the time I got to Richmond, the Churches through the City were ringing their bells. The chimes were resounding. It seemed as if all of Christendom was being called to Communion and Prayer. The day was Palm Sunday. There was just a light breeze that morning. The air had that hint of balminess that bespoke a much warmer day to follow. This Sunday could have been any Sunday. Everything seemed as calm and controlled. You could sense that all of Richmond was preparing to go to Church. The finest clothes were being put on now. Young boys fussed with their stiff collars, while the girls smoothed out each wrinkle of their Sunday dresses. Women arranged their most beautiful hats, while men in suits looked at their pocket watches and clicked their tongues that time was awasting. The firing of the cannon to the south seemed so muffled and distant. The day was Palm Sunday. I was not triumphantly entering Jerusalem upon the back of an ass; I was a lowly, dirty, and grimy Lieutenant of a badly defeated army, informing the commander-in-chief of the disaster.

I wanted to go directly to the White House. I came up Hull Street by the warehouses of tobacco. Behind the warehouse the spire of the Methodist Church reached heavenwards. I crossed the James River by Mayo's Bridge. Across the river to my immediate left hand side, were the struts of the railroad bridge for the Richmond and Danville Railroad. I could see trains crossing the river and pulling into the yard on the far banks of the river. Beyond the railroad bridge, loomed the red brick three story buildings of the Tredegar Iron Works, where most of the Confederate cannon were made. As I entered the city proper, the Gas Works were there on my right hand side. I went up 14th street. Trinity Church appeared on my right, with the Exchange Hotel on my left. I knew that I was near the Capitol building. I turned left on Franklin

Street, and right in front of me was the State Court House Building. Soldiers were scurrying everywhere. Although it was Sunday, the city was a beehive of activity. People were trying to find any cart or wheel barrow, or anything with wheels to haul their goods out of the City. Church bells were ringing. The workers in the State Capitol were hauling files out by the box load. I asked a soldier where the President was.

"Hell, Jeff Davis is at his home." He spit a chaw of tobacco on the ground.

"Where's that?"

"Don't you know'd anything?" The soldier looked at me as if I were a child.

I decided to pull rank. "That's 'sir', soldier. I am a lieutenant, and you will address me with respect." It was a mistake.

"I don't care if yer Jeff Davis hisself." He spit again and turned away.

I pulled my horse's head to start moving again, when another voice called out. "The White House of the Confederacy is in the Court End neighborhood. That's at the corner of Leigh and 13th Street, sir." A young boy saluted me, while he pointed the direction. He could have been no more than 13, but here he was dressed as private in the Confederate Army. It struck me that, if we were pulling boys of his age to serve, our nation was truly in dire straits.

"Thank you, son. God bless you."

"And you too, Sir."

When I arrived at the White House of the Confederacy, I was immediately struck by how bare and plain it was. I had expected some opulent palace, with massed white columns rising before a white planation house with a road of bent-over live oaks spreading their crowns and forming archways hung with Spanish Moss above the road and framing the view of the home. What was before me was anything but that which my imagination had wrought. It had been built earlier this century by and for a Dr. John Brockenbrough. It lacked any real flavor of style and artistry. What I approached was a three story box. The doorway was framed by two small columns that reached just barely above the door. The windows were symmetrically spaced two on either side of the door and five on the second and third floors. I could not believe my eyes. Then as I rode a little bit closer to the home, I realized that I was looking at the back of the building and that the front, which seemed to face a grassy lawn or oak, was far more in line with my fantasy.

Clerks were hauling box upon box of files from the Confederate White House. There was no thought of Church here. Yet, I could see from the state of confusion that reigned and the lack of urgency in the clerks' movements that the message still had not gotten through to those denizens of our Government. I shouted to one of the clerks, "I have a message from Lee for President Davis. Where is he?"

"Well, I reckon he's gone to Church." He lazily sat back on a couple of boxes of files, as if he had all the time in the world to answer me.

"Which one? Where is it? It's urgent that I speak with the President!"

"Why, he always goes to St. Paul's Episcopal Church over on 9th and Grace Street. Ain't that a pretty name for an address of a Church?" The clerk smiled at me as if he had revealed the secret of the Holy Grail to me.

"Thank you," I said curtly and proceeded to find St. Paul's Episcopal Church. Riding to the Church, which was directly across the street from the Capitol building renewed my faith in my fantasy architectural abilities. The Church's front was graced by as many columns as would befit the most beautiful temple in Athens. Its spire was not only tall, but also it was beautiful in its symmetry and grace. Four wreathed circles stared out from four of the eight faces of the octagonal spire. The whiteness of the tower was crowned by a grey cupola.

As I entered the Church, the Sexton stopped me. I certainly presented a picture that would despoil any church. I was covered with dust from my ride. My face was grimy and black with powder from tearing cartridges with my teeth. I am sure that my lack of proper bathing toilet in the past several days allowed my aroma to permeate from my unwashed, ragged, and bedraggled uniform. He balled his fist. He thrusted his fist to the mid-point of my chest to halt me. "What are you doing here?" He inquired. He stood in front of me blocking my way. His demeanor was that of a man who would not be trifled with. He stood there his face stony calm and unbending.

My attire and my personal hygiene contrasted sharply with cleanliness of the church with its perfectly stained oak paneling on the walls, the highly polished rosewood pews, and the glistening sunlight streaming in the large windows

The Congregation began to sing, "Jesus, Lover of My Soul." I saw the President stand to sing. The President was dressed in a fashionable black wool suit, his white shirt immaculately pressed and starched, and his traditional black tie.

"I have an urgent message for the President." I panted as by now I was out of breath from all my exertions.

Then I heard Dr. Charles Minnigerode intone to the Congregation, "The Lord is in His Temple; let all the earth keep silence before Him!"

Looking over his shoulder and then glancing back to me, the Sexton asked me in hushed tones, "Can it wait until communion and the service are over?" I was impressed that his tone was so even and exceedingly calm.

"No, sir, it cannot. I must speak with the President now!"

"I cannot allow that." Even, calm, impassive, he presented himself and made it clear that he would not a allow me to enter the Church.

"Sir, can you take the President a message? It is most urgent."

Within a few minutes, I had written a message to the President. While I was writing my message, a clerk from the White House came in with a telegram for the President. The Sexton took my message and the telegram down the aisle to pew number sixty-three where the President sat listening to the service. He unfolded the messages. The President's face, which had been beaming with Christian joy just moments before, turned ashen. The President stood up and quickly walked down the aisle, as he did so a few staff officers and couriers who had been in the Church stood up and marched to the aisle and formed a phalanx behind and following the President.

Davis stopped before me. His face was lined with complete disbelief and incredulity. "Lieutenant, is it true what Lee said? Is the situation beyond all hope? Must we evacuate the Capital today? Now?"

I nodded 'yes' sadly and slowly. "I was there, sir. The Yankees have broken Lee's lines in several places, and there is only the barest chance that he can reunite the Army and continue the fight."

"Oh, my God!" the President gasped. "Then, it is true. May we pray to the Lord to help our Nation and our Army in this crisis!"

The President and his staff rode away to the White House. I followed behind to see if there was anything else I could do to help the President.

By the time I got to the White House, the scene was far different from what it had been about a half hour ago. Clerks and officials were moving with haste. Files were being upended and papers were being burned in the streets. People, tears streaming down their faces, were crying out in the streets.

Davis began barking orders and directing the situation. Davis ordered that the more than $500,000 in gold and silver bullion, coins, gold nuggets, ingots, gold plate, jewelry, and Mexican pesos, be taken to the Danville railroad line and placed onto box cars to be removed to the new Capital.

Within minutes, the panic started. The Banks were mobbed with people wanting to take their money out, even though it was a Sunday. People and soldiers alike searched around for any wheeled conveyance to haul personal valuables from the City.

Then someone in the Treasury thought it would be wise to burn the paper currency of the Confederacy. Wheel barrels emptied out of the building, and great piles, nay mountains, of ones, fives, and ten dollar bills were set on fire, creating bonfires. Families ran to the train stations, screaming and yelling demands to be put on trains leaving the City. Others, knowing that virtually none would make it out on the trains, began a mass exodus of the City on foot or horseback, fleeing to the west. Voices were raised in swearing, crying, moaning, and wailing, which form a counterpoint to the cacophony of the howls of animals, being whipped, such that mules were braying, horses were neighing, and nowhere was there silence. As dark started to fall upon Richmond, some people chose to bolt themselves inside their homes, trusting that their locks would keep out the looters and bandits that seemed to rise, like a misty fog, out of the gutters of the streets.

All day, I worked at the White House, loading wagons with files that would be needed, burning those files that were not needed. I carried out anything and everything any official ordered me to do.

All of sudden, it was 5:00pm. The president was still in his office doing paperwork. I ran to his office. "Your Eminence, you must get out of here, now!" I was struck by the irony that I, a Lieutenant, was ordering the President, my commander-in-chief, around. He stood up, straightened the papers on his desk, as if he were leaving the office on any normal work day and would be back tomorrow to finish what he could not get done today.

CHAPTER 43:

FIRE AND SWORD

Day of wrath and doom impending.
David's word with Sibyl's blending,
Heaven and earth in ashes ending.
Oh, what fear man's bosom rendeth,
When from heaven the Judge descendeth,
On whose sentence all dependeth.
- **Dies Irea**, *13th Century, Unknown, but attributed to Thomas of Celano*

April 2, 1865 7:00 PM

Even with all of my prodding, it was not until around 7:00pm, that President Davis made his way to the train station to board a train for Danville. He had earlier kissed his wife, Varina, and his children, Jeff Jr., Joseph, and Winnie, goodbye so that they could board an earlier train.

For about an hour he stood in his office. His left hand absent-mindedly stroked his signature goatee. He stood ram-rod straight still in his Sunday best black suit. Unlike lesser men, he did not loosen his tie to undertake his work, but remained always a formal figure. His face had the greatest cast of sorrow upon it. He had lived a life that seemed dogged by tragedy.

While he was in the army, he had married the daughter of his commanding officer, Zachary Taylor. He deeply and completely loved Sarah Knox Taylor, but within three months of their marriage she lay dead, while he was struggling to hold onto his life through the fever that had robbed him of his wife. It took him many years to recover from her loss. Later, he had married Varina Banks Howell, who was the granddaughter of a former Governor of New Jersey. She was nearly twenty years younger than he was. She had borne him six children of whom three, all sons, had died during childhood, including his son, Joseph Evan, who had been born just before the war and who fell from a balcony of the White House of the Confederacy. So, his life had been marked by great personal tragedy; now, it would be marked by great defeat and possibly by execution as a traitor.

He jammed a cigar in his mouth and turned to leave his office. Unlike most men, he did not look back as he reached the door. He strode through the White House and to the waiting carriage.

With the departure of the government of the Confederacy, the City authorities thought that they would negotiate a surrender of the City to the Federal forces. The barest hint of the City falling into Yankee hands was enough to turn this already tragic night into one of thorough catastrophe.

Ardent secessionists, rather than face the hangman's noose, decided that this was the moment to abandon Richmond. All order collapsed.

The loss of order was punctuated by explosions set by both the retreating Army and the local militia. The City Council, thinking that they were acting in the best interest of the citizens of Richmond, ordered that all alcohol, some 300 hogsheads of whiskey in particular, be dumped on the streets and allowed to run down the storm gutters.

The wafting smell of liquor brought out every low life, bandit, thief, drunk, client of whorehouses, and looter, as if a clarion call had been sounded in the wilderness. The crowd formed almost instantly. Every imaginable form of cup, goblet, and drinking vessel was put to use, as well as anything else that the imagination might conceive would allow the user to scoop up some of the amber treasure that was flowing through the streets. Others just got on their haunches and lapped or licked the liquor from the stones of the street in a wide-eyed malay. Of course, a crowd once imbued with spirits began to run amuck. The devil's merriment was heightened, when prisoners escaped from their jails, and joined in the Bacchanalian frenzy. Looting and sacking of dry good stores, jewelry stores, restaurants, warehouses, and the homes just recently abandoned went unchecked as the local authorities controlled no forces that would dare to restrain the violence and evil that was being perpetrated. It was an unbridled carnival, wanton sinning, unleashed humanity at its lowest dregs, entering into every form of debauchery and license. Evil ruled the night. Rather than Richmond being pillaged by the Yankees, Richmond was being pillaged by its own Confederate citizens!

But then, as one imagined nothing more horrific could happen, the fire broke out. The Militia had been ordered to torch the warehouses where tinder dry leaves of tobacco were stored. The tobacco flamed and flared instantly and the conflagration swirled into the air igniting wooden warehouses. A strong southern breeze started blowing. The wind carried the sparks north and then throughout the City alighting here and there where the finest whiskey ran through the streets making blue flames dance and soar. The moon, which was on its downward slope towards the west, became obscured with smoke.

Richmond, a city built of wood, was dry and ripe with some of the buildings bearing timbers that colonial hands had hewn from the then-abundant forests. Building after building exploded, as they became fuel for the conflagration. Everywhere the blaze expanded. Some of the looters turned arsonist and added to the holocaust and inferno. The sound of the crackling fire as it ate its way through the ancient timbers rose ever greater in volume. The sound became a howling hurricane, as if every freight train in the world were passing by the City. The heat was intense.

I tried to fight it and was joined by some men, Vicee. But there were never enough of us and there were little or no means to fight this vast arena of orange glow. The smell of burning was overwhelming, for it was the smell of searing human flesh, of fat sizzling as the flames consumed the people hiding in their homes, too afraid to come out for fear that the looters would kill them and steal their possessions. The falling buildings created thunderous waves of noise. The ground shook while mighty giants were felled. Then avalanches of bricks cascaded upon hapless whites and blacks, as the City died. Voices cried out from beneath the smoldering rubble, but there was no one now to hear them and come help them. Screams rent the night. Moaning seemed to come from all quarters. Ash fell, choking breath-stealing ash.

I made for the Mayo Bridge, which I had crossed just hours before on my errand to warn the President. When I reached it, I saw South Carolinians jamming barrels of tar on and under the bridge while the last soldiers of the Confederacy marched across towards the west and reunion with what remained of Bobby Lee's Army. A sergeant asked me to supervise the destruction of the bridge to prevent the Union Army from catching up with us. I waited until the last man was across. I saw an engineer, who was a Captain, who had told the men how to place the barrels. I felt that I was usurping his command. I went to him. "All over, sir. Goodbye."

The engineer turned to his men. "You heard what the Lieutenant said. Blow her to hell!"

I did not look back, although I knew all of Richmond was burning. I put all the screams, the voices crying out from the rubble, the explosions, the smell of crisp flesh being burnt, the streets running wild with liquor, the destroyed files of the Confederacy, the burning of millions of dollars of currency-all of it, out of my mind.

My old world had been swept away with fire and sword. God's mighty hand had visited His destruction upon the earth, destroying one Confederate city after another, leaving none standing. We, as a nation, had been humbled by God. We must now accept His divine punishment. We had no choice but to submit. We had to get down upon our knees and pray for our salvation. Our only hope was in Him.

Within my heart, I could feel a peace descending that I had not felt for a long, long time. I was serene and calm. I knew what I had to do.

I rode to rejoin my men, the Hampton Legion, and await my fate. I had come through the holocaust. I was Orpheus, who had descended to Hell to reclaim Eurydice. I would fulfill my vow. I would return to you, Vicee. I would return to South Carolina. I would live with you, my wife, and raise our child, George Carson. I would look to the future, and I would trust in the future. With God's guidance and strength, I would rebuild my world - whatever it took.

CHAPTER 44:

EPILOGUE

The evil that men do lives after them; the good is oft interred with their bones.
-William Shakespeare

James Augustus McEachern
Seven days later, on April 9, 1865, James A. McEachern surrendered with Company G of the Hampton Legion at Appomattox. A rooster of his company at Appomattox is set forth as Appendix I, below. A timeline of his military records is set forth as Appendix II, below.

James had three more siblings born after the action of this novel. Sister Caroline Emma, nicknamed "Carrie," was born April 6, 1865. His brother Angus was born May 1, 1866. His last sibling was born on April 21, 1867, and was named Sarah Adele, but was known to all as "Della."

He had one son with Victoria Clifton Ham, George Carson McEachern, who was born on December 13, 1864. James Augustus McEachern died on April 12, 1874, at the age of 34.

As we have noted, he was wounded twice during the war. He never really recovered from these wounds. After the war, his health deteriorated such that by age 34, he died of what had not killed him on the battlefield in 1862 and 1863. He was survived by his son, George Carson, and his wife, Victoria.

What was his legacy? Well, surely his son went on to live into the 20th century. The son saw the world expand as the railroads grew across the continent and brought forth a vastly different country from that which his father had fought for only a few years before. He became a conductor on the railroads, heard about the first flights of the brothers Wright at Kitty Hawk, NC, and saw Theodore Roosevelt become president after another mournful assassination. Teddy as President pulled America kicking and screaming into the 20th century and forced her to become a world power confronting Japan and Russian in Portsmouth, taking on the Kaiser over Morocco, sailing the White Fleet around the world, digging the Panama Canal, busting the trusts, and enacting laws that established the Interstate Commerce Commission, the Food and Drug Agency, and so much more. But the son died in 1925, during the roaring twenties, leaving his son to become the first to go to college. He died on his son's birthday not knowing that the same son would someday become a doctor. That doctor went on during a world war to experiment with penicillin as a way to combat rheumatic heart disease.

So is a legacy those we beget? Perhaps.

What is the legacy of a man? Most of the time, it is things we never thought of, never knew that we had started or put in motion. But each man fits as a cog in that vast machine that is life on this planet Earth. What he did, who he touched, what he saw, what he felt, is known only partially to us who have come after him. The real substance of a man is known in all of its details by God, and by God alone. But for those of us who have come after, we are indebted to those who came before for all that they did. For without them, we would not be here and our world would be very different in their absence.

George W. Tucker
After A. P. Hill's death, Tucker, the faithful courier, attached himself to Lee's staff till the end of the war. Tucker was thereafter by Lee's side

carrying the 3d Corps flag. He later carried the white flag of surrender on the fateful morning of April 9, 1865. Tucker accompanied Lee to the surrender at Appomattox. After the War, he returned to Baltimore and is buried in Loudon Park Cemetery.

Sidney F. Cole

After the war, Sidney F. Cole moved to the north. In 1870, he and his wife, Frannie, returned to Timmonsville, S.C. There, he became the town magistrate, and, perhaps, because of multiple stints as a nurse in Confederate Hospitals, he established a business as a pharmacist. After Frannie died, he married Ida Timmons on August 15, 1894. On December 12, 1895, he died and was buried in Byrd Cemetery in Timmonsville, S. C.

Samuel McGowan

After the War, McGowan returned to Abbeville, South Carolina, where he had studied law before the War. He was elected to Congress, but he refused to take his seat. Later, he became a leading force against the carpetbagger movement that was influencing the State Legislature. Finally, he was elected in 1879 to the South Carolina State Supreme Court as an associate justice, which positon he held until 1894. He died in 1897, about two months before his 80th birthday.

James Fitz James Caldwell

Caldwell initially became a teacher after the War. He was a member of the Board of Trustees of the University of South Carolina until 1877. He married Rebecca Capers Connor in 1875, and was a devoted husband until she died in 1911. In 1870, he opened a practice of law. He had banks and railroads as clients. He ran for State Senate in 1890, but was defeated in a close election. In 1903, he ran for the position of associate justice of the South Carolina State Supreme Court, but was again defeated in an election. He also pursued a career of writing, including poetry and fiction, publishing a novel about the Reconstruction entitled, The Stranger. He died in 1925 at the age of 88.

Wade Hampton

During the War, Hampton's childhood home, Millwood was burned by General Sherman. Although offered the nomination for governor of South Carolina in 1865, Wade Hampton refused to accept the nomination and actually ran against the nomination. Later in 1868, he became the head of the state Democratic Party, but after the Radical Republicans swept the election, he ceased all political activity until 1876.

In 1874, his second wife, Mary Singleton McDuffie died. In 1879, his namesake son, Wade Hampton IV, and the last survivor of his five children by his first wife, Margaret Preston, died. In all, he had five sons and four daughters.

Completely opposed to the Reconstruction policies of the Republican Party, in 1876, Hampton ran for Governor. In order to assure complete privacy of his campaign, he took as his headquarters a famous brothel in Columbia, Gracie Peixotto's Big Brick House. The election was accompanied by much violence. After the ballots were cast, both parties claimed victory, and rival governments were established for a period of six months until the South Carolina Supreme Court ruled that Hampton had won. He was proclaimed the "Savior of the South."

He was reelected in 1878. Shortly after his reelection, he was thrown from a horse, and his right leg had to be amputated. Although he refused to be a candidate, his party elected him to the United States Senate the day after his leg was amputated. Nonetheless, he resigned his governorship and served two terms in the Senate. In the 1890's he served as United States Railroad Commissioner.

He died in 1902.

Evander McIvor Law

After the war, Law administered the extensive agricultural holdings and railroad interests of his father-in-law's estate in Alabama. In 1881, he moved to Florida, where he opened a military academy based upon The Citadel model, which he administered until 1903. In 1905, he became a Trustee of the Summerlin Institute and a member of the Polk County Board of Education. He also was the editor of the Bartow Courier Informant newspaper until 1915. He died in Bartow, Florida, as the last surviving Confederate major general, and is buried there in Oak Hill Cemetery.

John B. Gordon

Returning to Georgia after the War, Gordon ran for governor in 1868, but was defeated. Not done with politics, he became a Senator in 1873 and won reelected in 1789. He resigned his position in 1880 to cries of corruption. Nonetheless, he won the governorship of Georgia in 1886. In 1891, he was elected to the Senate again. He wrote his memoirs, which were quite popular. He died at 71 years of age, while visiting his son in Miami, Florida in 1904.

John B. Magruder

After the War, Magruder entered the military service of Emperor Maximilian I of Mexico as a Major General. After Maximilian was deposed in 1869, he settled in Houston, Texas. He died in 1871 and is buried in Galveston, where he had fought and won his greatest victory.

Joseph E. Johnston

After the War, for a time Johnston struggled to make a living. He became the President of a small railroad. After about a year and half, he founded a small insurance company in Savannah Georgia. In time, the firm grew until he had about 120 agents working for him. He wrote his memoirs, but they failed to sell. In 1877, he moved to Richmond, Virginia, and ran for Congress. He served one term. He became Commissioner of the Railroads under President Grover Cleveland. His death was tragic, for he served as a pallbearer for William T. Sherman, the man who had defeated him. Out of respect for Sherman, he would not wear a hat, although a cold rain was falling. Days after the funeral, he caught a cold, which progressed into pneumonia, which caused to his death.

James Longstreet

Longstreet's embrace of the Republican Party during Reconstruction made him a pariah in the South. Whatever his merits as a general (remember Robert E. Lee had called him his 'Old Warhorse'), were cast asunder by this political decision. President Johnson refused to grant Longstreet a pardon, even though Longstreet's application was endorsed by his old friend U.S. Grant. Johnson also refused to restore Longstreet's civil rights, saying that "There are three persons of the South who can never receive amnesty: Mr. Davis, General Lee and yourself. You have given the Union cause too much trouble." Nonetheless, Congress did restore his civil rights in 1868.

Initially, Longstreet went to New Orleans with his family, and became a cotton broker. Although he was considered for the position as Secretary of the Navy under President Hayes, he became the Deputy Collector of Internal Revenue and Postmaster of Gainesville, Georgia. In 1880, he served as ambassador to the Ottoman Empire under the Hayes administration. He then served as U.S. Commissioner of Railroads under Presidents McKinley and Theodore Roosevelt.

Interestingly on April 9, 1889, the 24th anniversary of the surrender at Appomattox, his home burned down, and he lost most of Civil War papers and memorabilia.

Probably, because of his change of political party, he became the target of other Confederate veterans of the War, who blamed him for the loss at Gettysburg, and, thus, the War. He fought back with his pen, writing many articles and a book in his defense.

In December of 1889, his wife of 41 years died. She had borne him 10 children, of whom five survived into adulthood. But scandal dogged him again when he remarried a woman (Helen Dortch) who was age 34, when he was 75. Helen outlived him by 58 years, dying in 1962. She was the last wife of any Confederate general to die.

Braxton Bragg

During the War, Bragg's planation in Thibodaux, Louisiana was confiscated and was used to house freed slaves. Thus, Bragg and his wife were forced to live with his brother after the War. In time, he became the Superintendent of the Waterworks in New Orleans. Thereafter, Jefferson Davis offered him a job at the Carolina Life Insurance Company, where he worked for four months before becoming dissatisfied with the job. He was offered a position with the Egyptian Army, but rejected it. He then was employed by the City of Mobile to improve the harbor, the bay and the river, but soon quarreled with various leaders of the city. Next, he became the Chief Engineer of a railroad in Texas, but left after quarreling with the Board of Directors. He died suddenly in Galveston Texas in 1876 at the age of 59.

Robert E. Lee

Although Lee was not arrested or punished after the War, he did not regain his citizenship until 2016, long after his death. He became the President of Washington College (now Washington and Lee University), and served until his death in 1870 at age 63. Lee did not write his memoirs, nor did he intrude into politics. When Grant invited him to the White House, Lee went and became an icon of unity for the nation. Ironically, Lee reportedly spoke of A. P. Hill on his death bed, as had Thomas Jonathan Jackson.

Union General James H. Wilson

Wilson was transferred shortly after Riddell's Shop to the western theatre, where he became one of the few Union Generals to defeat Nathan Bedford Forest. After Lee surrendered at Appomattox, Wilson led the chase after fleeing President Jefferson Davis, whom he captured in May 1865. He also pursued and captured the Commandant of Andersonville Prison, Henry Wirz. After the War, he returned to civil engineering and became a railroad executive. He fought in the Spanish American War in Cuba as a Major General and in the Boxer Rebellion as a Brigadier General. When he died in 1925, he was survived by only three other Union generals.

Hampton Legion Flags

The Flag of Company G, given by the ladies of Stateburg and presented by Dr. Nelson Burgess, is now in the Confederate Relic Room & Museum in Columbia, South Carolina. Nellie Gunter Elmore of Alabama is credited with finding the flag, which may have been in Captain Spann's son's possession.

The Confederate Flag, presented by the ladies of Matanzas, Cuba, Flag of the Legion, also is now in the Confederate Relic Room & Museum in Columbia, South Carolina.

Few other flags of the Legion have survived.

APPENDIX I

Roster of Men Present at Surrender at Appomattox of Company G, Hampton's Legion

Officers:
McEachern, James A., 2nd Lieutenant
Zimmerman, D. Jr., 2nd Lieutenant
Bailey, J. W. Sergeant
Owens, JJ.
Langston, R. W. Corporal
Golding, J. F.
Simmons, G. H.

Privates:

Axon, M.
Anderson, J. J.
Anderson, J. G.
Ballard, J. R.
Dorothy. J. W.
Denins, J. W.
Cope, W. D.
Easely, A.
Fripper, D. W.
Grimsley, J. A.0
Hodge, T. J.

Lee, J. S.
Mitchum, J.
McDonald, D.
McKay, L. P.
Nipper, A.
Pitts, C.
Reynolds, T.
Shayler, J. D.
Simmons, A. E. H.
Spires, G.

APPENDIX II

<u>Timeline of Service of James A. McEachern in the Militia and then the Army of the Confederate States</u>

January 1861 joined the Claremont Rifles
April 1861 Claremont Rifles detailed to Charleston S.C.; camp on Sullivan Island near Ft. Moultrie
July 15, 1861 Claremont Rifles becomes part of Hampton's Legion
August 19, 1861 Enlisted Columbia, SC 1 year term Company G (Captain James G. Span Commanding), Infantry, promoted to 2nd Corporal
Stationed at Camp Butler, September–November 1861
October 1, 1861 Promoted to 1st Corporal
Stationed at Camp Wigfall on the Occoquan, November–December 1861
Nov and Dec 1861 on Muster Rolls
January and February Muster Rolls-records are missing
March and April 1862 on Muster Rolls
Promoted to 3rd Sergeant April 25, 1862 during the reorganization of the Army
May and June 1862 Muster Rolls-records are missing
Wounded In Action, May 31, 1862 at Seven Pines
Stationed near Leesburg, VA July–August 1862
July and August 1862 on Muster Rolls (Reorganized April 25, 1862 Yorkton, VA.) (Due $25 Continuation and $50 Bounty)
Stationed near Fredericksburg, VA September–December 1862
Sept. and October 1862 on Muster Rolls
Nov. and Dec. 1862 on Muster Rolls

November 5, 1862-Promoted to 2nd Sergeant

Stationed near Petersburg, VA January-February 1863

Jan. and Feb. 1863 (Elected 3rd Lieutenant January 26, 1863; Absent on Furlough of Indulgence; Returned March 2, 1863)

Stationed at camp near Suffolk, VA March-April 1863

March and April 1863 on Muster Rolls

Stationed at camp near Richmond, VA May-June 1863

May and June 1863 on Muster Rolls

Stationed at camp near Petersburg, VA July- August 1863

Stationed near Chattanooga, TN September-October 1863

Sept. and October 1863 on Muster Rolls

Elected 2nd Lieutenant January 29, 1864

Commanded Company at Riddle's Shop- June 13, 1864

August 13, 1864, 25 day leave

August 27, 1864, 25 day leave

Sept. and October 1864 on Leave, caused not stated, on Muster Rolls as Mounted Infantry

Stationed near Richmond, VA September-October 1864

November 1864 Roster Report

December 26, 1864, On an inspection Report, Gary's Cavalry Brigade, commanded by Major Edward M. Boykin 7th Regiment, SC Cavalry

January 1, 1865 Inspection Report of Inspection dated December 8, 1864

Parole of Prisoners of War, April 9, 1865, Appomattox Court House, VA

APPENDIX III

Some Notable Civil War Generals Who Were Descendants of Scots

Confederate:
Robert E. Lee
Thomas Jonathan Jackson
John B. Gordon
John B. Magruder
Albert Sydney Johnston
Joseph E. Johnston
Jeb Stuart
Nathan Bedford Forest
George Smith Patton (grandfather of George S. Patton, Jr.- WWII General)

Union:
Ulysses S. Grant
George Brinton McClellan
Winfield Scott
Irvin McDowell
James B. McPherson
Arthur MacArthur (father of Douglas MacArthur)